Sadomasochism

From the AIDS Awareness series:

How can you write a poem when you're dying of AIDS?
(ed.) John Harold

'This is a moving anthology. So many pieces mention people going away, leaving a room, parting, missing one another, but there's also much about renewal and reunion, in dreams or reality, and about hope and love; it's very inspiring.' Anthony Sher

Positive Lives: Response to HIV – A Photodocumentary
(eds) Stephen Mayes and Lyndall Stein

'An exciting demonstration of how powerfully photography can communicate one of the most critical global challenges of our age.' Richard Branson

From the Women on Women series:

Daring to Dissent: Lesbian Culture from Margin to Mainstream
(ed.) Liz Gibbs

'Radical, readable and feisty, this new collection of essays from very different dykes give us all the courage to insist on our difference and the energy to dissent.' Patricia Duncker, University of Wales, Aberystwyth

Challenging Conceptions: Planning a Family by Self-Insemination
Lisa Saffron

'This pioneering book will be invaluable for lesbians contemplating motherhood.' Angela Mason, Executive Director, Stonewall

Portraits to the Wall: Historic Lesbian Lives Unveiled
Rose Collis

'In this all-too-slender volume, Collis has captured the danger and exuberance of some dozen historic lesbian lives. The book is well researched and accessible, journalistic and witty.' Fiona Cooper, novelist

Sadomasochism

*Painful Perversion or
Pleasurable Play?*

Bill Thompson

CASSELL

Cassell
Villiers House
41/47 Strand
London WC2N 5JE

387 Park Avenue South
New York, NY 10016–8810

First published 1994

British Library Cataloguing-in-Publication Data
A catalogue record for this book is available from the British Library.

ISBN 0–304–34307–2 (hardback)
      0–304–34305–6 (paperback)

Typeset by Yorkhouse Typographic Ltd, London
Printed and bound in Great Britain by Mackays of Chatham

Contents

Acknowledgements

THIS work could have not been completed without the help of numerous people, especially: Chris Tame, who shares my tendency to stick my neck out for others when no one else will dare do so; the Countdown to Spanner campaign; Adrian Parsons, who supplied the court judgments and media reports; Roy Wolfe, who tracked down everything ever written on the subject; Jason Annetts and Dawn Clark for reading various drafts; Sean Egan, who sorted out the computer problems; the British Museum North Library; and Dan. Regards to: Colin Laskey; Steve and Roz at Cassell; Richard Green; Kenny Plummer; Zak; the girls from Brazil; Kathryn; Eddy Holland; Mr McKechnie's class at Portsdown; and to the Kando Bongo Man and Diblo.

To Monica

Also available from the Cassell Sexual Politics List:

Coming Out of the Blue: British Police Officers Talk about their Lives in 'The Job' as Lesbians, Gays and Bisexuals
Marc E. Burke

'Marc Burke's path-breaking study helps give a voice to the previously hidden pains and dilemmas of lesbian, gay and bisexual police. It will become required reading for all those who wish to understand this controversial issue of the 1990s.' Ken Plummer, University of Essex

Safety in Numbers: Safer Sex and Gay Men
Edward King

'In the proliferation of writing about AIDS, *Safety in Numbers* stands out for its careful analysis of one of the most important areas of all – the need to develop and support effective prevention programmes for those most at risk. This book will play an important service in helping to save lives and combat homophobia.' Dennis Altman

Speaking of Sex: The Limits of Language
Anthony Grey

' . . . beautifully written in his usual easy and felicitous style. The plea for sex respect should convince anyone; but it was his chapter on love I found especially moving.'
Francis Bennion, author of *The Sex Code: Morals for Moderns*

Broadcasting It: An Encyclopedia of Homosexuality on Film, Radio and TV 1923–1993
Keith Howes

'Its range, rigour and thoroughness are breathtaking. More impressive still, it's a great read – fun, insightful and surprising.'
Richard Dyer, University of Warwick

Male Impersonators: Men Performing Masculinity
Mark Simpson

'Discussions of masculinity have hitherto been characterized by a timid tone of pious apology – here at last is the antidote to that all-too-sombre debate. Sharp, astute and decidedly spunky, Simpson's essays are guaranteed to amuse, provoke and illuminate.' Andy Medhurst, University of Sussex

Introduction

Spanner: The Non-existent Crime

DURING 1990 and 1991, the sensational trial of fifteen men accused of running 'a perverted sex-ring' propelled sadomasochism into the headlines; and, once the House of Lords had denied the defendants' appeal two years later, the sexual habits of hundreds of thousands of harmless people became a criminal offence. Anyone who puts a nipple clamp on their spouse, any cabinet minister who spanks an actress's bottom, or even star-struck teenagers who give their date a love bite, could now find themselves charged with assault. As a result, SM devotees, people who like to dress for sex, and prefer erotic role-play games to the missionary position, now have to keep their proclivity a secret; but they are not the real losers. History demonstrates that whenever the authorities seek to control the sexual habits of its citizens, the results are counter-productive; and this case, destined to become another landmark in the long, tortuous history of British sexuality, is no exception.

The fifteen members of this so-called 'perverted sadomas-ochistic sex-ring' were nothing of the kind. The defendants were merely a group of gay friends, who from 1978 sometimes got together, in two and threes, to have sex. Over time, some of them began to experiment with SM sex, obtained some equipment, and eventually began to videotape themselves. Some of the tapes were copied and distributed amongst the friends. Other than by occasionally introducing a new friend, the group members tended to keep themselves to themselves.

The police investigation into the group, codenamed Spanner, began when detectives in Bolton got hold of four of the tapes. Having convinced themselves that they had found a 'snuff movie', the police got very excited and decided that, if they brought the dangerous international-satanic-ritual-child-abusing-snuff-movie-making gang to justice, the public might be disinclined to ask why the police were interfering with Her Majesty's mail in the first place. To this end, the police raided the friends' houses and dug up their gardens in search of the dead bodies. They found none; nor any other evidence of a devious ploy.

Despite looking extremely foolish, the police went ahead with a charge of conspiracy to corrupt public morals to get 'a result'. They had to; this investigation into nothing had not only cost the taxpayer over £500,000, it had diverted police attention, time and resources from serious crime. However, by the time the Spanner case (*R. v. Brown*) came to court, the nature of the prosecution had completely changed. The fifteen defendants now faced charges under Sections 20 and 47 of the Offences Against the Person Act 1861; and the court was going to decide whether hitting a penis with a ruler, dripping 'hot' wax on to a penis, strapping someone with a cat-o'-nine-tails, caning the buttocks, strapping the buttocks with a belt, amounted to 'the infliction of actual bodily harm and wounds'.

The charges were ridiculous. By concentrating upon a number of one-off acts, the prosecution attempted to mask the fact that the members of the group were doing little more than what hundreds of thousands of married couples and lovers, be they heterosexual or homosexual, cabinet ministers or ordinary people, do every night of the week: add a bit of 'slap and tickle' to their sex play. Indeed, over the previous twenty years the number of magazines, books, clubs and organizations devoted to discussing and exploring the origin and nature of SM sex-play had dramatically increased. While most only dabbled with special clothing, sex toys or even canes, paddles and straps, others were becoming extremely adept at using these accoutrements in imaginative ways. Likewise, the public's interest in tattooing and body jewellery, from nipple rings to labia rings, had dramatically increased; and the use of items from ice cubes to 'hot' wax to increase and enhance the body's erogenous sensations had even become the subject of numerous feature films. Yet here was the law, having failed to find any evidence for their snuff movie theory, charging a group of friends for doing what millions of others were doing too. Spanner was going to be a test case to outlaw kinky sex.

The charges certainly made the defendants think twice about what they had done. Yes, a couple of the group *had* developed a taste for stronger forms of SM, but as they were consenting adults, any technical offence committed could easily have been dealt with by issuing a caution, and everyone could have been more thoughtful and careful in the future. Unfortunately for the defendants, not only did the police want 'a result', their advisers had other reasons for going after SM sex and making it a crime: they wanted to see if they could get away with extending the definition of assault under English law, and find another excuse to pry into the citizen's private life.

The real crime

On the best advice they could have received from counsel, the defendants pleaded not guilty, and prepared their rebuttals. It was believed that the prosecution would have to prove that there had been a hostile act or intent and a lack of consent, and that the assault charges were inappropriate given the sexual nature of events and because no one had been hurt. There was, however, one tricky problem to overcome: as they were gay, the defendants' acts were technically illegal under the 1967 Sexual Offences Act, which forbids gay men from having sex if a third party is present.

As it turned out, Judge Rant, the initial trial judge, did not appear to be too interested in that. By his ruling in court that consent was no defence to a charge of assault, the defendants were forced to change their pleas to guilty; and when they were formally convicted on 19 December 1990, they found out why the judge had made that ruling. His comments included a declaration that it was the role of the court to draw a line between what was and was not acceptable in a civilized society, and that as sadomasochism was 'degrading and vicious' it was on the wrong side of the line. It was SM sex which was on trial, rather than the defendants, and nothing but a guilty verdict would do. This decision, upheld at the Court of Appeal eighteen months later and then confirmed in a split (three to two) decision by the law lords in March 1992, raises two problems for a *really* civilized society: the judges' beliefs concerning SM sex bore no relation to what happens; and their legal justifications for making consenting activities like spanking an illegal assault were dubious.

By dismissing the two appeals, the law was drawing a very strange line: if people spank each other for mutual pleasure they are guilty of an assault, but if a teacher beats a pupil against the child's will, the teacher is not guilty of an assault. The House of Lords even reinforced a teacher's right to do this a couple of months after the final Spanner judgment. The decision also raises questions about how legal judgments are made. The convictions were justified on the grounds that sadomasochism involves violent sex acts, when nothing could be further from the truth.

In denying British couples or friends the right to spank each other for sexual pleasure, the appeal judges offered three inter-related justifications. First, they asserted that the essence of sado-masochistic activity is the infliction and reception of pain. Second, that inflicting such pain amounts to an assault in English law. Third, that no 'victim' of such an assault can consent to being assaulted. Not only is the third justification absurd, given the popularity of contact sports; its validity in the Spanner case obviously rests upon the first two assertions being correct. Yet the first justification is completely erroneous and the second only became a legal 'fact' by virtue of the Spanner judgments; their lordships could have easily decided otherwise.

Sadomasochism, let alone SM sex play, has very little to do with pain. On the contrary, whatever 'blows' are used in sex games, using spanking or nipple clamps, such acts are experienced mentally and physically as a form of pleasurable arousal-enhancement rather than pain. As pleasurable sexual arousal can hardly be analogous to a harmful assault, SM should not have been subject to an assault charge in the first place, and the second justification logically falls.

5: Spanner: The Non-existent Crime

Some SM devotees complained that the first two justifications made no sense at all, given that contact sports like boxing also involved inflicting and receiving pain; but this inconsistency could never be the real problem with the judgments. Although the definition of assault used in the Spanner judgments *would* apply to sports like boxing unless these sports were recognized as exceptions to the assault laws, the real problem is that the contemporary exceptions have never been explicitly listed in either case law or statute, and that mutually gratifying SM sex was neither an exception nor an assault before the Spanner judgment. In other words, the Spanner case, the appeal, or the law lords could not *confirm* that SM sex was or was not an exception to the law of assault, because this was an open question. By declaring that *consensual* SM sex was not an exception, the judges were making a distinction for the first time in history between the right to use real force in the name of sport and various forms of force to create sexual pleasure. As we shall see, the only way the judges could continue with their charade was to adopt a very selective interpretation of precedent-setting assault cases; but they also pulled a legal 'fast one'.

Section 20 of the 1861 Act specifically says that to be guilty of an assault you have to 'unlawfully and maliciously wound or inflict grievous bodily harm upon another person with or without a weapon or instrument'. Given that SM actions are consensual and designed to increase a partner's pleasure, it is highly contentious that the active partner is being malicious. As SM acts range from spanking to inserting rings through nipples, one would have to find a clever means to label them wounding or grievous bodily harm when they hardly differ from legal acts like getting an ear pierced and a firm massage. The only real difference is the sexual intent and the area of the body involved. Likewise, as acts like spanking take place in circumstances of sexual arousal, and are not experienced as pain, SM usually involves far less bodily 'harm' than many legal acts, such as the infamous practice of ramming an elbow into the face of an opponent on the soccer field. In order to get round this problem all the judges used the fact that because the defendants had pleaded guilty to the charges after Judge Rant's ruling, they had admitted that they had wounded and caused actual bodily harm to each other! This 'fact' was then used to circumvent both various legal definitions concerning consent and assault, and legal precedents like the *Donovan* case, which if followed logically would have required a not guilty verdict, whatever the judges thought of SM sex. The Court of Appeal's judgment penned by Lord Lane, for example, asserted that, as the defendants' intention had been to inflict pain and suffering, that amounted to a sufficient degree of hostility to constitute an assault, subject to the question of consent; but as the defendants had admitted that wounding or actual bodily harm had occurred, it had been correct to use the 1861 Act, and Judge Rant had been right to deny a consent defence to an act of assault.

In order to convince the public that SM sex was a threat to society, and justify this blatant piece of legal 'jiggery-pokery', Lord Lane offered a highly dubious definition of what really occurred. The constant use of the term 'sadomasochism' as opposed to the devotees' own terminology, 'SM' demonstrates that the court was determined to impose its own meaning upon reality. Contrary to his assertions: there is no such thing as a 'sadomasochistic libido'; as SM does not inflict 'pain', it cannot cause 'hurt', 'injury' or suffering; people cannot be divided into the sadomasochistically inclined and non-inclined; rooms containing a riding crop and straps do not constitute a 'torture chamber' unless one shares Lord Lane's vivid imagination. As for his bizarre diktat that those who use such instruments are 'sadists' and that the 'masochists' were their 'victims', it makes no sense at all, given that the vast majority of the defendants were in the habit of switching roles. Each and every one of these definitions had one purpose: to deny the defendants recourse to the obvious caveats open to them in Kenny's *Outlines of Criminal Law*, and Archbold's *Criminal Pleading Evidence and Practice*:

> even the most complete consent, by the most competent person, will not suffice to legalise an assault which there are public grounds for prohibiting. Thus consent is no defence, criminally, for any assault that involves some extreme and causeless injury to life, limb or health; or even one that constitutes a mere Breach of the Peace, nor for any assault likely to cause bodily harm (whether extreme or not) and not justified by good reason, e.g., sport, lawful chastisement.

7: *Spanner: The Non-existent Crime*

As a general rule it is unlawful to strike a person with such a degree of violence that bodily harm is a probable consequence. There are, however, two well recognised exceptions to this general rule: [i] blows given in the course of a friendly athletics context; [ii] blows given in the course of rough but innocent horse play.

In short: SM would be acceptable as long as there was no *de facto* injury or breach of the peace and there was good reason for the action, such as 'rough horse play'. Yet, by laboriously defining every act as injurious, and thereby suggesting that 'sadistic' sexual gratification could not be a good reason, Lord Lane was deliberately undermining the viable consent defence and avoiding any comparison with similar acts which did not lead to prosecution.

There are two reasons why this and the later House of Lords decision worry me as a criminologist. First, it is difficult to come to any other conclusion than that the Spanner judgments amounted to legalizing prejudice and moral beliefs about various forms of sexual pleasure, rather than the application of the law as it stood; and that these show-trials will enable 'society' to pretend it is doing something about violent sex crime by criminalizing people who enjoy 'kinky sex' rather than catching the real criminals. Second, the law of assault has been extended without recourse to a debate in Parliament. Lord Lane's decision in the Spanner case followed a previous belief of his, outlined in an Attorney-General's Reference, that it should be immaterial in borderline assault cases whether or not the acts occurred in private or in public, or whether or not the participants consented, because judges should decide if the acts charged were *in the public interest* or not. This drastically reduces citizens' rights to decide for themselves what they are allowed to like or do, even when it harms no one at all; and that cannot be right. Once one places in context the alleged 'violence' that occurs during SM sex, by realizing that one commits a battery simply by bumping into someone in the street, and that the law happily allows you to kill another person as long as the 'sport' is regulated, the Spanner decision is ridiculous. When one adds the manipulation of legal precedent, it should be considered a scandal.

The way the law of assault has been devised means that while the law is quite clear that one cannot assent to an assault, the circumstances of that consent can sometimes have an important bearing on whether or not the action should, initially, be defined as an assault. Although judges like to pretend that they deal with the question of assault before the issue of consent, it is frequently impossible to do this, precisely because one would have to make decisions about 'good reasons', 'horse play' and so on, first. This was exactly the situation that all the judges faced in the Spanner case. The precedents available to them also laid down a way out of this dilemma in borderline cases: let the jury decide. The judges, however, took it upon themselves to decide. Yet they not only refused to clarify what the 'good reason' for an exception was, they insisted that the law did not have to supply such a definition in borderline cases – the very time when logic suggests that we need one. The judges were using their power to place sex acts in a criminal category, without defining the boundaries of that category! The Spanner judgments are, therefore, a perfect example of why the law is still an ass.

The real reason why no definition was offered, the advised procedure was ignored and precedents were inverted was that maintaining consistency in the law of assault would have required the judges either to uphold the appeal or to remove exception status from several 'sports'. It obviously makes no sense at all to allow a malicious rugby player to hide behind the label 'sport' when smashing in an opponent's face, while simultaneously outlawing mutually pleasurable spouse-spanking; unless, of course, one wants to criminalize the increasing British interest in kinky sex. Despite conceding that the private and pleasurable nature of the Spanner SM sex acts puts 'these offences into a different category from the type of assault with which the Court is ordinarily concerned', and consequently reducing the sentences, this was clearly Lord Lane's intention:

> *We take the view that the function of the court is to mark its disapproval of these activities* . . . We are prepared to accept that the Appellants did not appreciate that their actions . . . were criminal and that the sentences upon them therefore should be comparatively lenient. *In future, however, that argument will not be open to a Defendant in circumstances such as these.*

9: *Spanner: The Non-existent Crime*

As the same sentiment was voiced in the subsequent appeal to the House of Lords, kinky sex is now illegal. The fact that the case involved a group of homosexuals as opposed to a heterosexual married couple is irrelevant; spanking or slapping one another, even in fun, is a criminal offence.

Even if one has no interest in SM sex this should be of considerable concern; because it is one of the major reasons why Britain is suffering from a rising crime rate. The Spanner judgement and many recent laws, from the 1984 Video Recordings Act to the 1994 Criminal Justice Act, which empowers Trading Standards Officers to peruse your video collection, are designed to criminalize harmless people who are easy to 'catch', while the real crooks and gangsters, who take more effort to bring to justice, get away with their crimes. As a result, the police's and courts' time is being wasted, because their increased activity will have no effect on the *real* crime rate. For some reason, the powers that be would rather waste your tax money imposing their hypocritical moral standards upon you, by policing your sexual and viewing habits, than stop you being mugged or murdered. Gay people and horror movie buffs have known this for years; and it is time everyone else knew what is going on too.

Since 1977, various moral groups have attempted to justify restricting the public's access to sexually orientated material by promoting a child pornography panic, claiming that there was a link between sales of soft-core pornography and sex crime, and insisting that no one would even dream of having non-procreative sex outside marriage unless they had been sexually 'abused' or had read de Sade. Despite the government's passing half a dozen laws which further restricted the public's right to view or do, sex crimes rocketed, and the public have lost confidence in the authorities' ability to deal with the problem. But even though these laws were passed following exaggerated claims about dangers and solutions, and were counter-productive to say the least, members of the public had the opportunity to voice their opinion or get their MP to do so. The same cannot be said for cases like Spanner where the increase in censorship and control is obtained outside the public arena by the police and the courts which are not accountable.

10: *Sadomasochism*

The origin of Spanner can be traced back to the determination of the Scotland Yard Obscene Publications Squad to promote an official set of sexual norms in Britain, and to find yet another justification for their existence. The Squad was not having a good time during the 1980s. Growing public acceptance of innocuous sexually orientated material, and a recent Customs Service clampdown on continental material, left the Squad with little to do following the video nasties furore. Despite a fourfold increase in operation costs, during the 1980s, prosecutions were down 75 per cent. In order to keep going, the Squad spent the first half of the decade raiding legal soft-core porn warehouses, and the second half jumping upon any moralistic bandwagon demanding more and more Parliamentary proscriptions against anything and everything they did not like. If the Squad had had their way we would not be able to buy even the hilarious comic *Viz* or sex education videos.

Having made themselves look ridiculous by their continual harassment of gay literature and assertions about widespread satanic ritual plots, the police seized upon the Spanner videos as a means to prove their conspiracy theories. They saw the prosecution of people they did not like as a desperate battle between the forces of civilization and an international gang of devious satanic sadomasochistic serial sex killers, threatening to take over the world. Detective Superintendent Michael Hames then promptly took advantage of the judgment to fuel his demand for even more powers to check the contents of the public's video collection, by claiming that the Spanner group ended up making their movies because illegal material was not 'hard' enough for porn addicts, and asserting that 'sadistic' pornography was becoming so bizarre, violent and widespread that it would eventually lead to real deaths being filmed. The Spanner fifteen were, therefore, merely fall-guys offered up as proof for a decade of police scaremongering propaganda purloined from drive-in movie plots; and the case was a show-trial, covering up the absurdity and self-indulgence of Britain's anachronistic moral police and the authorities' duplicitous hypocrisy.

As the Spanner case broke, I was half-way through preparing an extensive academic account of the battle over pornography and other forms of sexual expression that had preoccupied Britain and the USA since the 1960s. Initially the coverage of Spanner, and the *Modern Primitives* case which followed, merely played a bit-part in that saga. However, once the Law Commission announced that it was considering criminalizing 'sadomasochistic' acts between consenting parties, I realized that not only did the Spanner case prove that the law knew nothing about SM sex but that the authorities were also prepared to waste a lot of time and money covering up Spanner's origins with one of the most absurd judgments recorded in British law.

The law hoped to get away with this because 'sadomasochism' has invariably received a bad press, being instantaneously linked with contemporary serial killers who are also supposed to be motivated by an eighteenth-century anti-religious scribe called the Marquis de Sade. The fear and loathing invoked by this man's name amongst the ignorant and judicial classes is remarkable given that de Sade's real claim to fame was his opposition to the death penalty in Revolutionary France.

Knowing, as I did, that SM devotees have nothing in common with serial killers or child murderers, and even less to do with de Sade, I wanted to say so publicly. That desire increased once Ray Wyre, with whom I had just shared a TV studio, tipped me off that my detractors had abandoned their previous slanders that I was a porn-producing, white-slaving baby-eating satanist, in favour of the 'fact' that I was obviously a gay sadomasochist all along. Clearly, the prurient classes now believe that having the same sexual proclivities as the Spanner defendants should be a capital offence. Fortunately, Cassell were amenable at just the right time. This book is the result; and I thank them for it.

This polemic against criminalizing SM sex explains how and why SM has never had any connection with the malicious violence to which it is linked by people who are convinced that sex should not be fun. In doing so it will reveal why, though I am not a gay sadomasochist, I would not care if I was and why no one else should care either. It does so by contrasting the contemporary nature of SM sex games with erroneous beliefs about the psychology and nature of 'sadomasochism', and by popularizing what numerous academics have known for some time.

12: *Sadomasochism*

The argument is divided into three parts. The first traces the origins of our mistaken beliefs about 'sadomasochism', and demonstrates that those who believe 'sadomasochists' are 'addicted' to inflicting or receiving pain have no grounds for doing so. The second part compares the evil propaganda of those who wish to outlaw SM sex with neutral academic research in order to highlight the wide disparity between the myths about sadomasochism and the reality of a popular sexual preference known as SM.

I had originally intended to use the third section to reveal the way in which contemporary SM devotees organized their activities. Between 1984 and 1993, as part of ongoing research into contemporary sexual minority practices, I attended several functions organized by SM devotees. I was shown their equipment and costumes, and how they were utilized. Several devotees explained their fantasy histories to me and how they had realized them. No doubt many people would be surprised, if not horrified, to think that someone could and would want to become a professional 'voyeur'; but then they would not want to know what minorities get up to anyway. Thankfully, not everyone agrees with them, and sexual anthropology has a long respectable history. Following the careers of young models or strippers, swingers and fantasy realizers, and those who supply professional services, offers one far more understanding than interviews packed full of platitudes and apologies. The only real difference between studying sexual minority interests and other subjects *ethnographically*, as it is called, is that the subject matter involves sex. The fact that everyone is 'terribly interested' if you spend a day with train-spotters, a weekend with fundamentalist Christians or a month in a crofting community, but everyone drops their jaws the moment you spend a day working as a 'barker' in a London peep show or a night talking with performers in a São Paulo live sex show, also tells you a lot about British attitudes to sex. To be sure, sexual ethnography can sometimes be embarrassing, and there are all sorts of ethical problems to consider, especially when getting to know people off 'the scene'; but how else is one to avoid relying solely upon the sensational media accounts or the occasional drama played out in court? Social anthropologists following the lives of criminals, drug users or bizarre religious groups have similar problems too; but they can usually tell you far more about them than the media or the police.

Since the law lords' judgment, however, discretion about SM activities in Britain is advisable, and several devotees I was speaking to suggested that a chapter on the law would be far more useful. Consequently, the third section of the book is now devoted to a detailed criticism of the Spanner judgments, and reveals how the legal precedents were deliberately manipulated to criminalize a harmless set of sexual pleasures. By way of recompense for the omitted material, I have carefully selected some other sources listed in the guide to further reading.

Along the way, I take issue with several key theories of SM from the past. However, because of a restriction on the length of this volume, this should not be considered as an exhaustive academic review. For reasons that will become clear, I prefer to use the term SM rather than sadomasochism. It reflects the way that those who actively engage in sexual acts which may appear violent or domineering to non-devotees perceive themselves. I believe that the terms 'sadist' and 'masochist', if they are to be retained at all, should be reserved for people who get a vicarious kick out of inflicting pain or harm upon others and those who get their kicks out of vicarious suffering. When the terms 'sadomasochism', 'sado-masochism', or 'SM' appear in the text, their use reflects the terminological choice of the person whose views I am discussing at that point. During the 1970s, for example, some devotees and a number of academics used the non-pejorative annotation S/M to describe the activities they were studying. As SM devotees know more about what they are doing and thinking than anyone else, and their current preference is SM, I also use that term.

I have no doubt that those who feel uneasy about the idea of dressing up for sex in highly stylized fetish clothing and engaging in acts of control and restraint will not enjoy this book. They will complain that this book is partisan and not academic. I willingly plead guilty on both counts. It is partisan because I seek to debunk the justifications for persecuting harmless people; and the book is not academic because it's about time the public knew what SM is really all about and resisted the attempt of vested interests to mislead them in order to cover up their own failings.

Chapter one

Sadomasochism?

ALL three Spanner judgments were justified by the assertion that sadomasochism is a violent form of sexual gratification. Without this definition the judges could not have denied SM devotees the right to a consent defence. While none of the judges consulted any sources for their pejorative beliefs, they clearly thought that they spoke with authority and certainty. Yet, when one looks at the origins of the term we find what it describes has little in common with what the judges were implying.

What's in a name?

The truth and reality of any phenomenon is rarely found in a dictionary definition, or in references to historical examples that 'look' similar. The meaning of all human phenomena depends upon whatever meaning people want to give it now, irrespective of what others have thought in the past, let alone any innate quality the phenomena possess. This is certainly the case with sadomasochism, for a review of past definitions of sadomasochism, let alone SM sex, reveals that the judges were simply making up their connotations as they went along.

From the very beginning, those who defined what sadomasochism is drew a clear distinction between people who enjoyed what is now called SM sex and those who maliciously sought to harm others, and agreed that one could not draw a firm distinction between sadists and masochists. Popular beliefs to the contrary rest upon selective adaptations of the early theorists' moral judgments rather than their data, which ironically failed to establish the validity of the terminology chosen. It would be wrong, however, to place all the blame for this misunderstanding upon detractors, who will obviously exploit what fits their preconceptions while ignoring the rest; until relatively recently, many devotees suffered from similar misconceptions derived from their desperate search through classic texts to make sense of their feelings when faced with moral condemnation. Maria Marcus's *A Taste for Pain* (1981), for example, which recounts her search for a reason for her desire to be dominated, is typical in that, having painstakingly pored over every theory she could find, she stopped the moment she found one she could accept. Likewise, the Greenes' *S/M The Last Taboo* (1974) provides a lengthy justification for 'sadism' culled from Havelock Ellis, because they were convinced that he had provided a justification for their proposition that 'sadism' was quite harmless. In undertaking this kind of search, Marcus and the Greenes were not so much discovering the real meaning of sadomasochism as inventing one; and that is precisely what every work on the subject to date has done.

This obsession to discover the meaning of feelings and 'the real' you is, of course, not restricted to SM devotees. Many people hold to a common belief that everyone has an essential good self, a private self, waiting to be rediscovered. Despite its widespread appeal, particularly amongst the middle classes, this theory is a fiction. The feeling that one has an essential self is produced simply by one's failure to be honest with others because of a desire to maintain public approval whatever one is really thinking and doing, owing to the belief that others may not approve of your 'real self'. Compared to everyone else, SM devotees do have a good excuse for engaging in this social 'schizophrenia'. When one realizes the kind of problems gay people still have in being open about themselves in public, 'coming out' as an SM devotee, especially after Spanner, is not always advisable. SM devotees, like gay people before them, however, have begun to confront and challenge the pejorative label of sadomasochism thrust upon them, because it bears no relationship to their SM experience. In doing so, they are being far more honest about their feelings than most people. SM devotees have realized that some of the problems erroneously associated with the sadomasochist label stemmed from the failure of people to be honest about their feelings, and that it is frequently the attempt to suppress one's desires that leads to difficulty. They have also realized that it is only when enough people admit to various kinds of sexual feelings that a serious search for the origin of such desires can begin; any theory which precedes the open acceptance of a sexual desire will be handicapped by the inability to differentiate between the effects of the true feelings and the person's concern about fear of public denunciation. If the rise of the open gay community demonstrates anything, it is that one is more likely to get closer to the meaning of an experience amongst those who have found it possible to live out their private desires or 'selves' within a community of like-minded souls rather than from an isolated individual in a psychiatrist's chair.

Incredibly and ironically, there should be no need to do this in the case of sadomasochism; for when one reconsiders the classic studies by Krafft-Ebing, Ellis and Bloch, one sees that the definitions and meanings on offer were never closed or fixed for all time. Our belief that they were, and that people are either 'sadists' or 'masochists', is merely another consequence of the Freudian crusade to turn minority sexual desires into pathologies and secular sins; which contributes nothing to our understanding of anything, let alone sadomasochism.

Patriarchal perversions

Richard von Krafft-Ebing (1840–1902) was a forensic psychiatrist. As Professor of Neurology at Stuttgart and later Vienna University, he studied diseases of the brain and the nervous system; and his major medical claim to fame was working out that general paralysis of the insane was caused by syphilis. Krafft-Ebing was also a moralist and condemned most forms of sex. Being the director of a mental hospital, he took the opportunity to 'study' the relationship between mental illness and sex, and published *Psychopathia Sexualis* in 1886 to enable doctors to spot the criminally perverse and lock them up. To avoid the possibility that 'normal' people would also develop sex 'madness' by reading the book, he wrote the descriptions of sex in Latin; but, because it was the only comprehensive source available at the time, it became extremely popular, and Krafft-Ebing found himself spending the rest of his life 'improving' and expanding the text. Consequently, the *Psychopathia Sexualis* established many of the definitions and meanings about sex we still use today. What many fail to realize, however, is that it really only describes the manifestations of various sexual 'abnormalities' and does not explain their origins. Krafft-Ebing was already convinced that all mental and emotional 'aberrations' were caused by a weak congenitally determined 'bodily constitution'; a secular version of the 'sins of one's forefathers'. Apart from this simplistic belief about heredity, like most of his contemporaries Krafft-Ebing also confused the sexual ethics and ideals of the time with what was 'natural'. As far as he was concerned, social factors could only enhance an inherited deviant sexual trait. Not that this conviction stopped Krafft-Ebing opposing secular trends he did not approve of, by linking them with perversions. He believed, for example, that lesbianism was increasing at the turn of the century because of novel reading and the use of pedal-powered sewing machines! His explanation of sadism and masochism were almost as bad, but they were not what many think they were.

As far as Krafft-Ebing was concerned, sadism was the 'experience of sexual pleasurable sensations (including orgasm) produced by acts of cruelty, bodily punishment inflicted on one's own person or when witnessed'. Consequently, while sadists may have had 'an innate desire to humiliate, hurt, wound or even destroy others in order thereby to create sexual pleasure in one's self', being a 'sadist' did not necessarily involve hurting anyone, and could involve transferring one's own feelings of pain into sexual pleasure just as easily as experiencing sexual pleasure when seeing something hurt. This core idea, that sadists could hurt themselves, and Krafft-Ebing's further insistence that elemental sadism was present in lovers' and newly-weds' teasing, biting, pinching and wrestling, means that contemporary usage is at odds with the original definition.

British judges' belief that Krafft-Ebing discovered the stereotypical 'sadist' follows from his speculation that there *might* be a continuum between this 'normal' sexual 'horse play' and 'the most monstrous acts of destructions' found in 'extreme' forms of sadism; not that he could offer any evidence to establish this link. The case histories he offered of 'sadists' mostly amounted to nothing more than an interest in flagellation. They would invariably describe how, having seen a beating, the alleged 'sadist' would devise numerous means to copy the act. In Krafft-Ebing's much quoted 'Case 39', for example, the man's sadistic perversion amounted only to searching for a woman who would let him spank her during their love-making, after once observing his fourteen-year-old sister being chastised.

Apart from the fact that the constant references to these 'traumatic' experiences in his cases would help to undermine Krafft-Ebing's theories about inherited traits, the personal histories constantly failed to demonstrate his belief that 'sadistic' desires were a substitute for sex. It is very easy to draw a clear distinction between those who wished to indulge themselves and others as *part* of love-making and the theoretical 'sadists' who got their vicarious kicks from flogging animals or children.

Krafft-Ebing's evidence was invariably at odds with his explanations because he was always trying to squeeze his data into feeble theories rather than utilize the data to construct a viable alternative. His major stumbling block was his delusion that, because his patients' fantasies preceded any personal experience, the desire must be present at birth.

Having decided that sadistic satisfaction was a substitute for intercourse, it was almost inevitable that he would believe masochism to be a form of impotence:

> By masochism I understand a peculiar perversion of the physical vita sexualis in which the individual affected, in sexual feeling and thought, is controlled by the idea of being completely and unconditionally subject to the will of the opposite sex; of being treated by this person as by a master, humiliated and abused. This idea is coloured by lustful feeling; the masochist lives in fancies, in which he creates situations of this kind and often attempts to realise them. By this perversion his sexual instinct is often made more or less insensible to the normal charms of the opposite sex – incapable of normal vita sexualis – being physically impotent.

Not that he had any evidence for this; he simply purloined the idea from Leopold van Sacher-Masoch's novel of a man's impotent and slavish denial to a dominating woman, *Venus in Furs* (published in 1886), and then ascribed as much power to the imagination as he denied the sadist.

Despite these weaknesses, Krafft-Ebing was not completely blind; he considered the possibility that 'sadism' and 'masochism' were symbiotic, and noticed links with fetishism. His most important insight, however, was that masochists appeared to enjoy any kind of 'maltreatment' rather than physical pain. Indeed, 'pain' appeared to have little to do with it, and Krafft-Ebing was adamant that jaded libertines who undertook a beating to obtain an erection were not 'true' masochists. Unfortunately, Krafft-Ebing's attempt to differentiate between, and create a typology of, three forms of sadism and masochism merely created more confusion.

The most popular form, 'mental' or 'psychic' sadism-masochism, did not involve any attempt to realize one's fantasies because the sexual arousal invoked was a prelude to masturbation. The second, 'symbolic', form did involve acting out fantasies of dominance or submission, especially the latter, but the wish to be humiliated, embarrassed or degraded, rather than suffer pain, did not necessarily involve orgasm, as 'Case 64' demonstrates. The patient sought out a prostitute who would

> undress him, tie his hands and feet, bandage his eyes, draw the curtains of the windows. Then she would make her guest sit down on a sofa and leave him there alone in a helpless position. After half an hour she had to come back and unbind him.

The infliction or reception of pain was found only in the rarer third, 'physical', form. This, because Krafft-Ebing suggested that it could occur with or without sexual intent, has led to numerous problems with definitions since.

Krafft-Ebing's use of the same term to describe both non-painful sexually motivated dominance and submission games, and very painful non-sexually orientated, dominant and submissive acts which provided a completely different kind of pleasure for the active perpetrator, followed from his belief that the two conditions *could* be associated. Unfortunately, numerous cretins, and British judges, have read this to mean that the two conditions *must* be the same thing, even though Krafft-Ebing never managed to justify linking the two tendencies.

The major problem a logical mind would face both with Krafft-Ebing's original definitions and with his explanation of this hypothetical link was that they are both completely dependent upon a Victorian stereotype about male and female sexual responses, which has long since been discredited. If you do not accept the stereotype, you cannot accept Krafft-Ebing's explanation of the link or his definitions.

As far as Krafft-Ebing was concerned, males were always the motivator, whether as beater or beaten. This sexist anachronism was obvious in his attempt to explain sadism:

> In the first place, sadism, in which the need of subjugation of the opposite sex forms a constituent element, in accordance with its nature, represents a pathological intensification of the male sexual character; in the second place, the obstacles which oppose the expression of this monstrous impulse are, of course, much greater for woman than for man.
>
> It seems probable that this sadistic force is developed by the natural shyness and modesty of women towards the aggressive manners of the male, especially during the early period of married life and particularly where the husband is hyper-sexual. Woman no doubt derives pleasure from her innate coyness and the final victory of man affords her intense and refined gratification. Hence the frequent recurrences of these little love comedies . . .

In other words, sadism was a pathological form of the 'natural' heterosexual relationship found in those who have inherited the trait; a fact proved, once again, by the occasional appearance of the sadistic impulses before the necessary external experiential factors came into play. Either way, Krafft-Ebing's model meant that men were always dominant partners and had stronger sexual appetites than their wives; because women, 'if physically and mentally normal and properly educated' were not supposed to have any sexual desire.

21: Sadomasochism?

As a woman's 'love' was essentially spiritual rather than sensual as well, once she became a mother, a female's sex life was largely a means of proving her affection towards her husband. Women really had sex to have babies, and if left to themselves would not do so for any other reason.

Yet when it came to the exact nature of the pathology, Krafft-Ebing suddenly hedged: it *might* follow experiences of sexually pleasurable sensations; there again, it *might* consist solely of the 'innate desire'. The only thing he was convinced of was that the inherited tendency was paramount: not everyone had the potential to be a sadist. What really puzzled him most was why, if these 'sadistic' feelings could exist without the sadist injuring anyone else, the sadistic 'impulse' sometimes became focused upon other people and could even end in murder. The answer he offered was also dependent upon the 'natural' gender-determined sexual 'horse play' which inadvertently provoked extreme sadism – although he required an archetypal wife-beater, not found in his case studies, to prove it: 'Where the husband forces the wife by menaces and other violent means to the conjugal act, we can no longer describe such as a normal physiological manifestation, but must ascribe it to sadistic impulses.' Why we should do so Krafft-Ebing does not tell us; but, convinced that he now had the key to the explanation, he offered the belief in a close relationship between the emotions of love and anger as proof, and readily swapped the terms lust and cruelty for love and anger when it suited him. Ironically, while the theory of a continuum between lovers' 'horse play' and sadism made sense to him, the scene he offers as proof undermines it all: 'at the moment of most intense lust, very excitable individuals, who are otherwise normal, commit such acts as biting and scratching, which are usually due to anger.' Not only does this imply that biting and scratching would not occur at any other time, it ignores the fact that they are more frequently accomplished by the supposedly sexless female. To then link these actions to male 'lust murderers' who 'during the most intense emotion of lust' inflict 'a real injury, wound or death' upon the victim, is to invert reality, call a fanciful speculation a logical step and rely upon the sexist concept of 'normal' gender relationships for a third time.

22: Sadomasochism

In the intercourse of the sexes, the active or aggressive role belongs to man; woman remains passive, defensive. It affords man great pleasure to win a woman, to conquer her; and in the art of lovemaking, the modesty of woman, who keeps herself on the defensive until the moment of surrender, is an element of great psychological significance and importance. Under the normal conditions man meets obstacles which it is his part to overcome and for which nature has given him an aggressive character. This aggressive character, however, under pathological conditions may likewise be excessively developed, and express itself in an impulse to subdue absolutely the object of desire, even to destroy or kill it.

To put it another way, what Krafft-Ebing was asking us to believe is that very randy men who biologically inherit a latent sadistic urge have it brought into the open during the early stages of marriage by coy wives, who, once they give birth, provoke and flame the latent sadism in their partners!

While a Victorian patriarch like Krafft-Ebing could be excused for producing this theory, contemporary popularizers and judges cannot be excused for relying upon it. They would have to believe both in the sexist stereotype upon which the definition and origin of sadism relies and in the concept of inherited 'impulses'. Ironically, they would then have to accept that sadism was not only 'an excessive and monstrous pathological intensification of phenomena – possible, too, in normal conditions in rudimental forms – which accompany the psychical sexual life particularly in males' but also 'due to an awakening of a latent *psychical disposition*, occasioned by external circumstances which in no way affect the normal individual'. And that would mean accepting that sadism is a rare congenital or moral abnormality in which sex actually plays a very marginal part.

Ironically, Krafft-Ebing, as we shall see later, was on much firmer ground when speculating about a possible relationship between lust and cruelty, in which

love and anger are not only the most intense emotions, but also the only two forms of robust emotion. Both seek their object, try to possess themselves of it, and naturally exhaust themselves in physical effect on it; both throw the psycho-motor sphere into the most intense excitement, and thus, by means of this excitation, reach their normal expression.

But while it might be true that

> When the association of and cruelty is present, not only does the lustful emotion awaken the impulse to cruelty, but vice versa; cruel ideas and acts of cruelty cause sexual excitement, and in this way are *used by perverse individuals*

it does not follow that

> it is clear how lust impels to acts that otherwise are expressive of anger. The one, like the other, is a state of exhortation, an intense excitation of the entire psycho-motor sphere. Thus there arises an impulse to react on the object that induces the stimulus, in every possible way and with the greatest intensity. Just as maniacal exaltation easily passes to raging destructiveness, so exertion of the sexual emotion often *induces an impulse* to spend itself in senseless and apparently harmful acts. To a certain extent these are physical accomplishments; but it is not simply an unconscious excitation of innervation of muscles, which also sometimes occurs as blind violence; it is a true hyperbole, a desire to exert the utmost possible effect upon the individual giving rise to the stimulus.

This is simply a moralistic assertion. Yet even if it were true, sadism being an inherited pathology, most people simply would not advance to this destructive state; they simply would not have it in them. As these pathological perverts were rare, even if sexual excitement, being a strong emotion, provoked destructive emotions so that a cross-transference of excitation lead to destructive behaviour, such events would also be rare, and the individuals concerned quickly expose themselves.

Given his gender stereotypes, it was hardly surprising that, when it came to the far more common masochists, Krafft-Ebing could not fathom out at all, and had to admit defeat:

The number of cases of undoubted masochism thus far observed is very large. Whether masochism occurs associated with normal sexual instincts, or exclusively controls the individual; whether or not, and to what extent, the individual subject to this perversion strives to realize his peculiar fancies; whether or not, he has thus more or less diminished his virility – depends upon the degree of intensity of the perversion in the single case, upon the strength of the opposing ethical and aesthetic motives, and the relative power of the physical and mental organization of the affected individual. From the psychopathic point of view, the essential and common element in all these cases is the fact that the sexual instinct is directed to ideas of subjugation and abuse by the opposite sex.

But directed by what? There seemed so many forms:

In masochism there is a gradation of the acts from the most repulsive and monstrous to the silliest, regulated by the degree of intensity of the perverse instinct and the power of the moral and aesthetic counter-motives. The extreme consequences of masochism, however, are checked by the instinct of self-preservation, and therefore murder and serious injury, which may be committed in sadistic excitement, have here in reality, so far as is known, no passive equivalent. But the perverse desires of masochistic individuals may in imagination attain these extreme consequences.

As the label 'perverse instinct' explains nothing, Krafft-Ebing was forced to fall back on another nineteenth-century stand-by explanation, and recorded that masochists 'are given to excesses, particularly masturbation, to which the difficulty of attaining what their fancy creates drives them again and again'. Masturbation, while having no role in directing sadism, was a perfectly acceptable reason for the reinforcement of subjugation fantasies, because male masochists were obviously weak-willed characters. Apart from not showing enough moral fibre, or exhibiting the right ethical and aesthetic standards in their behaviour, their masochism was 'unnatural' because men were supposed to have domination impulses, and not go around consciously behaving like women. Unfortunately for Krafft-Ebing, as most masochists' sex and fantasy lives were separate, his evidence did not fit the theory. He was completely baffled, for example, by his 'Case 57', who revelled in the idea of being mastered, and avidly read *Uncle Tom's Cabin* for inspiration; but having already made up his mind, Krafft-Ebing was hardly likely to look at the obvious social origins of his clients' sexual taste, and so lost the chance to discover why most masochists 'failed' to act out their fantasies and did not even bother to try to, even when obsessed, as 'Case 57', for example, found: 'The thought of a comedy with paid prostitutes always seemed so silly and purposeless, for a person hired by me could never take the place of my imagination of a "cruel mistress".'

Just as Krafft-Ebing's definition of sadism was undermined by his failure to prove the sadistic continuum, his concept of masochism fell apart, because he could not come to grips with the logic of masochistic fantasy. For him:

> the individual affected is controlled in his sexual feeling and thought by the idea of being completely and unconditionally subject to the will of a person of the opposite sex; of being treated by this person as a master, humiliated and abused. This idea is associatively suffused with sensual pleasure; such an individual revels in fantasies, in which he creates situations of this kind.

Yet, if masochists found the idea of subordination sensuous and created numerous fantasies about such situations, but rarely acted them out, masochism would amount to an acquired mental condition rather than an inherited active state; and Krafft-Ebing was only too well aware of the ramifications of this. Despite his suggestion that masochism may be a hereditary defect in *some* cases, he knew that its social origins meant that sadism might not be inherited after all.

Despite his beliefs about innate latent impulses, Krafft-Ebing's descriptions and definitions of the ideal type of masochism and sadism clearly constituted thought-processes. The only connection with innate conditions rested upon his positivistic belief that everything in the human psyche was ultimately reducible to biological and physiological processes. As this could not negate the role of fantasy, it is easy to see why this core contradiction between theory and evidence has constantly confused even the most intelligent readers. As Marcus noted:

> In one place he says that masochism is due to sexual response being pathologically high, so that everything, even pain, becomes a sexual stimulant; and in another place he says the opposite, that masochism is found in people who have lived too intensely and thus have blunted their senses to an extent that something extra in the way of titillation is needed for potency.

Krafft-Ebing could not get out of this ambiguous and contradictory mess for two reasons: his method, and his endearing inability to dismiss completely the role of the mind, free will and consciousness, despite his biologically determined theories.

When recording sexual 'abnormalities', Krafft-Ebing offered a definition of the 'condition', and then a series of subdivisions based upon his patients' genitals, head shape, height, build, heredity predispositions to disease, family antecedents and a mass of other futile data supposed to reveal the truth of the definition. He simply did not have the ability to utilize the content of the case histories laid out in this way. While naturalists using the same method record diversity as well as similarity, they would never claim to have explained their origins like Krafft-Ebing tried to. That generations of commentators and reviewers have neglected the absurdity of such methods follows from their simplistic adoption of Krafft-Ebing's definitions out of context. Yet, any case history chosen at random would quickly demonstrate how Krafft-Ebing's more articulate patients reveal far more about the prevailing form of analysis than about the origin of their own desires:

> I am thirty five years old, mentally and physically normal. Among all my relatives in the direct as well as in the lateral line, I know of no case of mental disorder . . . I have never masturbated in my life . . . in spite of its marked

pathological character, masochism is not only incapable of destroying my pleasure in life, but it does not in the least affect my outward life. When not in a masochistic state, as far as feeling and action are concerned, I am a perfectly normal man.

If people find his lists, descriptions and anecdotes confusing it is hardly surprising: Krafft-Ebing could not make sense of this mass of data either. His apparent contradictions are due to his lack of systematic analysis. Ultimately, he realized that as his patients exhibited no difficulty in choosing to indulge their proclivities or not as the fancy took them, he could not ignore free will. The only one suffering from a compulsion was Krafft-Ebing; he simply could not help himself making unscientific moral judgments based upon the limits of his cultural beliefs, whereby sex was for procreation and anything else was 'abnormal', if not dangerous. Consequently, the numerous lessons to be drawn from his case histories, which must be placed in their historical context, have been lost in the logic of Krafft-Ebing's selective theories. In reality these did rest to a great extent upon social factors, like trying to palm off contemporary cultural prejudices as science. When it suited his argument, for example, Krafft-Ebing did not hesitate to promote the ancient folk legend that Russian peasant women regarded a beating from their husbands as a sign of love. Likewise, he simply refused to believe that an advanced civilization which properly educated young ladies could ever produce sadistic women like Sacher-Masoch's heroines.

Consequently, once one realizes that Krafft-Ebing's theory really rested upon cultural influences – whereby the more 'elevated' the society is, the more greatly sexual proclivities differ between men and women – it's not too difficult to perceive that, whatever his patients were doing, Krafft-Ebing's account of sadomasochism could only ever reveal their reactions to stifling Victorian bourgeois sexual norms rather than any innate qualities that sadomasochism may consist of.

In order to discover the origin of the alleged impulse, and why the *idea of pain* could be sexually stimulating, one has to turn to Ellis and Bloch rather than Krafft-Ebing.

The power of the imagination

Havelock Ellis's claim to fame was his *Studies in the Psychology of Sex*, published between 1896 and 1928. Although he studied medicine, Ellis (1859–1939) did not practice but used the respectability conferred by a medical degree to promote the causes of sex education, birth control, divorce and homosexual equality. Unfortunately, despite these revolutionary pretensions, the *Studies* were rather boring, over-elaborate speculations about the 'sexual function' and dozens of other silly theories. They come alive only , and then only just, when discussing the origins and benefits of sexual 'deviations' which Ellis realized were common to relationships. In particular, Ellis was fascinated by the fact that some people appeared to find pain sexually stimulating; not least because he appears to have shared this tendency.

Ellis's theories on this subject were dominated by two ideas he shared with Krafft-Ebing: a possible link between the emotions of love (by which he meant sexual arousal) and those of anger and fear; and the relationship between the male's 'display of combativity' and the female's 'agglomeration of fears' when it came to having sex. Where he differed from Krafft-Ebing was in his recourse to the general arousal theory, which asserts that *all* states of arousal – be they anxiety, anger or sex – are physiologically indistinguishable; so that, for example, pain could stimulate sexual desire just as easily as it did anger or fear. Ellis thought that sadomasochism might emerge when a person's 'sex drive' was weak, and the emotions of anger and fear were effectively used as sources of sexual energy:

> Pain acts as a sexual stimulant because it is the most
> powerful of all methods of arousing the emotions . . .
>   In the ordinary healthy organism . . . although the
> stimulants of strong emotion may be vaguely pleasurable,
> they do not have more than a general action on the sexual
> sphere, nor are they required for the due action of the
> sexual mechanism. But in a slightly abnormal organism –
> whether the abnormality is due to a congenital
> neuropathetic condition, or to a possibly acquired
> neurasthenic condition, or merely to the physiological
> inadequacy of childhood or old age – the balance of

nervous energy is less favourable for the adequate play of the ordinary energies of courtship . . .

An organism in this state become particularly apt to seize upon the automatic sources of energy generated by emotion. The parched sexual instinct greedily drinks up and absorbs the force it obtains by applying abnormal stimuli to its emotional apparatus . . . the abnormal organism in this respect may become as dependent on anger or fear.

In this model, sadomasochistic 'pain' has nothing to do with an innate impulse; it is the means whereby the sensations aroused by a painful experience are transferred to a weak sex drive, which may exist for different reasons. It is only when the 'negative' emotions are very strong, so that they may overwhelm any erotic desire during the transfer, that the process becomes completely negative; but when this occurs the feelings that result would also be anger or fear rather than sexual. As we shall see later, this guess has been substantiated by modern psychological research; but this should not detract from the fact that as far as Ellis was concerned the process was both common and conscious; it had to be.

According to Ellis, far from being an aberration, sadism and masochism were part of everyday sexual intercourse.

At first sight the connection between love and pain – the tendency of men to delight in inflicting it and women in suffering it – seems strange and inexplicable . . . In understanding such cases we have to remember that it is only within limits that a woman really enjoys the pain, discomfort or subjection to which she submits. A little pain which the man knows he himself can soothe, a little pain which the woman gladly accepts as the sign and forerunner of pleasure – this degree of pain comes within the normal limits of love and is rooted, as we have seen, in the experience of the race.

Ellis believed that, in any physical force, from the possible discomfort of the initial act of penetration to a full-blown caning, the 'pain' involved was not only a transitory, natural, step to extensive pleasure, it was often directly experienced as pleasure. The more force was used, however, the more ground rules there had to be. For a successful masochistic transformation to take place, for example, 'the woman needs to be certain that she is not going to be hurt and that the pain is a clear token of love'. For a successful example of this, Ellis referred to one of his female patients who found 'pain' pleasurable as long as: she was absolutely sure of the man's love and had perfect confidence in his judgment; the pain was deliberately inflicted in kindness for her own improvement, as opposed to being accidental, or excessive; and that she was very sure of her own influence over the man. Sadomasochism was thus a combination of 'nature' and civilization.

Ellis was convinced that this human experience followed self-evident biological truths about all mammals, and had actually occurred from the time the male animal first pursued the female. Far from banishing such impulses as Krafft-Ebing supposed, Ellis thought it more likely that:

> the natural process of courtship, as it exists among animals and usually among the lower human races tends to become disguised and distorted in civilization, as well by economic conditions as by conventional social conditions and even ethical prescription. It becomes forgotten that the woman's pleasure is an essential element of the process of courtship . . . Thus various external checks which normally inhibit any passing over of masculine sexual energy into cruelty are liable to be removed.

In other words, if sadistic acts existed in civilized societies they did so because civilization had proscribed 'rough and tumble sex' and women's enjoyment of it. By insisting that women should behave in a delicate way, society had caused numerous problems, including converting what was a natural sexual relationship into a system of male dominance over the female.

While this made perfect sense to Ellis, and appeals to many of today's 'sexual radicals', this tidy little theory is dependent upon the core sexist stereotype, and is not without its contradictions either; the major one being that individuals exhibiting the sadomasochistic tendency did not neatly divide into a sadistic or masochistic category. Ellis's sensible way out of that latter problem was to ditch the bipolar division, which he thought was based upon a misreading of de Sade:

> The attempt to define sadism strictly and penetrate to its roots in de Sade's personal temperament reveals a certain weakness in the current conception of this sexual perversion. It is not . . . a perversion due to excessive masculinity . . . the most extreme and elaborate forms of sadism are more apt to be allied with a somewhat feminine organization.

Ellis also realized that to be a successful sexual sadist one would have to understand the masochists' desires. His own case studies, and a critical review of previous accounts, including Krafft-Ebing's, convinced Ellis that 'there is no real line of demarcation' between sadists and masochists; and he suggested that even de Sade could not be regarded as a pure sadist, given his masochistic experiences. As a result, Ellis became embroiled in the early debate over terminology, and backed those who sought a term to cover the dual tendency. Fere had offered sexual algophily and Notzing algolagnia; based upon the Greek 'algos' or pain, and 'lagneia' or lust. But neither term proved any more illuminating, and the original terminology still proved useful to Ellis in his attempt to create a typology of degrees of sadomasochism.

Ellis's typology offered a means of transcending Krafft-Ebing's awkward third category, and demonstrated that the more closely one looked at *active* sadomasochism, the less importance one could attach to the notions of cruelty and harm. Ellis thought it was obvious that sadists who became sexually aroused by violent thoughts, like the woman who fantasized about torture while inflicting bites upon her husband and the teenager who could orgasm only while thinking of flowing blood, were very different from those who had mastered their desires and carefully incorporated them into consensual love play. The latter exhibited two abilities not shared by the former. First, those who were sexually active always seemed to be able to switch between the sadistic and masochistic roles. Ellis was so impressed with this switchability that he offered it as the major proof that the tendencies were symbiotic. Second, he also noted that sadomasochists also demonstrated an ability to intellectualize their sexual 'perversion' and could control their feelings and desires, unlike those who were compulsive or manifested a non-sexually-orientated form of 'sadism'.

By examining the role of the human will and imagination, the very aspects that Krafft-Ebing ignored, Ellis not only isolated what separated out devotees from the others and effectively undermined the central role that 'pain' was supposed to play in sadomasochism, he offered a way out of Krafft-Ebing's quagmire. Speaking of one case study, Ellis noted that:

> From the first he has loved to invent stories in which whippings were the climax, and at thirteen such stories produced the first spontaneous emission. He has even written comedies in which whipping plays a prominent part. He has, moreover, searched the public libraries for references to flagellation, inserted queries in the *Intermédiaire des Chercheurs et des Curieux*, and thus obtained a complete bibliography of flagellation which is of considerable value.

This person has even turned a source of sexual stimulation into an academic exercise which he then used to help himself understand and increase the enjoyment of his proclivity. Contrary to Krafft-Ebing's belief, Ellis thought that all real devotees would want to realize their fantasies whenever possible, but that they would not leave the imagination behind once they did, because, as a contrived reality would rarely replicate their favoured fantasy exactly, they would have to adapt to circumstances:

> A situation appears to one in imagination and one at once desires to transfer it to the realms of fact, being oneself one of the principal actors. If it is the passive side which appeals to one, one would prefer to be passive; but if that is not obtainable then one takes the active part as next best. In either case, however, it is the realization of the imagined situation that gives the pleasure, not the other person's pleasure as such, although his or her supposed pleasure creates the situation.

This switchability not only made nonsense of Krafft-Ebing's core divisions, it meant that the proclivity was as cerebral as it was physical; and that realization opened up the possibility that sexual arousal could emanate from a transfer of the emotional excitement induced by a mental representation of one's fantasy as easily as any physical experience of 'pain'.

The essence of sadism-masochism, therefore, was not so much the enjoyment of 'pain' as the overwhelming of one's senses, or what Ellis called the 'joy of emotional intoxication'. Pain could still have a specific function, but

> Pain . . . largely constitutes a special case of what we shall later learn to know as erotic symbolism: that is to say, the psychic condition in which part of the sexual process, a single idea or group of ideas, tends to assume unusual importance, or even to occupy the whole field of sexual consciousness, the part becoming a symbol that stands for the whole.

In other words, 'pain' was only one of many ideas or actions which could be transferred into an intense emotional feeling in order to enhance one's sexual experience; and its imaginative use to this end demarcated those who utilized 'pain' for sexual pleasure, and those who held a cruel disposition. According to Ellis, this was true for de Sade, whose extreme fantasies were developed in solitary confinement. To miss or underestimate the role of the imagination in his work meant that one ran 'the risk of confounding de Sade and his like with others of whom Judge Jeffreys was the sinister type'. By making de Sade a typical instance of the group of perversions he represents, and adding his own observation that 'it is pain only, and not cruelty that is the essential in this group of manifestations', Ellis argued that we came nearer to the explanation of the phenomena. The masochist's experience of 'pain' had to be inflicted in love, and the sadist's infliction of pain was designed to be felt as love:

> we have thus to recognize that sadism by no means involves any love of inflicting pain outside the sphere of sexual emotion, and is even compatible with a high degree of general tender heartedness. We have also to recognize that even within the sexual sphere the sadist by no means wishes to exclude the victims' pleasure and may even regard that pleasure as essential to his own satisfaction. We have, further, to recognize that, in view of the close

connection between sadism and masochism, it is highly probable that in some cases the sadist is really a disguised masochist and enjoys his victim's pain because he identifies himself with that pain.

If Ellis was correct, this sexual 'pain' had nothing to do with cruelty whatsoever, being designed to engender pleasure; and many so-called sadists would really prefer to be masochists. 'Sadistic' cruelty was something else entirely. Ellis also reserved the term 'algolagnia' to the special class of cases in which the thought or the spectacle of painful acts provoked sexual stimulation in persons who identified themselves with neither party. To class them as sadists was incorrect, because they could just as easily be called masochists given that 'they reveal an undifferential connection between sexual excitement and pain, not developed into either active or passive participation'. As this group rarely indulged in sexual activities themselves, it would then become very easy to make a distinction between sadomasochists who utilized painful pleasures in sex games, those who gained some sexual excitement by watching violent acts and those who enjoyed inflicting pain upon others. When discussing the first group:

> It is scarcely correct to use the word 'cruelty' in connection with the phenomena . . . The persons who experience these impulses usually show no love of cruelty outside the sphere of sexual emotion; they may even by very intolerant to cruelty.

After all, those who attempted to activate their fantasies were generally highly sensitive children and the most tender of adults: 'The strong man is more apt to be tender than cruel, or at all events knows how to restrain within bounds any impulse to cruelty.' In contrast, the most extreme forms of sadism were invariably exercised by imbeciles, and the most elaborate amongst females.

In short, active sexual sadomasochism had little to do with pain, and everything to do with emotional pleasure. When pain was used as a stimulant it was only one amongst many other forms of stimulation used. Those who enjoyed cruelty for its own sake, like those who became aroused by watching violence, were a different breed; demarcated by their inability to switch, or even consider alternative, roles. As those who acted out their fantasies relied heavily upon their imagination to affect their pleasure, sado-masochism could hardly be a regressive urge born of some kind of atavistic primordialism or genetic immoral impulse; the intellectualism involved, and the way devotees gained command of their senses, would place it upon a plane above the simple sex urge. Talk of 'pain' therefore, was a nonsense, though it took Magnus Hirschfeld, the German psychiatrist and sexologist (1868–1935), to spell out what Ellis was talking about:

> The expression 'pain' becomes devoid of all meaning when that which normally causes pain induces in the masochist not pain or a sensation of discomfort, but, on the contrary a sensation of pleasure. We can avoid this paradox only by adopting, instead of the term 'pain-craving', the scientifically more exact term 'stimulation craving'. The masochist requires far more intensive affect of his senses than the normal person. (1971)

Sadism–masochism was a search for pleasure, not pain.

The truth does not hurt

I feel a little sorry for Iwan Bloch (1872–1922), the Berlin physician who specialized in venereal diseases. Despite inventing sexology, utilizing comparative analysis, and revealing the universality of algolagnia, which he defined as 'painful lasciviousness', Bloch is ignored by contemporary students. Yet without him, most popular accounts and explanations of Edwardian sexuality from 'corset discipline' to 'lust murderers' would not exist, because Bloch endeavoured to include everything he could cram under the label algolagnia from the practice of 'lathering' bodies in brothels to sexual kleptomania. Likewise, though Bloch's accounts, such as *Strange Sexual Practices* (1933), may look somewhat naive today, he worked hard to dismiss many contemporary sexual 'myths' and was one of his period's more critical thinkers. He quickly realized, for example, that 'lust murder' was far rarer than often assumed, having noticed that most of the examples offered were actually post-rape murders to eliminate the witness.

Bloch's motive was science, not sensationalism; and we would do well to emulate him; unfortunately he could not help being controversial. His contemporaries did not want to hear that 'sexual abnormalities', far from being pathological, were really quite common amongst 'ordinary' individuals, that they could be found almost everywhere, 'independently of time, place, racial conditions and cultural forms', and that aberrations and deviations were as essential to life as the 'sex impulse' itself.

As far as algolagnia was concerned, there does not seem much to choose between Bloch and Ellis at first sight. Bloch thought algolagnia was a natural desire. It was 'an elementary phenomenon of amatory activity', had its origins in our primeval animal instincts and merely reflected the 'indissoluble association' between pleasure and pain, even though some contemporary forms reflected social factors or some forms of spirituality. Bloch, who waded through a vast amount of anthropological and ethnological data to offer example after example to 'prove' his points, was also convinced that 'actual physical pain' was rarely involved, mainly because the algolagniac sought pleasure rather than pain.

> The pleasure anyone experiences in his own pain, or in that of another, constitutes the nucleus of all aloglanistic phenomena, and to cruelty as an intermediator in this painful lasciviousness there belongs only a secondary role.

Like Ellis, Bloch also believed that the true algolagniac sought satisfaction in sexual interaction rather than in substitutes or vicarious forms, and that it was the mental intensification required to secure pleasure which enabled one to separate algolagnia from the 'certain instincts deeply rooted in the soul of the people'. How and why this division occurred Bloch could only guess, but drawing upon de Sade's speculations for clues, he opted for a person's emotional experience:

> the principal cause of the actions in which cruelty becomes pleasurable is the powerful emotional disturbance, the violent excitement . . . 'All sensations increase one another mutually.' Anger, fear, rage, hatred, cruelty, increase sexual tension, and therefore also increase the pleasure of the discharge of that tension.

However, while both Krafft-Ebing and Ellis had toyed with the same idea when seeking the ambiguity between universality and individual forms, Bloch effectively reversed the order of events. As far as he was concerned, the person's desire for sexual pleasure came first, and the highly charged emotional circumstances which were then utilized to enhance that pleasure were related to other tendencies the individual possessed. But if Bloch's model was somewhat more simplistic than Ellis's, his observations and categories were far more socially orientated.

For Bloch, while not every manifestation of algolagnia involved sex, and fewer still were motivated by cruelty, every case had to be considered in its historical and social context. One of the worst examples of 'sadism' as opposed to algolagnia he came across was 'tropical frenzy': the 'condition' found almost exclusively amongst Europeans occupying positions of imperial officialdom with extensive powers, which the office-holder would never exercise at home, where the person would also hold to conventional morality and social relationships. When this power was matched with a personal belief that the indigenous population was an inferior race, the Europeans would indulge their 'impulses'. Similar tendencies, Bloch claimed, could be found amongst civilized people wherever they oversaw systems of slavery and serfdom.

In other words, the form algolagnia would take depended upon both the individuals and the circumstances they found themselves in; there was nothing in the core condition that made it necessarily harmful or dangerous; and in highly civilized societies the individual form would be determined by how that society organized its forms of sexual courtship,

Like both Krafft-Ebing and Ellis, Bloch believed that the form algolagnia took in society was primarily shaped by the way in which men and women dealt with the female's ability to withhold sexual pleasure from men despite her social subordination.

> The greater the sexual passivity and coldness of the woman, the more readily does she gain dominance over the man . . . In so far as man becomes the 'slave' and victim of his sensuality, does he exhibit a masochistic disposition; but, in so far as by his force and his intelligence he overcomes this sexual dependency, and by means of his

natural activity and energy displayed also in sexual relationships, behaves heedlessly and brutally to the woman, who has now become completely passive, does the sadistic element preponderate in him.

The possibility of a man becoming a masochistic wimp or a callous sadist did not, however, mean that either would occur; algolagnia could develop in any direction, and was one not two separate conditions.

From this we are able to understand how it is that sadism and masochism may often appear in the same person; they are only the active and passive form respectively of the algolagnia which lies at the basis of both of them, and in which the true essence of both these phenomena subsists.

Though such an explanation leads no nearer to the origins of algolagnia, Bloch had at least drawn attention to the way in which it was multi-causal in origin and situational in its manifestations. The most common form, flagellamania, for example, required a physical reaction for the stimulation to work, 'much assistance' from the imagination, a prior development of the passive or active side, and the initial arousal through 'some chance occurrence'; but the form it would finally take would also depend upon the historical and social context.

Amongst Bloch's other more interesting contributions to the debate was the assertion that passive algolagnia, which he defined as a 'desire to endure pain and degradation and abasement of every kind, for the purpose of inducing sexual excitement', was far more common than active algolagnia. He also used the testimony of professional dominatrixes to initiate several ideas that later became popular, including the suggestion that passive algolagnia was particularly prevalent amongst socially powerful men such as lawyers, judges and state officials for whom it acted as 'a kind of liberation from conventional pressure and the professional mask'. Bloch suggested that while women's physical masochism was far less common because of their greater 'command over their sexual impulse', many exhibited a physiological masochism of a more spiritual kind. On the other hand, he noted that it was not unknown for women 'of good position' to play the part of prostitutes, be it in brothels or on the streets, and that many more 'endured sexual relationships with men of lower classes, such as workmen, coach-men, etc. and . . . even seek sexual enjoyment with any casual member of the rabble they may meet on the streets'. Whatever way you looked at it, masochism in a civilized society appeared to be an indulgence of the bourgeois classes, took innumerable forms and need not involve physical pain at all.

A *non-existent condition*

While most people simply quote from the theories prompted by those responsible for 'discovering' and defining sadomasochism in order to support their prejudices, a serious application of the theories is not possible without an attempt to reconcile their differences. This is not difficult. The disagreements, for example, can easily be explained by their theories and the exact nature of their studies. As he worked with criminal types, subscribed to eugenic theories concerning heredity and character defects, Krafft-Ebing concluded that sadomasochism was an abnormality. As Ellis conducted a personal crusade against the sexual norms of the time, he suggested that civilization has distorted our natural inclinations and argued that sadomasochism was one of the results. Bloch's extensive research into the world's sexual practices encouraged him to speculate on the universality of such tendencies, and the importance of particular cultural manifestations.

The very fact that their theories are otherwise so diverse makes their similarities all the more significant. In one way or another, algolagnia appeared to be an exaggerated form of a natural tendency within sexual intercourse; there appeared to be a link between 'pain' and pleasurable sensations. Though these specula-tions rested upon somewhat sexist assumptions, especially the inference that sadomasochism was essentially a means of accommo-dating or indulging males' lustful thoughts, sadomasochism was definitely tied up with the human ability of emotional and physical sensation transference, especially that of turning thoughts of humiliation or 'pain' into pleasure. The individual's ability to do this varied, as the physical-emotional experience was partly determined by personal experience, situational circumstances, contemporary sexual practices and norms and the role of imagination. Though Krafft-Ebing held to a belief that the experience was also pathological, and dependent upon innate impulses, he could not really justify this belief. All three also agreed, in contradistinction to modern British judicial opinion, that sadomasochism did not consist of two distinct tendencies, that it did not necessarily involve physical pain, and that it required a high degree of imaginative and 'intellectual' input. While Krafft-Ebing insisted that there was a possible link between all forms of overt sadism, he could not substantiate this either; but Ellis and Bloch both offered good reasons why the ability to control desires and switchability could be used to distinguish clearly between sexually active sadomasochists and anti-social individuals who were motivated by cruelty or hate rather than by the desire to enhance sexual arousal. The reason why they could not be completely sure was that such cases rarely figured in the case files. Finally, even though Krafft-Ebing and Ellis were not aware of the ramifications, all three clearly alluded to the way sadomasochism was shaped by contemporary sexual practices and norms; which obviously meant that if the 'natural' relationship between the sexes changed, sadomasochism's manifestations would too. They were not fixed for all time. So little was actually known, and so much remained to be discovered, that it would be correct to say that 'sadomasochism' as such did not exist as a definite entity.

Looking back it is easy to be amused by the foolishness of some of their speculations, but it is indisputable that what these early theorists defined as 'sadism' and sadomasochism bore little relationship to the fears voiced by the Spanner judges. Their assertions appear to rest upon a couple of quotes from Krafft-Ebing, and a lot of half-baked Freudianism, which in the last sixty years has drowned out the early theorists' insights into the interaction between repressed desires, social conventions and the role of the imagination in sadomasochism by incessant psychobabble.

Chapter two

Psychobabble

OUR failure to distinguish between SM acts, a non-existent entity called 'sadomasochism' and the cruel vicarious 'sadist' follows from the lack of attention to the early theorists' clear distinction between violent cruelty and an intellectualized system of arousal transference which occasionally utilized pain as a stimulant. But the real problem can be traced to the power we grant to psychiatry. For, although psychiatrists have been churning out hundreds of papers about 'sadomasochism' for almost a century, it is highly debatable whether or not their theories and conclusions really concern sadomasochism, let alone SM devotees; and the damage we have allowed them to cause is incalculable.

Fraud

Just when Bloch and other sexologists seemed to be getting somewhere with their theories about sadomasochism, along came Sigmund Freud (1856–1939), a failed hypnotist and cocaine addict, whose 'talking technique' and extrapolations about clients' experiences based upon sexually violent religious myths made Mesmerism look positively scientific.

In any event, Freud's comments about sadism and his three attempts to explain masochism – *Three Contributions to the Theory of Sex* (1905), *A Child Is Being Beaten* (1919) and *The Economic Problem in Masochism* (1924) – were all shaped by his own preoccupations rather than anything said by his clients on the couch, or by an SM devotee. As a result, the more Freud said, the less sense he made. Far from enlightening anyone about people's sexual proclivities, Freud was actually inventing psychobabble: the tendency to talk more and more about less and less concerning people's mental states and motivations, without recourse to systematic research.

Freud's initial account, like most others, rested upon the stereotypical dichotomy between male aggression and female passivity in sex. He believed that the roots of active algolagnia could be found in the fact that

> The sexuality of most men shows an admixture of aggression, the desire to subdue, the biological significance of which lies in the necessity for overcoming the resistance of the sexual object by actions other than mere *courting*. Sadism would then correspond to an aggressive component of the sexual instinct which has become exaggerated.

So far, nowhere. Freud then considered contemporary popular usage and suggested that 'strictly speaking' only 'an absolute attachment of the gratification to the subjection and maltreatment of the object' could 'claim the name perversion'. But, as this threatened to make some sense, Freud quickly changed his mind; perhaps sadism was the result of the child witnessing 'the primal scene':

> If children at an early age witness sexual intercourse between adults . . . they invariably regard the sex act as some sort of ill-treatment or act of subjugation: they view it, that is, in a sadistic sense. Psychoanalysis also shows us that an impression of this kind in early childhood contributes a great deal towards a predisposition to a subsequent sadistic displacement of the sexual aim.

As that conveniently explained everything, even though he had no proof whatsoever that all sadists had witnessed such an event, Freud moved on to masochism. In its 'extreme form' the 'gratification is connected with suffering of physical and mental pain at the hands of the sexual object', and comprises 'all passive attitudes to the sexual life and to the sexual object'. Then it dawned upon Freud that if he simply copied everyone else he would have two problems.

The major problem he faced was that, psychoanalytically, masochism did not make sense. As all mental process in Freud's original model were governed by a principle of pleasure and avoiding pain, the masochist's desires were incomprehensible, and threatened the theory. To make matters worse, as everyone else was abandoning the bipolar division between sadism and masochism, Freud's whole model of psychiatry, based as it was upon immutable biologically determined gender patterns, was also under threat. Freud was in a mess; and it was hardly surprising given that he could delude himself that as 'certain perverted tendencies regularly appear in contrasting pairs . . . [this] . . . is of great theoretical value', without realizing that he had created that 'fact', through his own categorization system, in the first place.

As Freud did not want to start all over again, he decided that the easiest solution was to explain away sadism's origins as a transmutation of a death instinct, in which the variation in degree might be explained by 'the infantile connection between fighting and sexual excitement'. It sounded good, but it relied upon a feeble misrepresentation of others' speculations:

> That cruelty and the sexual instinct are most intimately
> connected is beyond doubt taught by the history of
> civilisation, but in the explanation of this connection no
> one has gone beyond the accentuation of the aggressive
> factors of the libido. The aggression which is mixed with
> the sexual instinct is, according to some authors, a
> remnant of cannibalistic lust – that is, a participation of
> the domination apparatus, which serves also for the
> gratification of the other ontogenetically older needs. It has
> also been claimed that every pain contains in itself the
> possibility of a pleasurable sensation. Let us be satisfied
> with the impression that the explanation given concerning
> this perversion is by no means satisfactory and that it is
> possible that many psychic strivings unite herein into one
> effect.

Given the work of Krafft-Ebing, Ellis and Bloch, the only person who would be satisfied with such an 'impression' was someone not competent to realize that if the 'striking peculiarity' of this 'perversion' was that the active and passive forms were usually found in the same person, the ramifications of the complementary observation that 'he who experiences pleasure by causing pain to others in sexual relations is also capable of *experiencing pain in sexual relation as pleasure*' would be pretty 'striking' as well.

So it comes as no surprise that, rather than ditch his model, Freud did what his followers have been doing ever since: blame the patient. In the *Three Contributions*, Freud insisted that the masochists had turned their sadism upon themselves, with a little help from the castration complex and guilt. As this made masochism a product of sadism his model was safe – for a time.

Ten years on, Freud changed his mind. In *Instincts and Their Vicissitudes* (1915), he now suggested that sadists were interested in exercising power over others; but *if*, for any reason, the sadist replaced the 'other' with himself, he would then develop an obsessional neurosis, and *if* the sadist then bumped into someone who also fancied the idea of acting out the sadist's initial interests, then the first sadist would become the second sadist's masochist. The discovery of this 'reversal into the opposite' just happened to coincide with another theoretical shift; Freud could now ignore the problem of the pleasure principle. The masochist, it turned out, was not really seeking 'non-pleasure' at all; since any strong excitation in an infant would produce 'sexual' pleasure, *if* this event was immediately followed by an unpleasant one, the infant would learn to seek the initial pleasure experienced through a repetition of the unpleasant event. Just like that.

By the time he then wrote *A Child Is Being Beaten*, which attempted to relate the development of an allegedly common 'beating fantasy' to his model of childhood sexuality, Freud had finally caught up with some of Krafft-Ebing's speculations:

> the influence of the school was so clear that the patients concerned were at first tempted to trace back their beating-fantasies exclusively to these impressions of school life, which dated from later than their sixth year. But it was never possible for them to maintain this position: the fantasies had already been in existence before.

But try as he might, Freud's attempt to link the three-phase beating-fantasy process – in which a disassociating child finds the beating, which occurs simultaneously with the repression of love of the mother, not only a punishment for the forbidden sexual relationship but also an erotic regressive replacement – to his more general theory ended in failure. He was finally forced to admit that 'little light is thrown upon the genesis of masochism by our [*sic*] discussion of the beating fantasy'.

Never mind: *Beyond the Pleasure Principle*, which appeared a year later, transcended all these problems by inventing the 'death instinct'. Everything could now be explained by the fusion of the libido and aggressiveness. As the pleasure principle could not possibly lead anyone to injure the object of their desire, there had to be a death instinct which ensured that those whose libido was narcissistic were not governed by the ego. This was all very convenient; and Freud showed that he knew he was pulling a fast one by hedging the explanation with numerous caveats. It was 'plausible', and:

> If such an assumption as this is permissible, then we have met the demand that we should produce an example of a death instinct . . . but this way of looking at things is very far from being easy to grasp and creates a positively mystical impression. It looks suspiciously as though we were trying to find a way out of a highly embarrassing situation at any price.

Yet Freud promptly ignored this understatement of the century when he completely rewrote the definition of masochism and made it a primary impulse which could evolve into two or four other manifestations depending upon which texts you read.

The first, primary *erotogenic masochism*, like primary sadism, was the product of a clash between the life and death instincts, which left traces of the carnage all over the place. Whereas the sadistic survivors hiding in the superego promoted a 'will to power' partially overcoming the death instinct, some of the fallout left in the physical organism interacted with the libido to produce the mutant 'primary masochism'. If the subject was then confronted with tension-producing stimuli, such as the kind of pain and anxiety experienced in infancy, the end result was a relatively unaggressive and nonsexual person, which Freud called 'woman', or an atypical and usually impotent male. Males who developed this feminine masochism were effectively being castrated, or copulated with, or giving birth through fantasies and behaviours involving gagging, being beaten or acting in a subservient manner. But if, as more often happened, an unconscious sense of guilt then prompted the masochist into self-destructive acts, the more numerous *moral masochists* emerge, and, as the original sexual aspect becomes detached, these people are left with a strong feeling of unconscious guilt which leads them to crave various forms of punishment.

In short, Freud's rationales for masochism are mystical, and look suspiciously as though they were simply a means to evade a highly embarrassing theoretical problem at any price.

The simple reason why Freud could not really understand anything about sadomasochism, and why his followers never have done either, was that psychiatrists simply refuse to accept that people might just use their conscious mind when developing their sexual desires; yet Freud even noted that

> In my patient's milieu it was almost always the same books
> whose contents gave a new stimulus to the beating
> fantasies: those accessible to young people such as the so
> called *Bibliothèque Rose*, *Uncle Tom's Cabin* etc. The
> child began to compete with these works of fiction by
> producing its own fantasies and by constructing a wealth
> of situations, and even whole institutions, in which
> children were beaten or were punished and disciplined in
> some other way because of their naughtiness and bad
> behaviours.

Like the psychiatrists who followed him, Freud considered that his patients were puppets guided solely by strings made of unconscious desires and fears pulled by a puppeteer called childhood trauma. As Freud could never envisage a child getting bored and cutting the strings, or becoming angry and striking back at the puppeteer, Freud thought he could catalogue the puppet's actions, write a new script and build a completely new puppet theatre complete with scenery and a light show so that the puppet could only ever play on the Freudian stage. Then Freud picked up a megaphone to draw an audience, and became the biggest mountebank in history, as the case of masochism reveals.

Behind all the babble that followed from his assertions stand Freud's stereotypical attitudes about masculinity and femininity, which were far worse than anything Krafft-Ebing relied upon. Freud was adamant that no man should ever really 'surrender' to a female; for to do so was against nature. *Female masochism*, on the other hand, was a 'fact' and, far from having anything to do with thousands of years of women's social subordination, re-codified and justified by Victorian patriarchal apologists like Freud, this 'inferiority' was not only 'natural' but Freud was convinced he had the psychological explanation of how nature turned out women the way it did. This made Freud very happy: the 'feminine type' as far as he was concerned was the least 'mysterious' of all forms of masochism, and was the most accessible to observation, because it was the end result of the normal psycho-sexual development. Once little girls discovered that their clitoris was smaller than a boy's penis, they developed envy, failed to work through their Oedipus complex, and ended up hating their own gender, by blaming their mother for making them girls. Oh, and by the way, that is why little girls do not masturbate. Meanwhile, if a little boy's death instinct is introjected and supplements the primary 'erotogenic' form, secondary forms of masochism appear, from a desire to be beaten to wanting to give birth, depending upon the influence of the oral, anal and genital phases of the boy's life. If the death-wish does not introject, then he grows up wanting to be treated like a naughty little child or seeks passivity in intercourse as a castrated female – hence the label female masochism. But while some of Freud's pupils, like Otto Rank, quickly saw through this assumption of naturalness and realized that women were pushed into behaving the way men wanted them to, they failed to see the more obvious problem with the whole theory.

Compared to the other early theorists, Freud had an extremely limited number of case studies and reflections to draw upon. Rather than attempt to consider the question of algolagnia after extensive observation and full consideration of its manifestations, he simply sought to force it into his wider model. By linking the sadomasochistic 'perversion' to the Oedipus complex, then to stages of a child's sexual development and the 'pleasure principle', he was seeking to 'prove' that the intriguing similarities noted by other definers were merely secondary elements of a core 'perverse' sexuality. In redefining sadism and masochism as a pathological throwback to our primeval heritage or inescapable childhood trauma, Freud could then ignore the implications of the dual tendency, and dismiss the necessity of the fantasy element as merely the means of bringing these dangerous traits to the surface. While this might please moralists, who completely miss the implications of the moral masochism category, everything for Freud was a perversion of a non-existent state.

At best, all Freud really achieved was to stigmatize sadomasochism at the very time others were trying to make society come to terms with itself. As the sociologist M.S. Weinberg (Weinberg *et al.*, 1984) once put it:

> Sadomasochism is a good example of the way a pathological condition is established by the medical community, for until it became a diagnosis it received little attention and was not even classified as a sin.

If sadomasochists had had a problem coming to terms with their desires within the Victorian sexual moral straitjacket, then after Freud, they also had to contend with being diagnosed as perverts, despite the fact that the use of numerous forms of physical and mental pain during sex has been acceptable as far back as the *Kama Sutra*, if not before.

Your turn

Given the ambiguous, contradictory and confusing foundation of psychiatry's analysis of sadomasochism, it is hardly surprising that nothing has made sense since. During the 1920s, everyone got in on the act, though the popular conception of sadomasochism which stuck probably stems from J. Sadger's *Contribution to the Understanding of Sadomasochism* (1926). Sadger believed that the 'condition' began early in infants. Those who felt the effects of a withdrawal of sexual stimuli, through toilet training, prevention of masturbation or castration fears, more than the positive pleasure it had given them in the first place became sadists. Masochism was caused by a rough parent cleaning the genitals, invoking castration fears simultaneously with pleasurable sensations.

By the 1930s, when Freud's followers began to quibble amongst themselves, several took their cue from Alfred Adler (1870–1937), who sensibly ditched all talk of pleasure principles and death instincts, and considered the way the human psyche was influenced by the need for dominance and affiliation. For a time this led to greater attention being paid to social factors such as the constant anxiety invoked by the clash between people's desire to dominate or control others in their search for autonomy and the contrary desire to be indistinguishable and dependent upon others. Sadism and masochism were seen as extremes in this continuum. The sadist, being frustrated and feeling exploited, humiliates and enslaves others as a self-demonstration of strength and to feel protected from the fearful unknown quantities of life; or, as Karen Horney put it, sadism was a neurotic need for superiority. Masochists accepted exploitation and humiliation to prove that they were not a threat, were uncompetitive and ever-loving, seeking to enlist others in the cause of protecting themselves against the unknowns of life. Horney, being a bit of a feminist, finally threw out the Oedipus complex too. In her *The Problem of Feminine Masochism* (1973), masochism became a means of loving the sadistic actions of the 'love object', and derived from the attempt to convince oneself that parental controls were an affirmation of love, rather than hate. The masochist had effectively developed a strategy whereby active suffering avoided the need to face the fears that feelings of passive weakness or insignificance would invoke. In this perspective, sadism and masochism were the means of adapting to one's socialization and the vagaries of life, rather than some obscure sexual tendency; and analysts spent a lot of time dealing with the far more common symbolic forms these tendencies can take in order to help the individual become less anxious or dependent.

The real breakthrough finally came in 1941 when Theodore Reik's *Masochism in Modern Man* finally caught up with Ellis and Hirschfeld. Despite simplistically asserting that sadists, being aggressive characters, really gained pleasure in their fantasies or actions against others, Reik reopened the original line of enquiry by suggesting that masochists were seeking pleasure rather than pain:

Pleasure is the aim, never to be abolished, and the masochistic staging is but a circuitous way to reach that aim. The urge for pleasure is so powerful that anxiety and the idea of punishment themselves are drawn into its sphere.

But any hope of a renaissance was dashed during the 1950s. By then it was becoming difficult to keep up with all the new theories. Bernard Berliner (1958) proposed that masochism was an attempt to preserve the pre-Oedipal oral level of object attachment, in the face of unloving and cruel objects. Far from being the child's sadism turned upon itself, it was a pathological way of loving a person who replies with hate and ill-treatment: an adaptive response to a cruel and harsh traumatic environment. Not quite, said R.M. Loewenstein (1957). Masochism could just as easily follow from fears of castration and object loss. Yes, by inviting punishment the masochist turned the dangerous unloving parent into a loving one, but one should never prioritize pre-Oedipal experiences, however influential, over the Oedipus complex's crucial effects. Yes, psychiatry has an obsession with monocausality, but people will have to accept that masochism is the repression of incestuous fantasies in which the subject tries to handle 'the forbidden' by enacting a scene of punishment, which amounts to a sort of symbolic castration threat. F.S. Friedenburg (1956) rewrote everything, and put it down to children's teething stages.

During the 1960s the haggling over whether, and which feature of, the pre-Oedipal or Oedipal stage was seminal got louder and louder, and the issue over dual or separate tendencies came to a head. The wooden spoon goes to S. Panken (1967), who was adamant they were separate phenomena, and trawled over imaginary rather than the real contradictions in Freud's earliest abandoned concepts, ultimately insisting: 'It seems highly questionable, however, that roles may be reversed with such ease.' Edmond Bergler (1961) thought that all neurosis in life followed from an initial form of 'psychic' masochism, a kind of infant megalomania, acquired in the first eighteen months. All infants experience the same fears of starvation, being devoured, being poisoned, being choked, being chopped to pieces, being chained and being castrated. They are, however, simultaneously dependent upon the mother who invokes these fears. As the infants' fury can hardly be directed against the source of that satisfaction, they turn it upon themselves in an attempt to gain their omnipotent control.

By the time women began taking to the streets in the early 1970s, psychoanalysis was finally, or so it thought, facing up to its sexist roots. Jack Novick and Kelly Novick (1991), for example, even came up with a female version of the beating fantasy. Young girls, apparently, despite suffering from intense libidinous wishes towards their fathers, also had a desire to be punished for these incestuous wishes. They then promptly ditched the beating fantasy in boys, reserving it for those with deeply disturbed ego and drive development.

Where this innate capacity for infants to know that their non-existent incestuous desires are morally wrong comes from, was never explained; but this awkward question can be avoided by opting for C.W. Socarides' concept (1958) of the 'demonic mother', whereby sadists suffer first from a pre-Oedipal fear of merging and fusing with their mothers and then from their subsequent guilt. Esther Menaker (1979) thought we should concentrate on the centrality of the ego, the person's desperate attempt to maintain self-worth, and the mothers' responses; they were as crucial to this ego development as they were for instinctual satisfaction. Alternatively, you can embrace N.C. Avery's scenario (1977), which proves that the solution to all problems is the simplest route, by seeing sadists as trying to control their fear of the loss of their Oedipal object, be it their parents' deaths, indifference or hostility. If you are getting bored, follow R. Robertiello (1970); imagine what 'must' actually take place, and throw in some real sex to hold the reader's interest. Female masochism, apparently, follows a girl's rage towards an uncaring mother; but, because little girls are not allowed to express their rage outwardly, they cunningly manipulate their fathers to do the deed instead. As long as you accept that it is inevitable that a small child will do this – that the child will be able to gain her satisfaction by making sure that she will get the opportunity to see her parents having intercourse, that the scene will be interpreted as an act of aggression against her mother, but that the child will simultaneously engage in mother empathy, so that a fusion between the child's sex drive and her sadistic interest in wanting her mother to be hurt takes place – this will explain adult sexual masochism in women.

The Reagan years were not much better; but it finally began to dawn upon some that their psychoanalytic perspective was in total disarray. Mollinger (1982) threw the cat amongst the pigeons by demonstrating that it was possible to explain all the clinical manifestations of sadomasochism whatever development stage was prioritized, though in order to do so requires an untenable leap of faith. Initially, infants do not realize that many pleasurable and painful experiences do not emanate from themselves, for they can not readily distinguish themselves from the world. Consequently, the infant would not understand that painful experiences would emanate from neglectful or hurtful parents; which would make it impossible for so-called sadistic or masochistically orientated events to be experienced in standard psychoanalytical terms: they would experience pain both as the victim and victimizer. Conversely, if the growing infant, still dependent upon adults, disassociates from their painful experiences and seeks to maintain a good interaction with adults, it is easy to see that, if aggressive behaviour is inhibited, what is called masochistic behaviour could easily follow. In the confusion of being both 'hurt' and 'loved' at the same time all sorts of psycho-dynamics could develop before the full realization that the self and others are separate, required for the Oedipal crisis, takes place. The only one to make any sense at all at this time was C. Brenner (1982), who, being intrigued by the idea that masochists invariably demon-strated elements of sadism at the same time, argued that the pathological forms seemed to differ from what was normal only by degree rather than in kind.

It was time to sort things out. So in March 1983 the Association for Psychoanalytic Medicine held a symposium on the nature of and cure for masochistic and narcissistic characters. Unfortunately, none of the babblers could even agree what they were talking about. While some of the Freudians wanted to look at sexually orientated fantasies, and ignore 'moral masochism', others tried to home in on people's non-sexually-orientated self-destructive behaviours which attempt to gratify the various problems that arise in their psychic development. Otto Kernberg (1991) was simply bemused by it all: as masochistic behaviour was fairly common, it was impossible to draw a clear boundary between 'normal' and pathological forms, let alone distinguish between the developmental features. What was the point, now that the term masochism had lost its specificity in psychiatry? While the symposium was hardly likely to listen to that idea, it had to admit that after sixty years psychoanalysis had yet to quantify what masochism was, let alone establish an agreed framework through which to explore the subject. The *American Psychoanalytic Association Journal*'s special issue on sadomasochism which followed the symposium could not offer a solution either. There are now so many papers, discussions, theories and propositions that it would take years to follow them all through. Psychiatric sadomasochism was anything the babblers wanted it to be. So, if you're stuck for a job, all you have to do is to pick and mix from the theories on offer, produce something of book length to impress your friends, make it virtually inaccessible to the general reader, pick upon a dead president or serial killer as the archetype of your 'new' theory to secure public attention, and bluff your way through the TV chat shows.

Get the perverts

As the psychoanalytic debates about origins became more and more esoteric, fewer and fewer people could follow them; and so the public was forced to rely upon an egotistical bunch of popularizers who did not care to follow the debates either: they knew that sadomasochists *must* be 'sickoes' and, as the public were completely ignorant of what was going on, they could say anything they liked to prove it. Textbooks, like Clifford Allen's influential *Psychosexual Disorders* (1969), failed to keep up with the debate; and most, like Joseph Tenenbaum's *The Riddle of Sex* (1935), merely repeated the babble from the 1920s. This was hardly surprising given that most authoritative reference works like

54: Sadomasochism

The American Handbook of Psychiatry and the *Encyclopaedia of Psychiatry* were still obsessed with the issue of pain.

The collective effect was that a jumble of unfounded assertions, which linked sadomasochism to death-wishes or instincts, over-emphasized the role of pain, insisted that such 'suffering' was needed for sexual potency and asserted that, because it was a compulsion, sadomasochism was devoid of any intellectual element. As far as the second-division babblers were concerned, sadomasochists were obviously immoral, and would progress from watching horror movies, through battering babies and sex crimes, to murder, unless they were stopped. Rape and 'lust-murder' became linked with sadomasochism because popularizers then labelled the likes of Fritz Harmann, Neville Heath, Brady and Hindley, and the Boston Strangler as sadomasochists. The public spent too much time watching B movies in which the white-coated 'shrink' would explain to the hero who had to save the heroine that sex-murdering perverts had missed out on one developmental phase or another and could express themselves only through being cruel to, and ultimately killing, their 'love object', because of some psychologically regressive identification between the heroine and the killer's mother.

This rubbish, like the original Freudian psychobabble which spawned it, had little to substantiate it, being no more than a moral imperative masquerading as 'science'. The problem was that these popular assertions conflated the real distinctions to be made between the harmless SM devotees and compulsive criminals. As the consensus held that all 'sadistic behaviour was murder in miniature' and an evil to be eradicated, while the babblers haggled amongst themselves over the pre-Oedipal factors, the popularizers' simplistic message that sadomasochists were dangerous people, who if given an inch would take your life, took hold, and became a self-fulfilling prophecy. Every despicable crime that involved any kind of sex act was redefined as 'sadistic', and any and every facet of the perpetrators' past life was redefined to fit the symptoms. For several decades anyone who fancied the idea of spanking someone else would fear they might turn out to be a serial killer, and anyone who thought they might like to be spanked dare not ask, in case they were murdered as a consequence. The moralists loved it.

On the couch

While the inability of the babblers to agree amongst themselves about the answers to simple questions like 'Is Peter Sutcliffe mad?' has steadily eroded the public's awe of psychiatry in general, there are several fundamental reasons why psychiatric theories about sadomasochism should never have been taken seriously.

First, the psychiatrists cannot agree amongst themselves what masochism is. At various times they have suggested that it is a form of manipulation, a plea for help, a method of making oneself lovable, the down-side of artistic creativity, and a religious expression. They cannot agree whether or not it is caused by a low sex drive, masturbation, reading pornography, low self-esteem or child abuse; or whether or not it is a form of moral superiority, is related to suicidal or homosexual tendencies, or amounts to a denial of aggressive impulses or is a defence against anxiety. Likewise, psychiatrists cannot agree whether or not sadism is caused by an increase in permissiveness, high levels of male hormones, masturbation, homosexuality, castration anxiety, fixations at numerous stages of psycho-sexual development, a neurotic need for superiority, blood lust and so on. Sadomasochism is simply what the individual psychiatrist wants it to be.

Second, these frequently ambiguous, and not infrequently contradictory, explanations reflect three main problems related to the babblers' methods: the collection of their data; their theoretical focus; and their concept of normality.

Having no concept of the need for a diagnostic review procedure, the psychobabblers cannot assess or compare their own clients' accounts with others. They do not possess the systematic data covering the age, gender, sexual orientation, beliefs, socio-economic position and so on which would enable them to extrapolate from their clients' experiences to the wider world. Many have not even realized that their 'clinical studies' rely upon a self-selective and unrepresentative sample of the population, such as those who voluntarily attend or are forced to attend analysis, and are completely unrepresentative of the rest of us. As each course of 'treatment' can take between three and four hundred hours, the number of 'patients' psychiatrists will see is very small, and no analyst will ever come across, let alone be able to study, more than a few representatives of any psychopathological type. As these unrepresentative samples will obviously consist of those who have difficulties accepting or adjusting to their proclivities, any inferences, generalizations and conclusions drawn about the many others who are too busy enjoying themselves to talk to a psychiatrist will inevitably be misleading. As we shall see, when it comes to sadomasochism, active devotees rarely even consider their proclivity to be a burden, and would never go to a psychiatrist. Consequently, it is impossible to accept the psychoanalytic truisms which appear in the American Psychiatric Association's *Diagnostic and Statistical Manual of Mental Disorders*, the DSM-III-R.

It has never even dawned upon the babblers, for example, that the only reason why sexual sadomasochism appears to be more frequent in males is that it is far more difficult for a woman to engage in such acts outside 'normal' relationships and roles than it is for males, because female sexual behaviour is far more socio-culturally inhibited and socio-economically restricted than it is for men. As most female SM activity takes place within couples, or on the 'swinging' scene, it would obviously remain hidden to psychiatry. Contrariwise, the simple reason why transvestism appears to be a male 'fetish' is that we place more sanctions on male dress than on female dress. Females can cross-dress without anyone complaining.

Part of the reason why psychiatrists cannot agree over definitions follows from their remarkable ability to find a 'recognized' mental disorder for any facet of human behaviour, and their inability to distinguish between the so-called 'symptoms' of a proclivity and the problems caused by society's reaction to it. During the 1950s, for example, psychiatrists were convinced that there was a link between alcoholism and homosexuality simply because a few people who could not come to terms with their sexual preference, owing to their fears about the social stigma they would face, turned to alcohol. Most of the symptoms that psychiatrists believe are innate or intrinsic to various sexual tastes are really ego-dystonic problems caused by the non-devotees' sexual socialization or their fears about the adverse reactions of others, which prevent the patients from accepting and coming to terms with their proclivity. American and German studies of self-identified sadomasochists who sought 'help' for their 'problem' have shown that they were invariably people who had found it difficult to integrate into either country's extensive sadomasochistic subculture, which strongly suggests that their 'problem' followed their feeling of isolation or refusal to accept their desires.

The lack of real data turned up by psychiatrists in contrast to sex researchers and sociologists, which I review in chapter 5, inevitably means that most psychological 'studies' are merely 'theoretical'; they usually consist of theories about theories rather than data. This is obviously a very thin basis for providing a realistic account of anything. Built up like a jigsaw puzzle over fifty years, the psychobabble on sadomasochism even fails to show any awareness of the mass of contradictions it has produced as a result; most psychiatrists do not even take account of others' theories when offering their latest missive. Take, for example, Henriette Klein's 1972 essay *Masochism*, which asserts that: 'Both [sadists and masochists] experience great anxiety with the sexual act and can never really feel free to enjoy it. They come to the act with anxiety and depart from it with added guilt.' Even if this was the case, Klein has obviously not considered the ramifications of Reik's previous suggestion about the dynamics of such events in *Masochism in Sex and Society*, whereby 'in the place of pleasure accompanied by anxiety, there steps anxiety-producing pleasure, resulting in the osmosis of pleasure and anxiety'. Before proceeding, Klein should have provided a good justification for rejecting Reik's caveat; for the failure to do so would always detract from the value of what Klein might have been able to prove.

This problem is compounded by the numerous theoretical differences which exist within the paradigm. Psychoanalysts are pretty lousy theorists anyway. Even when most believed in the death-wish, not one of them bothered to answer necessary questions like 'why doesn't the residual evolve into masochism in everybody?', before proceeding with their other assertions. The necessity to have done so becomes apparent when one considers the most bizarre of all the babblers' theoretical tautologies. The vast majority of the patients upon whom modern psychoanalytic theories are based have never ever demonstrated the slightest overt interest in active sexual sadomasochism, not even in their fantasies. The psychologists are invariably dealing with people who display the various manifestations of what Freud called moral masochism, and they then assert that there is some symbolic link with repressed sexual desires irrespective of what really appears in the case history. Sexual sadomasochism is thereby constantly being found pathologically guilty by *no* association with moral masochism.

To argue that the same psychological forces can lead some people to debilitate themselves in everyday social intercourse, others to engage in ritualistic spanking before sexual intercourse, and still others to viciously mutilate and kill people, is tantamount to failure. If psychiatrists cannot even determine which of their clients is an erotogenic, or feminine, or moral masochist, they are hardly in a position to claim that they can identify specific symptoms let alone origins.

This failure follows from the psychiatrists' dishonesty. While they like to point the finger at sexual sadomasochists, they tend to keep quiet about moral masochists and religious activists, who according to Freud would be just as 'sick'. Many analysts actually believe that they are, but deliberately obfuscate the difference to avoid offending the wider public. So they play safe by steering clear of the subject unless the authorities want an excuse to go after some marginalized religious cult, and focus attention upon the sexually active to take advantage of public prejudice. No wonder the only thing the psychologists hold in common is an unproven assertion that sadomasochism is a psychopathology, that is 'not natural'. They then utilize this consensus to push their own moral values, effectively promoting the very problems they claim to be solving.

Take the case of C.W. Socarides whose works *The Overt Homosexual* (1968) and *Beyond Sexual Freedom* (the latter is referenced in Mass, 1983) reflected his twenty-year crusade to cure homosexuality, which he seems to think is linked to 'sadomasochism', because they are both supposedly products of infantile drives. Sounding more like a deliverance minister than a psychiatrist, Socarides once blamed the sexually different for the threat of a nuclear holocaust:

> Man's crucial failure is that he has been unable to manage the 'beast' within himself. He has been unable to collect and integrate inner knowledge in order to employ it in the

capacity of love, for understanding the gratification of his instinctual needs in a way beneficial to himself and to society. When he regresses to the level of emotional thought, brute emotion, or even lower and further back in his primitive past to sheer hedonistic response (of either elemental pain or pleasure), technology becomes a dangerous toy in the hands of the beast of pride.

The problem with this explanation, as Lawrence Mass (1983) pointed out, is that, *if* Freudianism had correctly identified the real impulses at work, it is far more likely that the bomb would be dropped by someone who, because they had failed to gratify their impulses, would take their frustrations out on the rest of the world.

Finally, we get to the awkward question of normality. In order to condemn sadomasochism, psychiatrists are always adversely comparing it with what is normal, even though they have never come clean about what they think normality is. Klein, for example, tells us that 'Both the masochist and the sadist over-eroticize and over-emphasize sex in that sex looms out of all proportion to all else in life.' Yet Klein does not offer *any* standard by which we can test that proposition. Exactly how many hours a day is one allowed to think about one's sexual hobby before it becomes 'out of all proportion'? Do other people 'under-eroticize' sex?

At the very least, the psychiatrists hidden standard of normality would have to be an ethnocentric one, when it comes to sex, and sadomasochism in particular, because anthropologists Chellan Ford and Frank A. Beach's *Patterns of Sexual Behaviour* (1951) found that societies in which sex is naturally associated with biting, scratching, hair-pulling and so on also tend to believe that women 'naturally' take as active and as vigorous a role in sex as men do. Perhaps psychiatrists think these whole societies are over-erotic too.

No one seems to have noticed that those who talk most loudly about 'natural' social relationships, like marriage, have a habit of ignoring the role of biological bedrock in human actions. In the case of sadomasochism, it's amusing to see how psychoanalysts, who in most countries have to qualify as medical doctors first, can willingly accept the concept of mental addiction to pornography while simultaneously ignoring any possibility that sadomasochists are activating the body's natural endorphins which may stimulate the pleasure others may feel as pain. I have no idea whether sadomasochists are stimulated by endorphin release, as some contemporary masochists and fakirs suggest; but as I am not asserting the contrary, I do not have to.

Where do sadomasochists come from?

The obvious indication that psychobabble can provide no useful insights into active sadomasochism is its continual inability to answer simple questions about its own theories, let alone reality. A psychiatrist cannot even tell you what's the difference between a sadist and a masochist, or what the extent of sadomasochistic desire is in 'normal' people; let alone what the exact role of the Oedipus complex plays in all this. Yet, the moment one adds a little common sense and includes the social factors which psychiatrists completely ignore, it immediately becomes obvious that the most important factor in all so-called 'pathologies' is the simple imposition of one social group's beliefs upon other people's behaviour. The ridiculous mess that psychiatry has now bequeathed to society, for example, is perfectly illustrated by Bruce Naylor's account (1986) of emerging sadomasochism in children and adolescents.

Being a good psychotherapist, Naylor, from the Burlington County Special Services School District in New Jersey, became very concerned about children who 'act out' sadomasochism in the classroom, and has spent some time studying the phenomena, before 'sharing' his insights with us.

According to Naylor, eight-year-old 'Gary', who was hyperactive, suffered from enuresis, had an inability to concentrate in school, suffered from low self-esteem and engaged in aggressive behaviour towards other children, was obviously a budding sadomasochist. This trait was found in all his relationships: Gary's close friendship with another student, for example, simply alternated between bouts of fighting and exhibiting 'special fondness'. Fortunately for him, Gary was referred to a therapist who had an interest in curing sadomasochism, and was 'offered' several years' therapy in order to overcome 'his' problem. Gary certainly needed it, because, while he was in therapy, Gary even tried to 'provoke' the therapist into punishing him for misbehaving during the 'group counselling sessions' and when he was thirteen, during a period of several weeks' separation from his father, owing to the latter's temporary absence, Gary 'was so determined to recreate an emotional experience involving submission and suffering' that he burned holes in his own skin with a cigarette while telling the therapist that he had met a man who had paid him $20 to do it. What other conclusion could one come to, other than that Gary will end up volunteering to star in a homosexual snuff movie?

The first possibility is that the real fortunates have to be Gary's father and relatives, because the symptom checklist used to diagnose Gary as a sadomasochist was being used three years later to diagnose the likes of Gary as 'victims' of 'satanic abuse'. The second is that Gary's behaviour at school is no different from that of thousands of others who come from violent or neglectful households. Third, if Gary became a confused adolescent it probably had more to do with the fact that his father was a long-standing single parent who exercised frequent and harsh corporal punishment, and that Gary's desperate attempts to please, gain affection and approval, as well as make sense of his life, failed. Fourth, the fights with his peers, derogatory remarks about teachers and habit of pulling facial expressions, far from reflecting a wish for 'punishment', simply amounted to Gary's only means of expressing his dislike of the circumstances he found himself in. Fifth, the babblers were so busy trying to avoid seeing the obvious that they even put Gary's inevitable failure to complete school-work down to a desire to attract attention, rather than the fact that Gary had obviously lost so much time being punished at both home and school, and sitting around in useless 'therapy' pandering to a mis-diagnosis, that he inevitably fell too far behind to understand and complete new tasks.

It comes as no surprise, given his self-validating interpretation, that Naylor is convinced that Gary and similar children will try to get the therapist to punish them too. The most bizarre aspect of the diagnosis, however, is his reference to the cure. As long as the therapist 'resists', and offers the child an alternative 'response', the 'pathological bond' which holds the child in 'the sadomasochistic vice' can be weakened; and Naylor even has the example of Bob to prove it:

> The therapist was convinced that he overheard 11 year old Bob calling him an obscene name outside his office. The therapist felt himself becoming enraged and believed that he was completely justified in delivering a stern lecture and in sending the boy back to class instead of allowing him to remain for his therapy session. Afterward, uncomfortable about his precipitous actions, the therapist began to analyse the real reason for his own angry response. He concluded that he was responding to a 'call' from the child to enter into a sadomasochistic relationship similar to what the boy had experienced with his parents, who frequently punished him severely and continually threatened to kick him out of the house. The therapist retrieved Bob from the classroom and asked if he had been blamed and punished similarly at other times. Sensing a change in the therapist's attitude, Bob poured out feelings of rage and resentment over his parents blaming, punishing, restricting him to his room and physical beating. There was a notable improvement in Bob's behaviour after this and he treated the therapist with a great deal of consideration.

That Naylor could delude himself that any change in Bob's behaviour instantaneously followed the therapist's recognition that the child was craving further punishment, demonstrates just how single-minded and self-centred some therapists are. Far from suffering from early addiction to sadomasochism, Bob was clearly being ill-treated at home, and, having been constantly picked on and stigmatized by his teachers, felt hopelessly trapped whatever he did. Bored with the enforced 'therapy', Bob then showed his disapproval by swearing. The therapist's reaction, and the return to class, probably came as a relief to him. What is really incredible in this example, however, is not Bob's but the therapist's reaction. He instantly blamed Bob for his own failings, which included, at the very least, a short temper and authoritarian tendencies. Even when he was supposedly 'reflecting' upon his own attitude, the therapist still blamed Bob for making 'the call', rather than his own blatant shortcomings. If Bob now shows any 'consideration', it probably reflects the fact that the therapist finally listened to what Bob had to say, and Bob has worked out that the therapist may prove useful next time he is being ill-treated by his parents or teachers.

There is no mystery in these circumstances, or any need to consider some unresolved Oedipal conflict; merely a long overdue need to debunk psychobabble, and face up to the need to 'cure' most adults before they raise another generation of damaged children. This necessity to debunk the babble that tries to pass itself off as science can be found even in otherwise excellent therapists. Of all the psychiatric papers I have read, Janet Schumaker Finell's is one of the best; yet even her 'Sadomasochism and Complementarity in the Interaction of the Narcissistic and Borderline Personality Type' fails to see the obvious.

Finell (1992) has discovered that the need to gratify sado-masochistic desires is an important component of narcissist and borderline personalities. Both groups, who are amongst the most frequently diagnosed and discussed in contemporary psychoanalytic theory, apparently suffer from 'self-esteem, conflict-based, and developmental problems, and utilize primitive defences in their interaction with others'. They are obviously the kind of person you should avoid inviting to your party. But what sadomasochism has to do with their problems is a question that will bemuse anyone but a psychoanalyst. At best, the borderline type's real problems can be summed up as being interpersonally incompetent owing to their gross lack of empathy with anyone else. Normal people call them selfish, spoilt or a 'mummy's boy/girl'. And we have all had to deal with narcissists, who act out their seething aggression on the rest of us in the form of sneaky back-stabbing or, when possible, oppressing others. It's not surprising that Finell finds people suffering from these symptoms prove difficult to treat; the rest of us simply want to shoot them.

On the other hand, it's unlikely that anyone but a psychiatrist would suggest that we should label such people sadomasochists, just because it is possible to describe their odious traits in the following way: 'the narcissist tends to aggrandize the self through enforcing submission, helplessness and dependency in the other', while the borderline type 'devalues the self by attaching him or herself to another who are seen as powerful, dominant, and controlling'. The only possible connection between these descriptions and sex is that Finell's illustrative case histories debunk the idea that everyone else would get a rest if psychiatrists opened a dating agency to place each borderline 'masochist' with a 'sado-narcissist'.

Finell's case one, an unmarried thirty-five-year-old 'borderline' teacher, whose four-year, three-times-weekly, analysis is supposed to have been a considerable success, turns out to have been involved in a five-year stormy relationship with a 'sado-narcissistic' dentist (who else?) already. The psychoanalyst, of course, was not going to suggest that their problems stemmed from the fact that, while the dentist refused to commit himself to marriage or any serious involvement, the teacher was becoming increasingly frustrated at his refusal to do so, and that even when their relationship was going smoothly our 'borderline' was inevitably discontented. Doesn't Finell realize that 'borderlines' are never satisfied? Likewise, when case two, a narcissistic Mr F, sought treatment because he could not choose between his wife of twenty years and a lover of five, it should have been obvious that no cure was available. It is totally irrelevant that he married a 'clingy, dependent and helpless' woman, but could not find any release in his daily business, being extremely anxious and suspicious about colleagues; or that he bolstered his self-esteem by deluding himself that women were always falling for him and pursuing him, but then quickly fell apart when either woman in his life demanded signs of greater commitment. Mr F simply realized that he could not fulfil one's request without losing the other, and that meant he would lose his control over one or the other.

It is precisely because such symptoms of these types are standard that the really significant point is that neither case had expressed the slightest interest in SM sex. They never will, and devotees will avoid them both like the plague. SM sex would not provide a solution to their problems either; because the kind of people psychiatrists talk about when they throw around the label 'sadomasochist' are completely different from those who engage in SM sex. Consequently, even if we were mad enough to take psychoanalysis seriously, it could never tell us anything about the origin and nature of SM devotees.

Psychobabble

After seventy years of failing to collect any decent empirical data about sadomasochism, psychiatric knowledge of sadomasochism is non-existent. All we are offered is a mass of theoretical speculations premised upon a predetermined label supported by a dubious terminology used to babble on about a small and unrepresentative clinical sample. It is impossible to draw any meaningful conclusions about sadomasochism, let alone SM devotees, from what psychiatry has on offer. Indeed, once one reviews the historical origins of the psychiatrists' classification, discovers its feeble foundations, then considers the glaring weaknesses in the psychological position, it becomes imperative to ignore it completely. Despite psychiatrists having woefully failed to distinguish between the many varied activities that are inanely given the label 'sadism', and having slapped the label around willy-nilly, without a second thought, it turns out that most of the so-called sadomasochists they have 'analysed' have exhibited no interest whatsoever about expressing their desires sexually. What is really shocking, however, is that psychiatrists have clearly been selective in their application of their theories too.

As Leon Salzaman has pointed out, most babblers cannot even distinguish between the sexual and the moral masochist. He suggested that sexual sadism as originally defined was extremely rare, and that estimates have been inflated by including those who engaged in sex play that became rough and exciting, fetish practices and bondage games, which have nothing to do with the original conception. Sexually orientated 'masochists' are far less prevalent than, and should not be confused with, moral masochists who tended to berate, belittle or actively destroy part of 'the self' in order to obtain some psychic reward or relief of tension from guilt, helplessness or powerlessness. Their hope that their continued displays of apparent helplessness would somehow stimulate others into benevolent actions really is an infantile throwback, and enables them to avoid striving for real strength, pride and dignity by achieving a false sense of grandiosity through the covert power to control or manipulate their human environment. And in doing so, Salzaman gives us a clue or two as to those who oppose SM sex play.

Chapter three

Popular Fallacies and Fears

DESPITE decades of obfuscating psychobabble, the public show a remarkable ability to differentiate between sexual sado-masochism and 'sadistic' violence. It is possible that no one would worry too much about what people got up to in their bedrooms if it were not for the efforts and influence of various social groups, who ironically display the traits associated with moral masochists and simply cannot stop talking about sex in general, and violent sex in particular. A review of their ideas, however, quickly demonstrates that the complaints they have about sadomasochism follow from their belief systems about society and what they would like it to be like, rather than any threat posed by SM devotees.

Who cares?

Far from worrying about SM devotees, the general public are more likely to laugh at the idea of others who 'have to' wear fetish clothing or 'need' to be spanked in order to 'get off'. Knowing what real violence is, the general public can easily tell the difference between 'kinky people' who like to dress up for sex, and the 'sickoes' who violently force their wishes upon others. Consequently, while the public had little sympathy with the character played by Dennis Hopper in David Lynch's film *Blue Velvet* because he was a 'sicko', they merely thought that the lovers played by Kim Basinger and Mickey Rourke in 9 ½ *Weeks* were a bit kinky; and everyone had a laugh about ice cubes.

Indications of these common distinctions can be frequently found in the media too, even though since the Spanner case a couple of tabloid's have been snooping around 'exposing' private SM clubs or body jewellery specialists, trying to elicit public support for police interference. David Lister's account of the opening night party at Planet Hollywood, for example, poked fun at the choice of the restaurant's movie memorabilia

> that seemed to have been collected by a sadomasochism
> fetishist – Charles Chaplin's cane, the whip from *Basic
> Instinct*, the handcuffs from 9 ½ *Weeks*, the axe wielded by
> Jack Nicholson in *The Shining*. (*Independent*, 18 May 1993)

Only the week before, the *Sunday Telegraph* had illustrated a lead comment on the crushing defeat of the government in the Newbury by-election, entitled 'The Moment of Truth', with a Garland cartoon which depicted John Major stretched out on a dungeon rack, with the caption 'If it isn't hurting, it isn't working'.

Likewise, in popular usage the terms 'sadism' or 'sadist' are effectively similes for cruelty; 'sadism' is not even automatically linked to all vicious sex murders, as its failure to appear as a description, let alone a motive of actions, during Peter Sutcliffe's trial demonstrates. Yet *The Sun* did not hesitate to headline a Grenadier Guardsman's court martial for punishing raw recruits in training sessions as 'The Sadistic Sergeant'. In this context, sadism referred to his series of 'cruel punishments' which included being kneed in the thigh, punched on the face, kicked in the testicles, and the firing of live ammunition within yards of the recruits. Any form of cruelty legitimated by authority, from school teachers to Nazis, invites the same label, precisely because the general public wish to imply the possibility that the perpetrator gains some vicarious sexual 'kick' out of it, because they do not enjoy the real thing. The complaint by Lars Ullerstam (1967) that this popular usage renders the term 'sadism' meaningless is disingenuous; it simply means that the general public hold a diametrically opposed view to his own, and are far more selective in their use of the original meaning of the term than contemporary blabbers are.

Amongst large sections of the public, 'masochist' and 'masochism' have a much wider currency than 'sadistic', and the context in which they are used invariably implies something about the subject's sexuality. Although masochism can be used to denote anyone who would rather put up with unnecessary or unjustified burdens without complaint, rather than fight back when the option is available, sexual undertones are common. Even strong religious observance, especially in women, is frequently seen as a substitute for sexual activity. Despite great efforts, the politically correct have also failed to eradicate the commonly expressed sentiment 'I know what they need', voiced by people who are confronted with whingers and whiners of all types. Although it is unlikely that such beliefs reflect any knowledge about the Flagellants' particular religious motivation, or the *Catholic Encyclopedia*'s explanation about the relationship between orgasmic ecstasy and religious sufferance of extreme pain, religious beliefs can provide a useful base from which to explore contemporary public attacks on sadomasochism – not that de Sade's blasphemous attacks upon the faith have much to do with it.

Suffering

At the core of the contemporary Christian denunciations of SM sex acts is the perceived need to assert that suffering should be an atonement for sin, or part of God's plan, rather than be turned into personal pleasure. If the godless are allowed to enjoy playing with pain, it will detract from Christians' own suffering for their faith, or the power behind their warning to sinners that God's collective judgment will fall upon them.

Variants of both concerns can be seen in the frequent complaints about sadomasochism made by Mary Whitehouse over the last twenty years. While she is better known for her attacks upon pornography and TV violence, her theories about sadomasochism were far more important in her National Viewers and Listeners Association's analysis of the modern world.

Mary Whitehouse appeared on BBC's *Woman's Hour* on 5 March 1985 with the psychologist Glen Wilson in a debate about sadomasochism. After listening to the introduction, which featured a female 'psychotherapist' who catered for masochists at an SM club, Wilson suggested that SM was common, that the male clients referred to tended to treat it as a hobby in the same way that they would a model aeroplane club, and that fetishism was becoming more acceptable to the public, though he doubted that the phenomenon was increasing.

At first Whitehouse played the psychiatric card: she felt sorry for these 'adherents', and proffered the idea that the dominatrix featured must have had 'a pretty deep problem of insecurity'. If people have 'problems of that kind', which they must have or they would not do it, 'they need real help'. Temporarily forgetting that she was not talking about pornography, Whitehouse then told Wilson that Professor Sir Martin Roth and Professor Ivor Mills from Cambridge, 'working in clinical conditions there', were on record as 'expressing very great concern about all this type of material. It is counterproductive.' Even though the majority of people 'like that', with 'problems of that kind', might be able to 'laugh it off', there were always others who had profound problems which, 'if they are not dealt with properly, are going to lead on to very serious things'.

In short, the first reason to discourage all SM was that its social acceptance might encourage an oddball or two to succumb to an urge to do something nasty. It was not long, however, before the second, more fundamental, reason emerged. Whitehouse was very worried that SM was becoming far too common. A recent BBC adaptation of Tom Sharpe's novel *Blott on the Landscape* had shown a member of the English upper classes being caned by a female while tied to a bed; and Whitehouse could not contain herself. She thought it was 'quite incredible' that no one was protesting that such books and TV shows effectively normalized what is abnormal 'and must remain to be seen as abnormal'; presenting these 'needs' as something to laugh at was really dangerous, because once a society gets to the stage where everybody accepts it merely as something funny, 'you are back with your Weimar Republic . . . this is exactly what Hitler did, it's what Stalin did and if you go back far enough, it's what the Romans did when they became decadent.' If such programmes were allowed to continue normalizing these 'needs' they would soon remove the inhibitions in all of us; and then 'you really are opening the door to the most limitless and incredible possibilities'. Far from normalizing such behaviour 'we have to draw a line'.

In Whitehouse's world, of course, that line is already drawn. Everything is divided into expressions of Christian love and non-Christian lust. Nothing is ambiguous; there are no grey areas. Sex should be synonymous with love, which is a gift of God and is supposed to be restricted to the monogamous married procreative couple, because the reproduction that follows is the nearest humans can come to emulating and celebrating the creativity of God's Love. Apart from the fact that sex for pleasure deviates from this design, Freud had confirmed for Whitehouse that if people failed to sublimate their base sexual instincts, civilization would collapse. Civilization therefore had to rally round against the sadomasochistic threat, because, 'when sex is deformed, cheapened and exploited then the potential of life and *the whole social fabric of society deteriorates*'.

The Christian attack upon SM sex, therefore, is both a critique of all non-procreative sex, sex for pleasure, sex for fun, and the direct promotion of a form of sexual control. In her book *Whatever Happened to Sex?*, Whitehouse had argued that, along with humanism (the elevation of man without God) and communism, non-procreative sex undermines society's religious sentiments. By insisting upon a 'right' to have sex whenever they felt like it, a tendency much aided by the pill, non-Christians were profoundly affecting 'the human character and personality', and, consequently, civilization too. The 'new sexuality' of pornography, promiscuity and gay liberation had not only confused love with sex, but 'the tragedy was that bad sex drives out good sex', and 'when society itself devalues normal sex, affirms rather than discards sexual perversion in culture and in behaviour, then that society is indeed sick and carries within itself the seeds of its own destruction.' It does so, for Whitehouse and many other Christians, because they believe that God punishes societies which displease him; hence the reference to Weimar, Russia and Rome.

As far as Whitehouse was concerned, the permissive splitting off of sex from the family's font of love and civilization during the 1960s had led to a rising interest in sadomasochism during the 1980s, and Britain was asking for trouble. Sadomasochism, with its emphasis upon 'pain', not only prevented sexual intercourse *between men and women* from being a sacramental act and placed devotees in 'demonic bondage'; sadomasochistic desire itself apparently springs from people's 'deep fear of the void created by our rejection of God'.

The contemporary Christian attack upon active SM devotees stems, therefore, from what they believe SM sex represents rather than what it actually is. It is seen as the end result of the permissive 1960s which supposedly convinced everyone to regard sex solely in terms of 'physical lust', and a regression to our primitive origins channelling human creativity towards self-satisfaction at 'its most elemental and egotistical level'. SM sex is also a sign and consequence of God's displeasure.

The problem with this kind of Christian 'sign-watching' is that it invariably fails to fit the facts. According to Whitehouse, for example, the 1980s 'sadomasochistic society' confronted 'the abyss', for:

> when pornography moves – as it inevitably does – into the sphere of sadism and masochism, men continue to gaze like zombies at the soulless orgy, then one asks oneself, what will happen in this world, when men become increasingly dependent on *ever more extreme and decadent material*? Will we come to regard such things as acceptable, not only on paper but in real life? *If we can no longer be shocked by atrocious make-believe* will we, for long, be capable of being shocked by the atrocities of real life?

Unfortunately for Whitehouse, the answer is 'yes', for two reasons. First, far from being the endpoint of a process of ever more permissive pornography, SM immediately appeared as a sub-genre wherever hard-core pornography was decriminalized in Europe during the late 1960s; and, as I demonstrated in my earlier book *Soft Core* (1994), the amount of violent imagery has declined since them. In Britain, there is no evidence, either way, to demonstrate whether or not spanking, bondage and fetish magazines, whose content has not changed in over twenty years, makes up more or less of the total market. I suspect that it is growing slightly, but it is ironical that the Victorian period, when many Christians claim Britain was most blessed by God, produced so much SM literature. Second, only an ideologue would infer that the gap between SM make-believe and real atrocities is declining. On the contrary, as the public's support for initiatives like Live Aid and their protests over abandoning Bosnia to Christian fascism demonstrates, the allegedly immoral, ruled, classes who laugh at sadomasochism are far more concerned about real atrocities than the hypocritical governing classes, and even sections of the Christian community who think that the major problem confronting contemporary society is the declining sales of soft-core pornography.

The mistake that Whitehouse and others frequently make stems from the belief that 'sadistic' horror and pornographic movies automatically provoke viewers to copy what they see, and ensures that they will then go on to commit violent sex crimes. This is absurd. The fact that millions of people are perfectly capable of sitting through the 'sadistic' subtext Whitehouse finds in films like *The Night Porter, Fritz the Cat, Straw Dogs* and *A Clockwork Orange* without getting up at the end, picking up an axe or machine gun and causing mayhem debunks that claim. The reason the general public do not behave this way is that one cannot 'catch' sadomasochism, free love, violent tendencies or a desire to dress up in bowler hats simply by watching a movie. People who emulate a scene from a movie do so because they already want to do what they have seen. Christians who promote controls on this kind of material by alluding to an alleged effect, when they really want it outlawed because it does not promote a Christian outlook on life, are not only wasting their time, but are being dishonest and deflecting attention away from the real causes of the social problems they ideologically exploit.

Whitehouse is on much firmer ground when she suggests that as no one is without some evil intent or 'wild desire', such movies may encourage an existing intent. Yet, if we were to follow her logic and impose a blanket censorship on any material that any lunatic claimed inspired their evil deeds, the Bible would have to be outlawed before *Bondage Monthly* because of people like the Yorkshire Ripper. Restricting material on this basis is futile, as people denied access to one thing will always find another; it is also needless. Whether or not one believes in 'original sin', it is fairly easy to distinguish between those who attempt and succeed in controlling their selfish tendencies, and channel them into harmless activities, and those who do not or are incapable of doing so. That fact can, tragically, be easily demonstrated by simply contrasting the 1993 case of Colin Ireland, the social misfit turned serial killer, with his victims, who were drawn from London's inoffensive gay community. Ireland was *not* an SM devotee. He had no interest in and gained no sexual pleasure from bondage or corporal punishment; he merely worked out that by picking upon bondage lovers he had a perfect means to disable his victims. Far from being obsessed with sex or pornography, let alone SM, Ireland dreamed of becoming a 'somebody', loved seeing his deeds in print, and enjoyed baiting the police. He was a psychotic.

Likewise, while being correct to suggest that lust and depravity have historically been kept in check by various 'limits' which owe their origin to Christian values, Whitehouse has been known to over-emphasize sexual lusts while *ignoring* the far more destructive power and lust for power exercised by people. Consequently, while I do not disagree with her that society has suffered because sexual 'standards' and 'controls' have been under attack since the 'permissive 1960s', I do disagree that these 'standards' need legal protection. There is no logical reason why an act of fornication is infinitely worse than an act of greed, though it would be interesting to consider the reason why some Christians find the idea of spouse-spanking far more terrifying than an act of silent violence by a bureaucrat whose signature on a piece of paper can ruin the lives of hundreds of thousands of people at a single stroke.

This lack of reasonable justification for imposing sexually correct behaviour upon a population is matched by a core contradiction in the Christian argument anyway. Twenty-five years ago, Whitehouse liked to quote David Holbrook, who invented most of the 'feminist' criticisms of pornography. Holbrook believed that topless photos of young women amounted to an act of sexual violence, because he was convinced that such pictures were a manifestation of men's fear of 'femininity' and the 'hatred of women'. Holbrook was very perceptive: he could even spot sadomasochistic symbolism in the stage review *Oh Calcutta!* Yet, if sadomasochistic imagery was so prevalent back in the 1960s, and *all* pornography amounted to the 'sadistic' victimization of women, contemporary sadomasochism can hardly be the end result of a permissive process!

As for the idea that, of all the signs and judgments God could offer us, he in his wisdom decided that SM sex was more likely to convince us to return to the fold than any of the other horrors facing this planet today, it is laughable. No one needs *The Story of O* to prove how 'sick' our society has always been, let alone how 'perverse' we are becoming. If SM sex is a contemporary manifestation of Sodom and Gomorrah, the final stage of desensitization of the British public to violence, and the elimination of fundamental values which will inevitably lead to our rapidly impending destruction, how come God is letting the Dutch get away with it? Why do people believe that God is really going to be more horrified by a copy of *AtomAGE BondAGE* than by the million atrocities Europeans have committed in the Third World since the mid seventeenth century? Whilst I appreciate, and believe that others should too, the Christian crusaders' occasional attempts to sober up those drunk on relative values, the cure is frequently more disquieting than the hangover. Christianity is brought into disrepute by this kind of false prophecy. Whilst society should always look twice at anything that emerges in its midst, and examine what people are doing to one another, the Christians' same old war cry that society will collapse unless we agree to their latest demand for censorship or control has actually helped to create the mess we are in by directing public attention to false rather than real problems, and provoked a lot of prurience and sexual compulsion in the process. Whilst 'licence' without responsibility, as Mary Whitehouse keeps reminding us, is potentially harmful, it is nowhere near as harmful as blind obedience to dogma, the suppression of critical faculties and the promotion of puerile attitudes. When it comes to a choice between publication of another issue of *SIR Bizarre* and another Inquisition, it is obvious which poses the greater threat to society.

Psychotherapy

The Christians, of course, are not alone in their criticism of the so-called sexual revolution, or their assertions regarding the meaning of sadomasochism. Sections of the 'therapy' movement, the quack cures of the twentieth century, play a similar tune.

During the late 1960s, a group of second-generation followers of the revolutionary psychoanalyst Wilhelm Reich lambasted hippy types and students who were quoting Reich's work to justify everything from 'free love' to OZ magazine. This neo-Reichian attack upon 'sexual licence' and sadomasochism, which ran parallel to the Christian crusade, ultimately lies behind many of the therapy movement's contemporary beliefs without its practitioners even realizing it; and it is no surprise to find many of them joining forces with the Christian fundamentalists during the mini-inquisition to undercover satanic ritual abuse, but that's another story. Back in the late 1960s, the clearest expression of the neo-Reichian position was found in George Frankl's *The Failure of the Sexual Revolution* (1974).

Frankl believed that western society's widespread repression of the sexual libido leads either to the disassociation of our ego from our sexual drives completely or to various forms of sexual 'perversions', such as sadomasochism; and that it is the subsequent attempt to repress these perverse urges which produced chronic depressions, melancholia, anorexia nervosa, rigidity of mind or body or even catatonia. He then suggested that while the sexual revolution and pornography had enabled many to avoid these secondary displacements, as they could only partially satisfy infantile desires, people still failed to gain complete sexual satisfaction: only conversion to Reichianism could do this. Reich, in complete contrast to Freud, had suggested that the imposition of social and sexual morality during the rise of 'civilization' had impeded people's 'natural' sexual development so that a series of self-repressive mechanisms produced a widespread fear of the beneficial effects of natural orgiastic potency. Whatever strategy one took, be it abstinence or compulsive indulgence, the result was the same; people built up a crippling character structure which led to a fear of freedom and debilitating self-doubts. It was this perverse outlook which then accounted for so many of the so-called civilized world's problems. Any attempt to change the world without first having smashed one's own restrictive shell was therefore pointless. But while Reich had a brilliant, if sometimes a one-track, mind, those who took it upon themselves to further his work could not match his vision, and Reichianism quickly degenerated into dogma.

Frankl tried his best to enlighten the masses by pointing out that to a Reichian the worst social manifestations of 'sadomasochism' were selfish romantic longings and cultural aggression, rather than whatever people did in their bedrooms; and by warning that, while permissive sexuality *was* a rebellion against established morality, it could never really succeed in liberating the individual:

> The sexual fantasies of a revolutionary who wants to destroy in order to liberate himself become sadistic. He wants to free his incarcerated libido by blowing up the armour of his own body by making himself explode and also the environment in which he exists. He wants to tear the armour, the restrictions, the internalized symbols of law and order from himself in order to be free. Sadism in the service of liberation of the libido is one of the most basic manifestations of deprived and inhibited men. We have seen it operating among the romantics, and we see it here depicted in a brutal desublimated manner: the rage of the repressed who wants to smash the prison walls of inhibition.

As long as such insights were offered along with the rest of Reich's perspective, they could be used to explain why many self-styled revolutionaries ended up acting like fascists; and Frankl tried to do this. He extolled the virtues of, and the need for, orgastic potency, advanced by Reich in *The Sexual Revolution* (1951) and covered in detail in *The Function of the Orgasm* (1927), which, once achieved, supposedly enabled individuals to rediscover and find harmony in sexual love, and then extend their peace into the wider world; a sort of sexual-political Quakerism. Then came Lowen.

Whereas Reich's concept of love differed from the Christians', by being grounded in bodily functions and feelings rather than aesthetic ideals, Alexander Lowen (1976) effectively married the two. For Lowen, perfect love was expressed 'spiritually' as well as physically and mentally, and he went on and on about the need to stress one's respect for the other individual, the 'whole' person. This would hardly be required by someone who had already taken the Reichian road, because this kind of 'respect' would flow naturally from an orgasticly potent person. But, Lowen's near-neurotic emphasis upon such outward displays of 'respect' was so far removed from the healthy 'primitive' South Seas sexuality which had inspired Reich that Lowen effectively reintroduced the missionary position to the sexual revolution; and the further his popular paperbacks left Reich's original formula behind, the more Lowen's ideal of love sounded like an ascetic Christian's. Consequently, it was not long before the forms of natural sensuality recommended by Reich became regarded by Lowenites as more manifestations of a perverse sexuality. What the Lowenites failed to understand was that, in the 'natural societies' Reich alluded to, sexual experimentation, far from being repressed, was openly encouraged in daily life through the widespread use of sexual symbolism, and that everyone knew what sex was because of the group's sexually orientated rituals. That's why they did not invent pornography or sleazy strip joints. Every member of society would join in the rituals even if only as a spectator; and if sexual partners ultimately paired off in monogamous harmony, this was because everyone had passed through a childhood, and then adolescent, period of non-exploitative sexual discovery at their own pace and with others of their own age. The idea of taking 'advantage' of someone else sexually simply did not exist, as everything took its natural course, in its own time, and nothing was contrived. But by concentrating solely upon 'whole-person partner pairing interactions', the necessity of the complementary social eroticism was lost on the Lowenites, who, having left Reich's ideals so far behind, began to denounce anyone's attempt to reintroduce social sensuality in society.

The Lowenites were unable to differentiate between sexual exploration in a repressive society and what was a perversion from the real Reichian sexual norm. Extending foreplay, or obtaining further excitement by creating external situations of tension – sex in the open air, erotic stories and discussions with others, special techniques, sexy clothes, or games – which would compensate for the loss of natural eroticism, were dismissed by Lowenites as an obsessive search for greater sexual excitement. Even thinking about such things would increase people's guilt, frustration and anger, driving them compulsively on to the next level of sensual addiction, instead of the natural orgasm.

The most bizarre legacy of Lowenism is our current pre-occupation with sexual 'abuse'. Far from simply attempting to stop the sexploitation of children by adults, the modern therapy movement has attempted rigorously to control sexual exploration amongst the young themselves, and they have even reintroduced the Victorian obsession about 'self-abuse'. On the basis of the ridiculous assumption that *any* indication of sexual curiosity by children before their sixteenth birthday *must* mean that they have been sexually 'abused' by someone else, some therapists now spend all their time repressing children's natural inclinations. This, if Reich were right, would guarantee that the children would grow up to be as neurotic as the adults who repress or exploit them. Reich must be turning in his grave.

As a result, the neo-Reichians have merely provided a psychobabble version of the Christians' love-or-lust dichotomy. Not only have they ignored Reich's belief that the more sexual pleasure a non-compulsive people has, the more discriminating their attitude towards sex becomes; neo-Reichians cannot even match Mary Whitehouse's practice of drawing a clear distinction between an individual's practice of 'perversions', however defined, and the wider cultural context. Ironically, while many modern Christians promote the joy of sex, albeit within monogamous marriage, the neo-Reichians have ended up condemning almost any form of sensuality by denouncing it as sadistic or masochistic.

Once again, SM sex is being opposed not for what it is but for what a theory insists it means and represents. Yet, just as the Christians tend to ignore the logic of Freud's theory when it comes to their moral masochism, neo-Reichians forget that the form of 'sadomasochism' Reich warned against was not SM sex but people's slavish obedience to the social dogma of sex-fearing sadistic fascism.

Separatist feminism

Contrary to what they would have us believe, feminists who lambaste SM devotees are merely pushing another thinly disguised love-or-lust polarization purloined from the neo-Reichians or Christians. Rather than emulating the mainstream feminist tendency of encompassing historical origins and environmental factors in their explanations of social phenomena, the separatist wing of the women's movement subscribes to Holbrook's conspiracy theory about male plots to murder all women; and in tirelessly seeking to invoke a gender war it exhibits the most extreme form of 'moral masochism' that exists in contemporary society.

Although there were occasional references to a vague concept of 'sadism', borrowed from psychobabble, in their early attacks upon pornographic literature, the separatists' specific assertions about 'sadomasochistic society' emerged only when the wider women's movement began to question the purpose of social taboos about sadomasochism and other forms of non-procreative sex.

Once the separatists discovered that the very women they had hoped to convert to their sexually correct ideals were beginning to find that sex could be fun, the separatists' use of the label 'sadomasochism' to describe the major cultural manifestations of patriarchy began in earnest.

In propaganda like Laura Lederer's *Take Back the Night* (1980) and R. R. Linden's *Against Sadomasochism: A Radical Feminist Analysis* (1982), American separatists began to conflate sadomasochism *with* patriarchy; and their view was widely adopted in Britain. Bat-Ami Bar On, for example, insisted that:

> According to feminist theory, in our conduct we enact cultural ideas about acceptable behaviour by adopting given roles in a given situation. In the case of sado-masochism, the idea is the patriarchal view of sexuality in which *eroticism is connected with violence* . . .
> (Linden, 1982, p. 78)

'Violence' in this separatist sense does not refer to an SM sex act but to everything the male gender does. For Barry, Wagner, Bar and a gaggle of other separatist writers the 'cultural sadism' of patriarchy consists of marriage, the pill, and Valentine Day cards, as well as 'sexual slavery', rape and pornography. These all supposedly support a system of sadomasochistic violence against women by men. Indeed everything most people regard as normal behaviour is really 'sadomasochistic'. In short, as far as the separatists are concerned, sadomasochism is not an end-product of a clash between Christian morals and permissive sex: it is the means by which men maintain their dominance over women in patriarchal societies. As Stoltenberg, a male supporter of the separatists, puts it:

> For the male, eroticized violence against women results in the rarefication of his male sexual identity; his sexual sadism is the erotic correlative of his power in the culture over half the human race. *Male sexual identity is a meaningless construct apart from institutionalized and personalized violence against women.*
> (Linden *et al.*, 1982, pp. 125-6)

In 'separatist speak', 'institutional violence' is a metaphor for marriage, and 'personalized violence' is a metaphor for having sex. Given that separatists believe that every act of sexual penetration amounts to 'male' rape, they are hardly likely to differentiate between rape and pillage in an Anglo-Saxon village and a contemporary married couple playing sex games while dressed in PVC. Anything and everything in patriarchal society is an act of violence against women, and a sadomasochistic act at that.

The reason why no one apart from the separatists realizes this 'fact' is that everyone else in patriarchal societies has been brainwashed into behaving in a sadomasochistic way because of the availability of pornography *and* romantic fiction. Wagner asserts:

> Pornography is the propaganda which indoctrinates men into the sexual power they have over women and teachers men how to manifest that power. Patriarchy gives women a different medium that reflects our experience and educates us for 'proper' feminine sexuality: the 'cult of romance'. Through romance we learn to be passive, to wait and to submit to the pain and humiliation of loving someone who has power over us. (Linden *et al.*, 1982, p.24)

Once one realizes that innocuous Mills & Boon novels are apparently as guilty as a copy of *Tied up Tarts* in promoting sadomasochistic patriarchy, it is easy to see how the separatists can delude themselves that, while patriarchy has always been with us, its cultural sadomasochistic manifestations are increasing now. After all, it would be difficult to justify the theory that the dramatic increase in SM symbolism proves that patriarchy is engaged in a desperate backlash against the women's movement and promotes femicide – men's desire to murder women – when all you have as proof is the existence of a score of PVC and rubber fashion stores like Skin Two, a couple of feature films like *9 ½ Weeks*, and the decade of punk rock.

The real target in this separatist fantasy about a gender war is, of course, liberalism. As more and more women are able to take advantage of the growing opportunities for self-expression that the painfully slow, but steady, increase in equal opportunity affords them, the separatists have begun to realize that, despite all the books they have sold in the last twenty years, most women find this kind of feminism boring, and women who exhibit real self-esteem are hardly going to throw away what liberal society has to offer, in favour of spending their hard-earned cash funding the lazy separatists' gender war.

Rather than rethink their theory, the separatists simply became very angry, especially with women who have been 'duped' by patriarchy's educational, media and cultural indoctrination systems into believing they can exercise free choice, when really their oppression is secured through sadomasochistic practices like power-dressing and high-heeled shoes. Alert to the fact that SM devotees were simply exploiting these all-tolerating liberal principles to legitimize their overtly 'violent behaviour' against women, the separatists redoubled their efforts to alert 'wimmin' to the fact that sadomasochism was the ultimate outcome of the ethic of liberalism. Hilde Hein, in an essay *Sadomasochism and the Liberal Tradition*, then pointed out that liberalism is dangerous, liberalism is capitalism, and capitalism oppresses women, liberalism is survival of the fittest and women can't hope to compete, *liberalism is doing what you want to, but according to the feminists there must be limits: civilization is moral progress.*

By purloining Christian and Freudian arguments wholesale, and changing a few words around, groups like Women Against Violence Against Women spent the 1980s trying to convince anyone stupid enough to listen that, to impose these necessary limits, the 'wimmin's' counter-offensive must begin immediately otherwise sadomasochism would save patriarchy, and femicide would begin in earnest. Like millenarian Christians', the separatists' dire apocalyptic visions became more and more alarming as the decade progressed. Far from being an 'aberration', SM was now 'normal everyday stuff' infused throughout society. Nichols, Pagano and Rossoff believe:

> Violence has become idealized through television and film
> . . . This media violence more and more involves themes of
> bondage, leather apparel, whips and other images of
> sadomasochism, and it *is more and more sexual in content*
> . . . Along with fantasy violence, the media gives us fantasy
> sex. The 'sexual revolution' and 'personal growth
> movement' encouraged the ideal of sexual gratification
> without emotional commitment or even involvement
> between partners . . . *Gratification becomes an end in itself
> and any means to it are valid. Reduced to orgasm, sex
> becomes a commodity, one more thing to 'get'.*
> *However, such encounters, characterized by lack of
> feeling, growth or intimacy,* are not often satisfying on any
> emotional level . . . real life relationships pall in
> comparison to fantasy and frequently suffer as people set
> themselves impossible goals.
> (Linden *et al.*, 1982, pp. 142–3)

Anarchy was the inevitable result, according to Barry:

> Sade's life is a study of violent sexual excess . . . He
> quickly grew to detest any systems or schools that
> demanded control of his behaviour.
> To religion and its restrictive morality he reacted with
> atheism. To the governments and their legalistic restriction
> on morality he reacted with anarchism. His principle was
> that there should be no limit on his ability to act on
> whatever he chose for *his sexual pleasure.*
> (Linden *et al.*, 1982, p. 51)

Having failed to convince anyone but themselves, by the end of the decade WAVAW completely gave up on women who showed no signs of abandoning heterosexuality, let alone SM. They decided that the real problem was that because too many foolish women were suffering from 'a loss of self', and had succumbed to the liberal-capitalist-sadomasochistic-pornographic-patriarchal myth that women can enjoy anything men do, they were damaging the feminist cause. Nichols believed that women had to be made to realize that

> Ours is a destructive society, a society that corrupts us and must be resisted. This means that as part of the movement towards liberation, we need to look critically at our own thoughts and feelings, including thoughts and feelings about sexuality. *Sadomasochistic impulses are created and sustained by events and images within our society* and that sadomasochistic behaviour reproduces and therefore condones many of the power imbalances and destructive features of our lives. (Linden *et al.*, 1982, p. 137)

In order to ensure that women would realize this, whether they wanted to or not, the separatists then threw their weight behind the Christian crusade against pornography, alternatively asserting that no women would freely participate, but that those who did would end up as snuff movie victims. The end result was to demand legislation giving the police and trading standards officers the right to go through anyone's video collection to weed out sexually incorrect practices.

There are two major problems with these completely self-referential arguments. First, they depend upon a deliberate, but inconsistent, terminological obfuscation and ambiguity. A typical example can be seen in WAVAW's core ideological justification, and 'proof' offered to adherents, about the rise of this 'cultural sadism'. At the 1978 London Revolutionary Feminist Conference, WAVAW members Sheila Jeffreys and Sandra McNeill agreed that

> the massive boom in pornography of the last ten years can be seen as a backlash to the gains that women have made in this time. It compensates men for the threat to their status by providing them with *images of women as victims and slaves* in every newspaper and on every street corner.

Apart from the fact that anything that 'compensates' one for a loss can hardly be a 'backlash', the idea that 'page 3' models are somehow 'enslaved' demonstrates the ethereal and metaphoric nature of their evidence, and their simple inability to distinguish between the real origins and nature of underground hard-core videos, spanky magazines, top-shelf material and 'page 3' shows its weakness. If the proof that sadomasochism has increased depends upon redefining 'page 3' as the 'enslavement' of women, WAVAW are bereft of real evidence.

Second, this desperate appeal to civilized standards and the inevitable reference to de Sade, echoing the Christian critique, is really an attempt to shore up separatists' feeble theories about the male gender's innate attributes on the one hand and an attempt to control women's sexuality on the other. For, once lesbian SM devotees appeared, the illustrations and examples about sexual desires that groups like WAVAW had used for ten years to prove that there were essential differences between the genders, vaporized.

For over a decade WAVAW denied that women would or even could enjoy 'male' sex. Women were never masochistic let alone sadistic, they never had rape fantasies, fancied kinky sex or read any kind of porn. Everything from 'male' sex therapy to sexology, from condoms to the pill, were merely a means to induce women's complicity in their own oppression. Some of the more extreme separatists even asserted that women would not want to have sex, and would naturally constitute a spinsterhood, if they had not *all* been sexually abused by men when they were children. For separatists, all sexual variations, apart from their ideal forms of 'lesbianism', were 'perversions' and degrees of sexual slavery; and tolerance of sexual minorities, except their version of 'lesbianism', was yet another means to undermine women's ability to embrace feminism.

Once female SM devotees had 'come out', women had started making their own pornography and had begun to hold consciousness-raising meetings about sexual fantasies rather than the spinsterhood, WAVAW tried to hound the SM devotees, porn readers, sexual fantasizers and those who wore high heels out of the women's movement, denouncing them all as 'male identified' (the women's movement's ideological sin requiring excommunication), and then equated sadomasochism with every possible sin they could think of from 'racism' and 'anti-semitism' in order to justify their own form of fascism.

The supreme irony is that these feminist moral masochists, as I revealed in *Soft Core*, were often motivated by the fact that the idea of kinky sex turned them on, and felt they had to exorcize themselves! Consequently, because they have a problem with their desires, they refuse to accept that women who can accept their desires also prefer free choice to Stalinistic separatism, and do so because they realize that the separatists offer no solutions to the imagined, let alone the real, problems which follow from the vestiges of gender inequality in Britain. Blind to this simple fact, the separatists had to invent an excuse to cover their own, inevitable, failure: and sadomasochism still fits their bill.

Spot the difference

Incredible as the idea seems, the Christian, neo-Reichian and feminist denunciation of SM have a lot in common. All three belief systems insist that 'society' must set sexual 'limits' and boundaries, because far from being a small 'aberration' of the few, SM is suffused throughout our every thought, word, and deed. Their proof, however, merely consists of redefining every possible violent or sexual act as a manifestation of sadomasochism. All three belief systems denounce all forms of sexual gratification which do not appear to involve some form of undefined total emotional commitment, or appear to consist of a search for pleasure as an end in itself. Their proof that SM sex does not include any feeling of intimacy or satisfaction 'on any emotional level', however, merely amounts to an assertion that it does not. They believe that women are now being induced to enjoy their own destruction, but, like the (male) beasts before them, they are too dumb to know what they are doing, because everyone is either a slave to demonic bondage or sexual compulsions or penetrative patriarchy; and as a result the 'victim' is either dehumanized, orgastically dysfunctional or a male-identified woman. In order to remind us of the need for salvation, all three groups assert that sex has a particular purpose, be it the glorification of God, to gain orgastic potency, or a weapon in the gender war. Sex is not to be treated lightly, and certainly not for fun. In short, all three groups agree that SM is undesirable, and the antithesis of what perfect sex should be; and they have initiated media morality campaigns, therapy or a gender war to defeat SM sex.

The blatant weakness with all three complaints is that, as no distinction is ever made between what SM devotees get up to, and the 'anything and everything evil' that happens in the world, we are never offered any real reason to single out SM devotees for any special attention. As these detractors have never engaged in any study of SM devotees to justify their beliefs – which, by making SM the simultaneous cause and the symptom of all that is undesirable, does not make sense anyway – there is no need to take any of them seriously. The fact that SM sex is rarely attacked for what it is itself, but solely because it supposedly symbolizes something that these believers do not like, and allegedly inhibits the masses' conversion to the believers' particular faith, would further suggest that we should ignore the complaints altogether. There is, however, a good reason for not doing so.

One of the most interesting examples of the way in which Krafft-Ebing's single sadistic category and psychobabble came together with our three groups of detractors – in a Marje Proops article, 'A Tragedy of Degraded Sex', published in the *Daily Mirror* back in October 1985 – should make everyone take note. For Proops, '*Playboy* Culture'

> was a world of sexual licence. An evil world peopled by evil men who exploited women and by women who readily allowed themselves to be exploited. Decadent sex, drugs, alcohol, pornography and violence place the sixties squarely in history as the time when society sank to the depths of moral decline. And it was this sordid moment in history which provided the back drop for a crime that shocked even that near-unshakable society.

In referring to the murder of 1980 Playmate Dorothy Stratten, the article implied that *Playboy* had moved western societies from cheesecake to SM sex in less than two decades and was somehow responsible for the model's murder. Apart from the fact that *Playboy* had nothing to do with the woman's death, the article just happened to coincide with dozens of others promoting the same message emanating from moral pressure groups and the US Meese Commission, which was then conducting a crusade against the soft-core pornography industry. Every one of these articles was simply repeating the common assumption that men are essentially 'evil' or beasts for promoting hedonistic sex through pornography, sex therapy and sex manuals. This 'evil' supposedly appears in its most dynamic form in the link between violent and sexual impulses; the same suggestion that Krafft-Ebing made when considering the means by which the rare congenital sadists worked themselves up to a lust murder. Our three groups aim to universalize this fear in order to justify their attacks upon sexual beliefs and practices that do not conform to that of the 'moral masochist' in which one's own pleasure is sacrificed in the name of love, respect for the whole person, or spirituality, as a means to halt this deadly evil.

Although all three groups offer a different reason for an individual's innate lust – Christians, the Fall; psychotherapists, the genesis of early childhood; the separatist feminists, patriarchal male revolt against the moon goddesses – all three groups agree that no individuals can control their lust, and that the normalization of sadomasochistic sex leads to a general desensitization to ever-escalating forms of sexual violence. To celebrate or turn what are designated perversions into sex play is, we are told, to trivilize the horror of real acts of violence. This is why Mary Whitehouse refuses to treat it as a joke, neo-Reichians are desperate to get us all into therapy (or steal our children), and separatists want women to stop having sex with men. They all play off the fear that there is a direct link between SM sex play and a Nazi-style holocaust, in order to promote their belief that only the power of love stands between this inevitable outcome of male lust set free.

As SM devotees tend to keep themselves to themselves and not bother anyone else, these moral masochists hoped that their own attack upon sadomasochism would be taken as proof that a process of desentization was occurring in society, and that we were witnessing the last days – biblical end-time for Christians, the completely neurotic society for neo-Reichians, and patriarchal 'femicide' for the separatists. Unable to understand why their word did not have the power for others it had for themselves, they were unable to prevent themselves projecting their perverse fantasies on to society at large, and unleashed their search for snuff movies and satanic ritual child sex abuse, which contain scenarios far worse than anything even de Sade dreamed up in his isolated prison cell.

Unfortunately, though popular sentiment remained oblivious or dismissive of these three millenarian warnings, the cops moved in with Spanner. In the three court cases which followed, half a dozen judges turned to these moral masochists' nonsense to justify asserting that SM was unnatural, perverse and violent. So, before somebody else gets arrested, or accused of being the personification of evil, for dressing up in PVC, let us go and have a look for ourselves.

Chapter four

Sense and Psychologists

PSYCHIATRISTS and psychologists do not get on at the best of times; so it comes as no surprise that they do not agree about sadomasochism.

One of the most scathing attacks on psychobabble was launched back in 1971 by Eugene Levitt, the Director and Professor of Clinical Psychology at Indiana University Medical Centre, in *Sexual Behaviour*. As the interrelationship between sex and 'aggression' was universal, Levitt thought it ridiculous that high-frequency behaviour was being labelled atypical or pathological, while Freud's followers had contributed nothing to our knowledge about sadomasochism beyond elaborate word-spinning and semantic quibbling. 'Some of the speculations are peculiar, if not bizarre, and few seem to have a basis anywhere except in the writer's imagination.' Given that any act believed to work against an individual's welfare could be labelled masochistic, psychiatrists had simply extended the term to any life-style they did not like, from use of recreational drugs to political radicalism. The psychiatrists had even suggested that vegetarians were sadistically inclined towards animals! There had to be something better.

Spanking

Levitt reasoned that if one wanted to know anything about a phenomenon it made sense to begin with its common facets; and when it came to SM, spanking seemed an obvious choice, given that the use of belts, hairbrushes, paddles, shoes, open hands as well as whips and the rod being used on 'the butt' invariably turned up in case histories and sadomasochistic pornography. Levitt then suggested that the fun people got from spanking might have something to do with the butt being a secondary sexual characteristic. Apart from its display, like breasts and genitalia, being associated with sex, the butt and genitalia were enervated by the same third and fourth sacral nerves which made possible pleasurable sensations; so there was no mystery here. Once one then realized that because the butt was able to tolerate considerable surface trauma without serious pain it had become the traditional area of chastisement, it was hardly surprising that it could also be used by those who wished to play at misbehaviour or were seeking relief from guilt. As long as the stimulation was not so intense as to arouse responses like anger, which would compete with the sexual arousal, or too weak to have any effect at all, and as long as the individual concerned was already sexually aroused, or so inclined, the pleasure obtained from spanking was easy to explain. Levitt was at a loss to explain why SM devotees engaged in other acts, but as long as one took the same sensible approach the mystery would soon reveal itself.

Being Green

Three years later, Gerald and Caroline Greene, a British couple who had moved to the United States, produced a bestseller with an up-front exploration of the origin and nature of sadomasochism, which inevitably found most of the previous theories wanting. Unfortunately, the success of *S/M: The Last Taboo* (1974) probably had more to do with its extensive appendix containing extracts from 'the great works of S-M imagination' rather than anything else, because, despite their sensible criticisms of the current psychobabble, the Greenes offered little by way of an alternative.

Lambasting the lack of empirical data connecting devotees with sex crime, the Greenes castigated irresponsible clinicians for implying that all 'sadists' were potentially violent criminals, when many were simply happily married SM devotees. As far as the

Greenes were concerned, real SM devotees not only found sexual cruelty unpleasant but, unlike the clinicians, also believed in equality of the sexes. Far from recreating the power imbalances of real life in their games, or promoting new ones, devotees undermined the stereotypes upon which they rested. Havelock Ellis's client Florey, the suffragette who liked being whipped, had also revealed that 'masochists' tended to have high self-esteem, and that only highly imaginative people would seek out partners to join their submission fantasy lives. In contrast, the martyred wife and the moral masochist would have hardly any interest in SM; and 'sadistic' criminals did not either. They tended to have a mutilated upbringing, were antisocial, did not seek the free consent of a partner and suffered from fixations to the exclusion of all else. Most brooded on their fantasies and never found a partner, and when they had relationships, like Brady and Hindley, they never played SM games with their partner.

Sadly, rather than expanding upon these areas, the Greenes then attempted to beat the psychobabblers at their own game, and, drawing extensively from Ellis, offered elaborate but debatable answers to some of the more bizarre clinical speculations. Typical was the Greenes' suggestion that American men preferred Fem-Dom magazines because America destroyed 'its father' in rebelling against England!

They did, however, raise several important suggestions along the way. Chief amongst them was the revival of the idea that it would make more sense to explore SM's mental representations rather than the issue of 'pain', because the memory of seminal experience could only preserve impressions as a whole, whereas physical pain consists of a sensation and feeling which the memory can't easily replicate. Second, they suggested that SM was feared because in linking sex with the imagination it transgressed Anglo-Saxon culture's deep suspicion of any attempt to intellectualize the instincts. The most important point the Greenes made, however, was that all early commentators appear to have viewed the subject without any knowledge, let alone experience, of what SM devotees actually thought or did. Without such knowledge, speculation was futile.

Fetishism

Meanwhile on the British side of the Atlantic, Morris North had decided to do just that, and began to explore the world of sexual fetishism. His work was eventually published as *The Outer Fringe of Sex* (1981).

Although North was looking at the preoccupations of 1960s rubber fetishists, his study is of interest to us for two reasons. First, although his patients' major interest was rubber material, North claimed that they invariably fantasized about being dominated by women, ideally while being confined, bound, gagged and suffering some form of humiliation. Second, having trawled through the classic texts and the burgeoning number of rubberwear magazines, North's attempt to work out the relationship between fetishism, masochism, masturbation, fantasy, corporal punishment and an apparent inability to have 'normal' sex brought him into conflict with the central tenets of Freudian analysis of fetishism.

Freud originally suggested that a fetish was an item that appeared alongside the 'normal sexual aim and object', and 'ousted them completely'. The choice was perceived as a chance experience in early childhood; so that fetishism was quite common, involved some attribute of 'the beloved' and appeared when sex was unavailable or inhibited. Ultimately, it amounted to a substitute for the love object through an unconscious symbolic connection between the two. Fur, for example, could be associated with pubic hair. A fetish could become pathological only when it was prized more than sex and when it became detached from the particular individual with which it was apparently associated. Then, in 1927, Freud changed his mind. He decided that a fetish was a substitute for the penis all little boys expected their mothers to possess, and was a means to maintain their belief that all women really had a penis in order to relieve the male's castration anxiety.

Freudians did not like fetishists, who they believed were unwilling to be treated because they simply refused to see they had a problem. So for the next fifty years this deviation was subject to the usual babble. Alfred Adler (1933) asserted that the fetishist was a chronic masturbator. J.A. Hadfield (1967) put it down to the mother's hostile reaction to the infant male's erections when suckling, whereby the child began to perceive the female breast as evil and attempted to repress its desire for it – but would later become obsessed with breasts. It did not matter if the fetish object did not look like a breast, because the babblers decided that fetish material, like silk, felt like the breast to the infant, leather had the same body smell as the breast, and rubber combined both. Women, it followed, would never develop a fetish because they developed their own breasts.

Convinced as they were that men's instinctive drive for pleasure had to be sublimated in the cause of civilization, and that perversions were regressions to pre-civilized forms of behaviour, it never dawned upon Freud and his followers that the conflicts in his model, if they followed its own logic, were nothing of the kind. Any conflict would follow from the clash between the child's natural instincts and the attempt to force 'civilization' upon it through bizarre child-rearing practices, especially the repression of any sign of sexual exploration. By concentrating upon the mechanism of retarded sexual development in children who failed to negotiate the apparently steady sensational awareness of the oral, anal and genital phases of their upbringing, and then upon the problems in the child's psyche that followed, Freudians failed to consider that certain aspects of civilization might just be undesirable, and blinded themselves to the obvious. As most psychological problems appear amongst those who experience very strict upbringings, and 'perversions' among those trying to compensate for their conflicts, 'perversions', far from being regressions, would be the inevitable price societies paid for attempting to rigorously enforce civilized standards upon the child, and arresting its sexual development. As civilization advances not only would we expect perversions to increase in number, but women would suffer most. Indeed, women's 'unnatural' childhood retards their sexual awareness to such an extent that female fetishism is extremely widespread, and women are positively encouraged to sublimate through an attachment to 'finery', which if enjoyed by men makes them 'poofs' or 'perverts'.

What makes the whole idea absurd, of course, is that, being blessed with the sensation of touch, there is no logical reason why any human being would not find the feel of various materials extremely sensuous and stimulating. To imply that there is something odd about those who do so merely encourages 'civilization' to pretend otherwise, and places a double stigma upon those who dare to deviate from Freud's prejudice about ideal sexual relations, which meant restricting all sensuousness to the genitals, and Freud's belief that original sin was to be found in the failings of infants' reactions to their parenting. North also thought this absurd. 'Sociologically the perversions are the evidence of the casualties in the civilising process which people have been compelled to undergo.' North also realized that the essence of fetishism had to be culturally determined too; you could not have a rubber fetish unless someone invented rubber first. And these two insights enabled North to explore the conscious, as opposed to unconscious, origins of so-called perversions.

Rubberism

Two surveys conducted by firms specializing in rubber clothing through mail order advertising enabled North to uncover the fact that the vast majority of male rubberists had very respectable middle-class backgrounds. Out of the 325 replying to a West German company advertising in magazines like *Stern* and *Quick* in 1963, 232 were men. Of these, 86 claimed to be businessmen, 43 were in the professions and 61 were white-collar workers. Of the 93 women, 54 were models and 'photographic assistants', and 21 were in 'show business', 10 were 'artists', and 8 were housewives. How many may have been prostitutes is anyone's guess. A similar survey by an English firm produced the same result. Of 107 customers surveyed, the vast majority of the males classified themselves as civil servants, businessmen, medical practitioners, lawyers, teachers, students and creative artists. Of the women, ten claimed to be models, and one an actress. These results confirmed North's own profile, obtained from eight British firms, that the typical rubberist was male, between thirty-five and fifty-five years old, of good education, and middle-class. As he could not find enough female rubberists willing to go public, North assumed it was essentially a male fetish.

Rubberism, therefore, was clearly alive, if not well, long before the advent of the permissive 1960's. North found that devotees tended to be isolated, suffered from a considerable degree of guilt and shame, and experienced a scarcity of female partners. Unfortunately, he confused these social handicaps with the non-group nature of the activity and failed to consider the psychological effects of social stigma while trying to quantify the nature of rubberism, whose devotees had multiplied during the period between 1920 and 1939, when rubber mackintoshes and boots were commonly worn.

According to North, the typical rubberist engaged in the fetish without coitus, achieved ejaculation with the aid of rubber stimuli complemented by sadomasochistic thoughts or play. The male rubberist was invariably a 'masochist', who never adequately satisfied his needs because he worried that women would be repelled by the fetish or find it ridiculous. Consequently, their major outlets consisted of auto-bondage games, and 'verbal exhibitionism' through writing letters to fellow devotees in rubberist magazines and journals, and masochistic role-reversal fantasies. North also suggested that rubberists' pleasure came from the symbolic meanings they gave the material, rather than from enjoying its sensuous feelings. So, for example, rubberists associated their fantasy female figure's black outfit with the devil and wickedness, and crime and punishment. The mask of their dominant fantasy-figure was reminiscent of an executioner's, and the boots the rubberists wished to service denoted mastery. When it came to his own outfit, the rubberist utilized both male and female items, expressing what appeared to be a desire to experience both roles. North was adamant that the fantasy woman was masculine; while the rubberist's male role reflected his need to be protected from her; a point reinforced by our cultural use of rubber as protective clothing against rain, acid, electrical shocks and bed wetting. Proof of these speculations for North was to be found in rubberists' literature and fantasies.

The masochistic fetish in his fantasies is almost a criminal undergoing degradation ceremonies and stigmatizations that recall the whole history of the social treatment of the criminal. He has to be punished for something, but beyond the fact that it is something connected with sexual activity, we do not know what it is he is being punished for. In the role reversal of the sexes the woman becomes a dominant partner often represented as a mother figure or a substitute such as aunt, nanny, nurse or even wardress. They supply care, attention and affection, but also controls. The patient plays a child like role.

North then threw in a castration fear, supposedly reflected in the use of penis corsets and tying up the genitals, complemented by the typical 1950s conclusion that

> The ideal type of rubber fetishist is a latent type of homosexual with intense feelings of guilt about sex, probably derived from infantile masturbation, who can only achieve sexual satisfaction by appearing to a woman in the guise of a penitent, dressed in clothing that recalls childhood protection and dependence, and rendered not responsible for his present performances and actions.

This apparently followed the rubberist obsession that women were more dominant and sadistic in society than they really were.

This was twaddle. Although North alluded to the way that general unhappiness might follow from the fact that sex was still, then, a taboo subject, he failed to realize that everything else he noted, and more, could be explained by social conventions too. The devotees were clearly breaking fashion taboos, and the expectations of their middle-class wives might explain the devotees' fear about women's reaction. Situationally, the rubberists' failure to find female partners would explain its auto-erotic nature; which like the rubberists' fantasies might dramatically change once the interest could be shared. Given some of the wives' reticence to share their husbands' interests, it should hardly have surprised North that the rubberists found their fantasies more satisfying than the reality of their failed sex games. Yet there is no reason to believe that any of North's descriptions, let alone his own attempt at psychobabble, were intrinsic to rubber devotion. There was more than enough information in his account to provide a completely different, and far more rational, explanation.

North's Mr V, for example, was not only happily married to a wife who had no objections, but he had no desires to dress up as a woman, or be dominated by women, and he personally deplored the secrecy exhibited by other devotees, believing it was perfectly possible to be open about such desires. Likewise, Mrs B K, one half of a perfectly compatible couple in the era before 'swinging clubs', with no real need to contact anyone else, had a love of rubber which evolved through a series of 'submissive' sexual experiences. A 'playful move' by a boyfriend, enveloping her arms with the belt attached to her dress while kissing her, led Mrs B to having her wrists and ankles tied to each corner of the bed before sex. Being very much in love with her partner, and thrilled with the initial excitement of being held tightly while being kissed many times, led to a taste for more restriction. A joke about punishments when burning the toast then developed into an excuse for bondage sessions and tight lacing, soon complemented by a pair of black patent court heels from Gamba, London, high enough to make it difficult to walk, and the use of other garments, before experimenting with rubber.

Given these couples' ability to be perfectly at peace with themselves, the problems North uncovered amongst his rubberists appear to be related to sexual isolation, which can easily turn any proclivity into a compulsion, which then makes any later interaction unlikely to offer satisfaction, thereby maintaining the compulsion. If such people then found their way on to a psychoanalyst's couch, it's easy to see how these secondary social problems could be blamed upon their 'deviant' pleasures.

A typical case in point was North's senior medical laboratory technologist, at a large psychiatric hospital, whose other hobbies included antique collecting and art, gardening, shooting and religion. His taste for rubber began in the pre-war days with his mother's apron, and his own mac which he liked the smell of. But having been caught in the act of sniffing the mac, which was then thrown out, he had surreptitiously incorporated another in the house into his later masturbatory practices. His fantasies then began to fill up with women, unobtainable in real life owing to his age, who were powerful figures such as judges and wardresses, and who made him 'do things'. Keeping his proclivity a secret into adult life, his obsession grew to the point where he would purloin macs from 'ladies' saddlebags' (leaving behind their value in money), and would spend up to two hours before work every morning dressed in a woman's mac, with his feet tied together, watching passing women out of the window. Not surprisingly, he began to feel rather guilty about doing this, and every so often would throw away his collection in a futile gesture. In time, he met at work a 'nice normal girl' who turned out to be so nice that she persevered with their engagement despite her 'bitter disappointment' the day he confessed his weakness. She had hoped that married life would cure him. Sadly for her, being convinced that he was a worthless 'moral psychopath', our technician did not consummate the marriage, demonstrating that his obsession for rubber was not as strong as his conviction that he was 'abnormal'.

The couple's real problem, of course, was not a rubber fetish but their misfortune to come of age in the 1950s, when people were profoundly ignorant and suspicious of any sexual variations. A book like North's would have been seized and the author sent to jail while the middle classes agonized about sex in the closet. It certainly could not have helped that the technician's prospective mother-in-law also tried to convince her daughter that her future husband was a sexual pervert, not because of his rubber fetish, which she knew nothing of, but because he wore a beard! The nice girl's real problem was not rubber either. She was so nice (and her anticipation of the physical pleasure sex might offer so high) that she made special purchases of attractive nightdresses and make-up in order to pull her husband together. Having a positive attitude towards sex, even after she blew a short fuse when he announced that he would never be able to consummate the marriage, she even made strenuous attempts to indulge his fantasies, despite his unflattering responses. Although she got nowhere, her efforts clearly belie North's assertion that women were naturally revolted by fetishes. On the contrary, the wife had far fewer problems with it than her husband did; and her only disappointment stems from the fact that his silly beliefs about himself would prevent her having children, which she was convinced would emotionally fulfil her.

Not only have North's core 'symptoms', and the technician's experiences, become far less common over the last twenty years with the growing number of services, facilities and organizations available to contemporary rubberists, but North's other speculations are open to alternative explanations.

Rubber is a sensuous material. Black was merely the most common colour then. The fact that the rubberists could play around with the roles of their fantasies suggest that they were switchable rather than single-minded. Likewise, punishment and degradation fantasies could simply reflect the attempt to absolve themselves from guilt or shame, given the realization that their solitary games would look really odd to those not initiated and not aroused; after all, according to moral convention, rubber sex, like subservience to a woman, or solitary indulgences, is supposed to be degrading, especially when one ties up one's genitals to prolong erections and arousal. The rubberist's masturbatory fantasies, however, need not reflect masochistic tendencies, simply because the rubberist plays the role of a woman or submissive male. Such fantasies could just as easily be a simple projection, whereby the rubberist places himself in the role of an ideal partner. For those who adopted the role of the submissive male, their fantasies could also have replicated real childhood experiences with real female adults. Far from the rubberist over-estimating the number of dominant or sadistic women who exist in society, North under-estimated the extent to which dominant fantasy partners could represent the way in which mother figures, aunts, nannies and nurses appeared to small male children in those days, and may still do so. It is very easy to see how these adults' care, coupled with strict controls, could launch a boy into a rubber career, without recourse to North's 'heterosexist' inferences about latent homosexuality. North should have paid a lot more attention to his interviewees' references to nannies and prep school matrons.

If women apparently disliked overt 'perversions' or 'fetishism', they were clearly not adverse to invoking it; which was somewhat ironic given that their fears probably followed from their realization that kinky sex of any kind could undermine the procreative-wife role that they were supposed to play in society. Given the social background of North's subjects and the timing of the study, this would make sense. In the early 1960s, a husband with a fetish did not fit into the domestic ideal around which British post-war governments had rebuilt society, and would obviously conflict with many women's sexual socialization. To explore an interest, let alone develop one, would have placed most women at a disadvantage. The supposed threats that fetishisms and perversions posed, therefore, had little to do with the latent sadistic aggression psychiatrists alleged that these tendencies held, so much as with their rejection of socially determined norms. Now that women are able to be much more independent it comes as no surprise to me that they are also beginning to experiment.

Sadomasochists

Further light on the inevitable clash between social attitudes and sexual difference appeared during C. Gosselin and G. Wilson's studies (1980) of sexual 'deviants'. They sought to test the Freudian myths about fetishism and SM against the data they collected from an SM correspondence club (which issued a quarterly journal boasting informed articles by doctors and psychologists as well as testimonies, fantasies and contact adverts), and interviewing several females, some of who advertised in SM contact magazines.

They secured a sample of 133 male devotees with a mean age of 47, and 25 dominant women with a mean age of 33.7, who filled in an Eysenck Personality Questionnaire, and a Wilson Sex Fantasy Questionnaire, as well as supplying background data. The SM devotees had not experienced any more childhood corporal punishment than a control group, though their upbringings were marginally stricter. Over all, the devotees' rate of weekly orgasms and self-rated libido did not differ much from the control group either; and their slightly lower 'satisfaction with partner' score may have followed from the fact that only 57 per cent of the sample had steady partners, compared with 78 per cent of the controls. In contrast to North's belief, the SM devotees did, however, record high scores on their correlation between fantasy and reality satisfaction rating; and the women, who were more likely to be single, even gained greater satisfaction from their partners by having more orgasms than the controls did.

Contrary to the sensational stereotypes promoted by the moral masochists, the active SM devotees played their sex games only with someone else who understood the rather strict rules, and seemed perfectly happy doing so, as the case of Mr and Mrs B demonstrates. This couple, in their late twenties, had begun ritualized sex games in order for Mr B to overcome his low self-esteem, but it was not a one-sided relationship. Mrs B's previous socialization – 'a sort of emotional frigidity due to a lack of sexual confidence', together with a puberty filled with rape fantasies, not to mention a caning-induced orgasm potential – meant that one could hardly find a better-matched couple.

The SM acts recorded by the two psychologists were also extremely varied; and very few revolved around pain; exposure and risk games were far more common. The B's, for example, acted out a 'tart game'; 'One day my wife went down to the pub dressed like a tart; I went down later and picked her up like a punter. It was fantastic.' Those who did appear to enjoy painful acts readily had a habit of returning for more on subsequent occasions; though Gosselin and Wilson warned that, because many masochists were adept at passing off their fantasies as real events, care should be taken in taking them on face value.

In reality, SM devotees' fantasies were not that different from those of 'normal' people. Apart from the odd SM act, the major difference was that the SM devotees were more exploratory and included a greater amount of mate-swapping, being promiscuous, having impersonal sex with strangers, and using objects for stimulation. Contrary to expectations, however, they also scored highest on intimate fantasy themes, such as kissing and having intercourse with one's loved partner, which clearly implies that a great fantasy life does *not* detract from real intimacy; quite the reverse.

When it came to orientation, the predominantly masochistic outnumbered the predominantly sadistic by three to one; there was, however, no difference between these two in terms of libido and sexual satisfaction, though those with exhibiting fetish tendencies tended to have more masochistic fantasies, and the masochists tended to have even more fantasies.

The implication that devotees were perfectly 'normal', and hardly distinguishable from everyone else, was reinforced when they were subjected to Eysenck's tests. In *Sex and Personality* (1976), Eysenck offered a fairly good guide to people's mental state, which rested upon establishing three aspects of an individual's personality. First, extraversion versus introversion: the sociable out-going type of person who enjoys meeting with other people, the life and soul of the party, who does, however, tend to get mad rather easily, blows off steam and disperses it; compared to the quiet, studious person happy to be alone, who keeps feelings under control, is reliable and often has high moral and ethical standards. Second, neuroticism. At its extreme, this exhibits itself in the kind of person who worries a lot, is often moody, sleeps badly, over-reacts to stresses, and frequently suffers from vague illness which other people do not. In contrast, the non-neurotic persons tend to be calm, even-tempered, controlled and unworried; though they can be sometimes insensitive and unresponsive to others' problems. Third, psychoticism. This type ranges from the touchy, aggressive but socially acceptable tough-minded, through the manipulative and cold self-centred, to the blatantly anti-social person. Non-psychotics tend to be warm, gentle and more 'feminine' in their attitudes and behaviour.

An individual's personality tends to be a mix of these three variables; and, when it comes to sex, Eysenck has found that extraverts not only tend to be more outgoing and novelty-seeking in their sexual behaviour, with plenty of activity, excitement and social contact, but have intercourse more often, with different partners, in a greater variety of positions, than introverts. Psychiatrists have argued that the latters' problems in interacting with adult members of the opposite sex follow from poor looks, lack of social skills or unfortunate early sexual experience, involving hostility, rejection or humiliation; hence fetishism, bizarre activities and homosexuality. Eysenck, however, thought it far more likely that introverts' interests followed a higher level of arousal in their cerebral cortex, which lends itself more readily to a condition of notional fixation, so that they were more likely to be effected by guilt and consciousness, with consequent risks to their sexual development.

Be that as it may, Gosselin and Wilson found that SM devotees were more stable characters than the norm. The dominant

103: Sense and Psychologists

were closer to the norm when it came to extroversion, the predominantly submissive were more inclined towards stability than neuroticism and introversion. On the psychoticism scale the women scored higher than the controls for toughness and were extrovert, though their neuroticism score was no different from that of other women.

Of great importance was the fact that neither group displayed high psychoticism: a perfect guide to a person's selfish and violent tendencies. There was nothing pathological about the male SM devotees at all. They did not display particularly high guilt levels, and were no more obsessional than other people. They did not resort to impersonal and aggressive sexual acts if they had difficulties in finding partners. Those amongst the SM group with unrealized tendencies, of whom only 17 per cent achieved sexual satisfaction with their partners, tended to seek out professionals or other devotees.

Consequently, Gosselin and Wilson concluded that the major difference between SM devotees and other people was that the devotees seek to become specialists in their sex lives, start young and continue to devote time to developing and refining their skills throughout their lifetime: an important distinction when considering the insights behavioural psychology has to offer us about people with antisocial violent tendencies when it comes to sex.

Excitation transfer

During the last twenty years numerous behavioural psychologists have been considering the relationship between sex and aggression. Two of the world's leading authorities in this area, Dolf Zillmann (1984) and Park Elliot Dietz (1990), both find SM abhorrent, so their results are even more illuminating.

Contrary to clinical theorists, behaviourists have discovered that sexual frustration is not a major source of sexual aggression; for the sexually aggressive tend to be excessively violent in all forms of their behaviour. In contrast, Zillmann does not consider consenting sadomasochistic devotees particularly aggressive or deviant at all.

The reason why most people think SM is related to aggression and deviance is because the popular use of such terms is far broader than scientific enquiry can allow. For behavioural scientists, aggressive behaviour is, correctly, restricted to any and every activity in which a person seeks to inflict bodily damage or physical pain upon a person *who is motivated to avoid it*; and they also avoid terms like 'normal', 'abnormal' and 'deviant', because these are pejorative terms. In terms of social scientists' definitions of sexual practices in contemporary society, only a small majority of people would *not* be deviant. Zillmann further suggests that as long as a sexual act is victimless, the participants have informed consent, the acts do not produce distress and are devoid of hostility and aggression, regardless of their particular physical form, they could be said to be societally acceptable. Though he believes that more stringent ethical criteria may be desirable, this is not science as it defies consensus.

When it comes to the relationship between sex and aggression, which is central to Krafft-Ebing's theories about sadomasochism, behavioural science has since discovered the reason why people find apparently painful stimuli pleasurable. For while

> adrenal activity serves both sexual and aggressive
> behaviours potentially in a confounded fashion because of
> highly similar mechanism . . . the capacity for mutual
> facilitation is not derived from peculiarities in the
> evolution of the central nervous system. The elicitation of
> behaviour of the one kind is not assumed to trigger – by
> spillage of excitation of central connections – behaviour of
> the other kind . . . The capacity for mutual facilitation is
> viewed as the result of poor sympathetic differentiation
> between sex and aggression.

In other words, while the excitement produced in sexual arousal and aggression is similar, there is no biological reason for supposing that one would or could lead automatically to the other. In order for this to happen, the person must be motivated for them to do so.

In numerous cultures, especially pre-literate ones, where sexual initiatives have not been solely the male gender's province, sexual behaviour in which women tend to be equally active participants has often been complemented with seemingly aggress-ive acts such as biting and slapping. Yet, as there is no compelling biological reason for people's strong preference for excitement-laden sex, or for assigning a value to it when it comes to reproduction, as we have become more 'civilized', seemingly aggressive acts have become regarded as 'barbaric' and superfluous. On the other hand, according to Zillmann, nature ensures that monogamous coupling encourages 'physical habituation'. In other words, predictable gentle sex with one partner invokes boredom with sex. When it comes to reintroducing excitement, however, nature offers a cure that never fails:

> As the arousing capacity of novel partners is likely to fade and acute emotional reactions such as fear and guilt are improbable accompaniments of sexual activity, what can be done to combat the drabness of routine sexual engagements that is expected to result from excitatory habituation? Rough housing, pinching, biting and beating emerge as viable answers. In terms of a theory it is the controlled engagement of pain that holds promise of reliably producing excitatory reaction for transfer into sexual behaviour and experience. The excitatory capacity of acute pain is not in doubt. Moreover, pain is extremely resistant to habituation . . . Acute pain then always can be counted on to stir up excitement. It is the habituation fighter par excellence . . . [for it to work], however, pain must be secondary to sexual excitedness. It must be dominated by sexual stimulation. Only when thus domin-ated can it be expected to enhance sexual excitedness. If aversion becomes dominant experientially, it will motivate voidance reactions and impair sexual excitedness and consummatory behaviour . . . Although it is conceivable that pain, which under different circumstances might be considered intense, if not unbearable, could be employed as a facilitator of sexual experience, pain thus sets its own limits for employment.

The reason why 'rough housing' works this way is the phenomenon known as 'excitation transfer'. As Havelock Ellis expected all those years ago, the excitement generated in one area of the 'emotions' can be transferred to another.

The paradigm projects [in unrelated successive emotional reactions] the intensification of any emotional reaction that is invoked during the presence of residue excitation from antecedent reactions – with some specifiable exception. In [emotional reactions elicited by simultaneously present, yet potentially unrelated stimuli] it projects the intensification of any emotional reaction by sympathetic excitation due to stimuli other than those that elicited the emotional reaction proper. The paradigm is applicable to all emotional reactions associated with sympathetic dominance in their excitary component.

In plain English, if you are sexually aroused, it is very easy to use the sensation felt as pain in a non-aroused state to enhance your sexual excitement. Indeed, as long as one's sexual arousal is the pre-dominant sensation, it is difficult not to make this transfer. It is also physically possible to use any form of anxiety state to facilitate sexual responses, as long as it is not too threatening or really painful. This is why lovers often find that love-making after quarrelling and fighting is far more exciting than usual. Apart from 'making-up', genital vasocongestion (erections and vaginal readiness) will be increased. So it should come as no surprise that being spanked and so on has the same effect, particularly when the stimulus is deemed to be exciting. Numerous other kinds of stimulus can have this effect; but for Zillmann

It appears that there is no substitute for pain as a reliable stand-by for the creation of excitement, in case it is lacking. Pinching, scratching, sucking, biting, squeezing, pulling, shoving and hitting constitute the bulk of the arsenal for aggression-related arousers that can be exploited for the enhancement of drab sexual endeavours. In exploiting these means, receiving tends to work better than giving.

As SM devotees carefully refine these simple acts, by dressing them up in role-play, it is easy to see how they are deliberately manipulating various forms of *stimulation* in the service of sexual arousal; and how this consenting scene where the submissive's pleasure is carefully planned is obviously very different from a truly coercive act like rape, which involves aggressive action designed to inflict acute pain on a non-aroused victim.

The fact that SM fantasies also involve transferring thoughts and feelings about humiliations and pain into sexual pleasure lays to rest the common fear that a sadist could somehow get 'carried away'; for it is also obvious that dominant SM devotees derive their buzz from their role in creating the pleasure that the submissive partners receive, rather than any 'torment and suffering' they enforce.

Despite helping to explain the phenomenon, Zillmann would prefer people to avoid SM; because of a commitment to a particular form of 'family values', he finds any instrumental sexual experience, like SM, 'in extremely poor taste'. He has even attempted to negate the logic of his own research by asserting that SM is inadvisable because 'sadistic participants in sexual activities . . . are likely to disregard signals to limit the infliction of pain'; not that he offered any evidence or justification for saying so. In order to find out who might, we have to ask Dr Dietz.

Who's really sick?

The distinctions to be made between those who play at aggression for pleasure and those who get their kicks from real aggression can be clarified with the help of the forensic psychologist Park Elliot Dietz, because he has been preoccupied with sexual sadists for over two decades.

In contrast to those who engage in SM role-play, Dietz believes that sexually sadistic criminals can be clearly identified by the nature of their crimes. Unlike dominant SM devotees, whose aim is to arouse their partners, sexually sadistic criminals intentionally torture their victims in order to arouse *themselves*. As this is hardly likely to appeal to a voluntary consenting partner, the sexually sadistic criminal will spend a long period carefully selecting strangers for victims, will approach them under a pretext, restrain them, hold them captive, deliberately engender fear, rape them, mutilate them and ultimately murder them. Thankfully, contrary to sensational media accounts and TV shows, such people are rare. In the United States, for example, the National Centre for the Analysis of Violent Crime dealt with only thirty such people between 1984 and 1989.

One of the reasons why we tend to over-estimate their number, according to Dietz, is that the vast majority of so-called 'sadistic crimes' are nothing of the kind. The psychotic prostitute who mutilates her client's genitals, the schizophrenics who dissect their murder victims from pelvis to neck, and gang members who castrate people for showing an interest in one of the gang's 'girls' are not sadists; they are emotionally unstable. Although their crimes may shock us, criminals who engage in acts of sexual cruelty are invariably suffering from delusions or hallucinations and the like, rather than sexually sadistic motives. Dietz does not think that 'pathological group behaviour', like armed service atrocities against civilians or dictatorship police forces' sexual tortures, are really sexually motivated either. Criminal sexual sadists can be distinguished by their antisocial personality disorders, and acts of mutilation followed by murder, or murder followed by mutilation, and even cannibalism, are not necessarily indicative of either sexual excitement or sexual sadism. Sick people can hack up their victims for hundreds of different reasons, especially when it's a 'one-off'.

As it is fairly easy to work out what differentiates sadistic serial murders from the mentally disorientated and from perfectly normal SM devotees, the real problem that society faces is shown by the fact that, to return to the above example, none of the thirty American offenders identified by the National Centre was spotted by the psychiatric profession despite frequently crossing their path during military discharge or incarceration for earlier offences. For all their supposed insights and guidelines in their diagnostic manual, the DSM-III-R, not one babbler noticed anything odd about these antisocial psychotics at all. What is worse, the babblers even ignored the 'signs' when the offenders made it patently obvious. One, for example, referred by his mother at the age of twelve because of an obsession with the dangerous practice of auto-erotic asphyxiation (hanging oneself to obtain an erection), was simply told he would grow out of it: he eventually strangled three women. Another offender went to a psychiatrist because he was worried that his sexual assaults on women might lead to murder. In one session, as the offender described his fantasies of murder, the psychiatrist fell asleep. The offender walked out never to return and began his killing career. Another, arrested for enticing young boys to his home where he photographed them holding knives to one another and using tomato ketchup or ink to simulate wounds, easily absconded from the State hospital from which he was sent, and promptly murdered a young boy. Another was asked by a psychologist to write out his most bizarre fantasies as part of his therapy. The offender duly obliged with detailed descriptions of his actual crimes; but the psychiatrist just babbled on about the symbolic meaning of fantasies. Perhaps its time we took a long look at the psychiatrists as well as at serial killers.

According to Dietz, the killers, when they were profiled after arrest, failed to exhibit any particular common personality characteristics or social background; but he failed to record or cite what, if any, standard psychometric tests were used to determine this. This is odd because such tests are usually a good guide. Sex killers for example would score high on tests for beliefs and tendencies such as violence as a means for conflict resolution, lack of empathy for other people, excitement at danger and sexual guilt.

Be that as it may, the lack of shared social characteristics raises a big problem for those who promote mono-causal theories about 'sadomasochists' in order to justify censorship, deny lifestyle choices or appropriate public funds for their profession's pet projects. Fewer than half of the killers came from broken homes, which Dietz characterized by reference to infidelity or divorce. Standard assertions that the killers must have been physically abused or sexually abused in childhood did not hold up either: only 23 and 20 per cent respectively had been. Almost half were married. Fewer than half had been known to have any kind of homosexual experience, including childhood sex play, which Dietz, for some reason, thinks is important. Cross-dressing and minor sexual offences such as indecent exposure, never amounted to more than 20 per cent of the group either. Almost half had been educated beyond high school level. So background provides no automatic clue.

On the other hand, although the killers included a banker, a military officer and a cardiovascular technician, Dietz failed to spot that most tended to have low-level or potentially unstable occupations: amusement park train conductor, baker (two), bar tender, bar tender/nude photographic studio proprietor, bouncer/truck driver, construction worker, cook, chef, candy-maker, house-painter, labourer, ex-law student, logger, mechanic, TV repair man, security guard, upholsterer, construction contractor, musician, photographer, rancher, real estate developer/racing car driver, restaurant owner, and sales manager. This could indicate that there might be something in the difference between their current status and their aspirations. One had been a sheriff's deputy and ten of the others had military experience.

Given the extent of the practice, the figure of 50 per cent for recreational drug use is meaningless; and although many people would like to blame pornography, 50 per cent did not have any at all. Dietz's fear that avidly reading true crime magazines encourages antisocial behaviour did not receive support either; only nine demonstrated an excessive interest in police activity and paraphernalia, beyond what they needed for their crimes; which was lower than the twelve who appeared obsessed with driving, even when going nowhere in particular. So there was nothing singular in their general behaviour either.

But while there may be nothing in particular that links all the killers together, one can highlight seven common features in their criminal behaviour which definitely distinguishes them from harmless SM devotees.

The first difference is the relationship between the *modus operandi* and securing unwilling partners. All but one of these offenders appeared to have meticulously planned their crimes. In order to succeed both in the crime and in their attempt to avoid detection, they studied law enforcement procedures; studied and collected the weapons needed; constructed specific equipment to torture their victims; altered vehicles to be used in the abduction and torture — sound-proofing vans, disabling windows and door handles, and installing police vehicle accessories; prepared torture kits; collecting cameras and recording devices to keep records of their crimes; stocked up on survival provisions for travel to remote locations; conducted systematic surveillance of their victims; wore gloves to avoid leaving fingerprints; and took their victims to locations selected in advance. This cold-blooded *modus operandi* was complemented by conning their victims, the killers often openly approaching them under one pretext or another, including impersonating a police officer and other elaborate ruses. One even hired models legitimately, claiming that the photo sessions were for the covers of detective magazines. Most kept their victims alive in captivity, for periods ranging from twenty-four hours to six weeks. Twenty-seven of the offenders bound, blindfolded or gagged one or more victims, in an elaborate and excessive, unnecessarily neat and symmetrical way. In short, every action was directed at securing control over an unwilling victim rather than finding and entertaining a willing partner. While some SM devotees do collect an extensive range of pleasure-enhancing equipment, most simply need the odd restraining device, paddle, and a polaroid.

The second difference concerns the sex acts undertaken and forced upon the victim. The three most popular acts committed by these sadistic criminals were: enforced anal penetration, enforced fellatio, and violent vaginal penetration with various 'foreign objects' *rather than the penis*. In contrast, the numerous sex acts commonly associated with SM (covered in the next chapter) were very rarely used; and the vast amount of equipment they had, far from being utilized to enhance the victim's pleasure, or to replicate various SM scenarios, was simply used to restrain the victims.

The third contrast can be seen in the sadistic offenders' demeanour, during the torture that both preceded and followed the sex acts; twenty-seven of the killers are known to have maintained an unemotional and detached demeanour throughout their actions. There appears to have been no 'high' or pleasure equivalent to that in an SM scenario; merely further evidence of the killers' cold and calculating approach to their crime. In contrast to this lack of emotionality, most then kept personal items belonging to their victims in order to facilitate sexually arousing recollections of their acts.

Sadly, in the fourth case, every one of these criminals tortured their victims. The nature of the torture, however, appears to be completely unlike the symbolic acts in SM sex, being deliberately designed to inflict serious and permanent injury upon the victim rather than skilfully enhance their sexual arousal. The psychological humiliation, and physical degradation, not to mention the threats that accompanied such acts, were also 'for real'; these sadistic criminals delighted in ensuring that when these features were combined with the physical injury inflicted, they heightened the victims' fear. Dietz drew particular attention to the importance and role of generating and increasing the victims' terror in defining the sadistic killer. This evil feature of their approach was demonstrated by the lengths taken to ensure that the victims would remain conscious throughout their torture. Two of these offenders even resuscitated near-dead victims in order to cause them additional suffering before they died.

Fifth, while twenty-two of the thirty killers were responsible for at least 187 homicides and were suspected by the police of having committed another 120, the perpetrators' most popular choice of execution, despite all the possibilities open to them, was strangulation – an act that does not feature in consenting SM sex.

Sixth, when the perpetrators did not suffer from a sexual dysfunction, like retarded or premature ejaculation, they had committed previous sexual assaults including incest.

In short, real sexual sadists can be distinguished from harmless SM devotees by their *modus operandi* in securing unwilling victims; the lack of SM sex acts, skills, or intent; the pathology of unemotional detachment; their exhibition of extreme viciousness; and their high level of sexual dysfunction or previous record of sexual crime. The seventh difference? Unlike many SM devotees, none of these killers displayed the slightest tendency to switch and take the role of the victim.

The importance that Dietz attaches to the way in which the killers kept detailed records and numerous souvenirs of their offences should have been enough to convince the Spanner investigators that they were clearly not dealing with sexually sadistic criminals. Likewise, the police should have easily been able to make the necessary distinctions between those with criminal intent and the Spanner 'sadists', let alone the Spanner 'masochists' who were hardly terrorized strangers. This point is easily demonstrated by contrasting the Spanner defendants with Colin Ireland, the 'gay stalker' serial killer of 1993. While in his teens, Ireland already had convictions for burglary, theft and blackmail. He had spent two periods in borstal and, like many budding psychotics, had even attempted to join the Foreign Legion. Far from fantasizing about sex, let alone SM sex, Ireland fancied himself as a kind of 'Rambo' figure; his only compensation for two failed marriages and a series of broken relationships. Apart from his dramatic mood swings, which can be an indication of someone on the edge, Ireland began to talk openly to a girlfriend and acquaintances about his fantasies of killing people. Once he became obsessed with a prophecy that the end of the world was nigh; like several killers on the National Centre list, Ireland then threw his energies into 'survivalist' skills and dressing up in camouflage gear. In Ireland's case, however, even this was a failure. He was so hopeless at 'survivalism' that, far from living off the land, he would nip into the nearest town for a take-away. Having apparently practised, and got a kick out of, torturing and strangling cats, Ireland then picked his human prey from amongst the inoffensive clientèle of a gay leather bar: a choreographer of musicals, a mild-mannered librarian from Brent, an American sales director, a sheltered-home care worker and a Maltese chef. Once he had taken advantage of them, by tying these bondage devotees up, Ireland tortured them for their PIN numbers, and then strangled them. Having accomplished the deed, Ireland would then push condoms into his victim's mouth or nose, and burn the victim's pubic hair. In the case of his fourth victim, he set fire to various parts of the body, strangled the victim's cat and then stuck his victim's penis in the dead cat's mouth.

No amount of persecution of the SM community is going to stop someone like Colin Ireland; but it will ensure that it takes longer to catch him.

A psychodrama

In contrast to the psychiatrists, the psychologists raise important questions about SM, offer dozens of useful insights, and are able to differentiate between 'sadistic' criminals and SM devotees. Levitt's insight into spanking, the Greenes' suggestion that we should look at what devotees do while intellectualizing their sexual desires, and the need to consider the importance of social norms and isolation in creating many of the problems erroneously associated with the sexually different highlighted by North's study, need to be explored. The technician's experience, and North's observations about women's reactions to their husband's proclivities, can also help to explain the origin of current fears. The wives', and women's, apparent dislike of overt 'perversions' or 'fetishism' probably had more to do with the sexist role they were being asked to perform in society at that time. I do not believe it is a coincidence that the attack upon SM sex began at the very time women began to exercise their free choice and experiment. North could not quite grasp this point, nor the complementary fear that sadomasochistic fetishes were some kind of mental illness; his own socialization would not let him. Yet, as Thomas S. Szasz pointed out as long ago as 1974, as a real mental illness would consist of a brain disease or a neurological defect which would exhibit biological symptoms like a paralysis, the vast majority of designated 'mental illnesses' are no more than moral judgments about the patients' social beliefs or behaviour.

When it comes to sex, to call something a 'deviation', let alone a perversion, would also require an established and agreed 'norm' to exist. Yet the ideas of Freud and Krafft-Ebing upon which anti-SM scaremongering is based not only rests upon a ridiculous anachronistic sexist stereotype, but relies upon a delusion of grandeur. Like most other Victorians, Krafft-Ebing and Freud simply assumed that contemporary bourgeois practice was the natural and inevitable outcome of an 'evolutionary' process, whereby 'civilization' just happened to reach its ultimate form during the Victorian period. This common theme, running through everything from anthropology to zoology, not only dismissed the possibility of choice in favour of ethnocentric moralism, but led the authorities to enforce what they called a 'natural' order upon anyone who did not agree. The rubberists' problems in North's study followed from the public imposition of this moralism, as the contrast between the happily married couples and the technician with his religious obsessions demonstrates.

Thankfully, behavioural psychology does not let any relative moral standard prevent it from distinguishing between the many different kinds of people who have been labelled 'sadist' or sick. If Gosselin and Wilson's study is anything to go by, the current categories of sadism and masochism promoted by psychiatrists and upheld in out courtroom have no justification or basis in reality; they serve only to mislead the public. As this should have been apparent to anyone conversant with good medical diagnostic practice, whereby the greater the number of 'diseases' covered by a single 'symptom' the less likely it is that that symptom will have any diagnostic value, it is also fair to assume that the public were being deliberately misled. When it is then realized that the babblers' own 'bible', the DSM-III-R, emphasizes that to be designated a paraphiliac (a supposedly non-pejorative term for a 'pervert' taken from the Greek meaning 'besides' and 'love') an individual's sexual difference has to be his or her primary or major source of sexual gratification, it becomes apparent that the vast majority of SM devotees should not really be called 'sadists' or 'masochists' in the first place.

It is time that the public began to wonder why SM devotees are being deliberately associated with 'sadistic' killers, with whom they have nothing in common. There has to be more to this than the babblers' failure to possess the intelligence to conceive of new labels. Whatever the reason, as long as irrational psychiatry is allowed deliberately to promote the erroneous idea that there is some link between SM devotees and criminals, those who wish to exploit ideologically the evil acts of the emotionally disturbed or the calculating psychotics – who take out their morally induced psychosexual hang-ups upon unwilling victims – in order to imply that there is something dangerous about consenting partners who like playing mutually pleasurable sex games will not only maintain the confusion; they will ensure that the sadistic killer's carnage will continue. You cannot stop one Yorkshire Ripper by persecuting fifteen gay friends. Unfortunately, vested interests and moralists are more than prepared to allow that to happen rather than draw the lessons from behavioural psychology, because mainstream psychiatry's assertions about sadomasochism serves their moral agenda.

On the other hand, while psychology can tell us how pain can be transferred into pleasure, and make assessments about SM devotees' attitudes and actions compared to those of dangerous people, it still does not tell us much about the kinds of things SM devotees do, or why they do it. In order to answer those kinds of questions, and demonstrate once and for all that there is nothing inherently dangerous about consenting SM sex games, we need to review the work of sociologists and sexologists, the only people who have ever bothered to find out.

Chapter five

Defending the Indefensible

IT took sociology a long time to explore the world of sexuality; but once John Gagnon and Bill Simon had opened the door in the late 1960s every kind of sexual behaviour, and belief about it, was open to question. One after another the myths and unfounded assumptions which lay behind stigmatizing the sexually different were exposed for what they were: baseless nonsense serving the cause of moralistic persecution. And once homosexuality was freed from its ridiculous designation as a mental illness it was not long before attention turned to SM sex, and it was discovered that denunciations and interpretations based on the concept of giving and receiving pain were completely inadequate for describing what is really a very complex type of behaviour.

High heels and bondage

The sociologists took their lead from the anthropologist Paul Gebhard, whose 1968 essay 'Fetishism and Sadomasochism' undermined the idea of individual pathology by pointing to sadomasochism's cultural roots, and the futility of defining a widespread and diffuse sexual practice by reference to a few 'extreme' examples. Gebhard wondered why, given numerous examples of 'combative' mating amongst mammals and its positive neurophysiological effects, anyone should find similar kinds of sexual behaviour in humans strange, especially when society promoted so many forms of dominant–submissive relationships, and frequently valued social aggression.

What was really intriguing about sadomasochism was that it appeared prevalent in its organized form only in literate societies full of symbolic meanings; which meant that, far from being a manifestation of a base instinct, sadomasochism required a considerable amount of intelligence and organization. Detractors' explanations did not make sense either: if the psychodynamics of childhood, puberty and adolescence had anything to do with it, it was far more likely that masochism derived from the prohibitions and punishments handed out for sexual exploration so that masochists were relieving their guilt at the same time as seeking pleasure. Pain could not be the major factor, otherwise devotees would just as easily gain pleasure or sexual satisfaction in accidental pain. On the contrary, devotees seemed to spend so much time carefully organizing the 'scripting' of their activities in order to control and plan the nature and amount of punishment that sadomasochism looked more like a theatrical production than a simple act of sexual violence. Whereas 'sadists' had to develop an extraordinary level of perceptiveness to know when to continue and when to stop, masochists seemed to get as much, if not more, pleasure from the 'threats' and suspense involved as they did from any form of pain. Some enjoyed and obtained their gratification from reflecting back over events, some from the event, and others merely by the anticipation of the event. Many clearly did not like any kind of pain at all, but were turned on simply by the constraint or sense of helplessness in bondage games instead. If one was simply dealing with pain, what was the purpose of the incredible range of fetish items from specialized clothing to specialist devices, which provided either additional gratification or substantial pleasure in their own right through the ingenuity and creativity of the user? Some devotees even suggested that without love and tenderness sadomasochism was pointless.

Then there was all the 'unconscious' sadomasochism in society to explain too. The Institute for Sex Research, founded by the pioneer sex researcher Alfred Kinsey at Indiana University, discovered that one in eight females and one in five males were aroused by sadomasochistic stories; and it was possible that bottom-slapping and high heels had something to do with it too. At the very least, given the subtle appearance of numerous sadomasochist themes in the media, psychiatrists were clearly looking for a stereotypical abnormality that did not exist. Their 'explanations' hardly explained anything, and certainly not the phenomena they were supposed to be addressing.

In their stead, Gebhard suggested that widespread sadomasochism might follow from the frustrations of living in a social pecking order based around dominance and submissive relationships which, when matched with the perennial difficulties encountered in the search for sexual gratification, produced an endless source of combinations of sex and 'violence', not least because the pecking order alluded to the symbolism of sex to describe itself, and the symbolism of the pecking order to describe sex. As a result, organized sadomasochism would appear only in well-developed, complex civilizations with extensive symbolic meaning systems, in which some people sought to transcend the inescapable repressions and frustrations of life through the symbolism of sadomasochism:

> Sadomasochism is beautifully suited to symbolism: what better proof of power and status is there than inflicting humiliation or pain upon someone who does not retaliate? And what better proof of love is there than enduring or even seeking such treatment?

I can think of several; and while Gebhard raised several useful questions, there are obvious problems with his account.

First, as with the psychiatrists before him, Gebhard's definitions of sadomasochism were too flexible; being whatever his argument required them to be. Second, repeating the unproved assertion that sadomasochistic women were rare, he underestimated the effect that social sanctions may have for women so inclined; and despite alluding to the role of fantasy where many people's desires remain because of lack of opportunity, Gebhard did not allow for tangential manifestations such as unattached 'cock-teasers' as they are known, or wives who delight in humiliating their 'ineffective' husbands. The major conundrum, however, was caused by Gebhard's concept of cultural influence. By suggesting that sadomasochism's ultimate existence can be traced to socially sanctioned and symbolized violence on the one hand, but then arguing that the psychodynamics of the individual masochist's experience rested upon a social taboo against violence on the other, he was burning the candle at both ends. While it would be perfectly possible, in a complex society, for one to reach a similar end by different routes, in this case the way in which diffuse social influences worked would need further elaboration before being taken for granted. Nevertheless, the psychobabblers' spell had been broken, and sociology moved in.

How many?

Trying to establish how many people have the potential to indulge in and enjoy SM sex is difficult; the estimates vary so widely. As far back as 1929, Hamilton's marriage habits survey turned up a figure of 28 per cent of males and 29 per cent of females admitting that they derived 'pleasant thrills' from having some form of 'pain' inflicted upon them. The Kinsey studies discovered that around 24 per cent of men and sadomasochistic stories. A survey by Hariton (1972) into married women's fantasies came up with 49 per cent fantasizing about submissive scenarios during sexual intercourse, with 14 per cent doing so frequently. A mid-1970s independent agency poll funded by *Playboy* of 3,700 representative students from twenty colleges found that 12 per cent of female and 18 per cent of male students had indicated a willingness to try master–slave role play, or bondage sex; 2 per cent had actually tried and liked such activities. Hunt's 2,000 respondents offered lower figures: 8.4 per cent of males and 2.1 per cent of females had obtain sexual pleasure from an act of domination, with the number for submissive acts being 2.5 and 4.6 respectively (Hunt, 1974). In complete contrast, a study of male college students, by Greendlinger and Byrne (1987), has claimed that a staggering 80 per cent enjoyed the idea of being tied up and forced to have sex by a woman!

Consequently, while extrapolating from such studies is difficult because their definitions of SM acts vary and the figures differ so widely, it is clear there are millions of people who have SM-like fantasies, and quite a few who would like to play-act them out.

German contacts

The first major study to see what kind of person took the plunge was Andreas Spengler's (1977). By checking out those who had identified themselves as sadomasochists by advertising in German contact magazines during the mid-1970s, he really put the pressure on the psychobabblers' definitions.

The only thing these devotees had in common was their high standard of living, social status and education. Those who were married tended to keep their proclivity secret, rather than force it upon their wives, even though, unlike gay men or bisexuals, they therefore faced greater problems finding willing partners.

Whatever their sexual partner preference, none of these devotees was compulsive either. The frequency of their SM experiences was extremely low: only 20 per cent indulged themselves as often as once a week. With a mean score of five SM experiences a year, no one seemed to suffer from any uncontrollable urges, let alone a dependency upon sexual 'painful' acts. Everyone could, and most did, enjoy other forms of sexual activity. Likewise, only 13 and 16 per cent respectively adopted an exclusively dominant or submissive role; and when it came to the use of any kind of painful stimulation, the more extreme the practice the rarer it was. The devotees' most common preference was simple bondage complemented with corporal punishment. Even fetish clothing was used only by 50 per cent of the sample, uniforms by 16 per cent, and rubber by 10.

When it came to fantasies, there appeared to be a link between the number and frequency of SM experiences and SM sex fantasies. No one seemed either to fit the serial killer stereotype – brooding away, psyching themselves up for the inevitable frenzied attack upon an innocent. While 10 per cent worried about their desires, 90 per cent, being perfectly happy, had never even considered going to a doctor or psychiatrist about their sexual preference. The biggest burden anyone faced was the problem of social stigma; and it is extremely pertinent to note that the 10 per cent who felt negatively about their SM fantasies were invariably those who were not integrated into Germany's extensive sadomasochistic subculture. Like North's rubberists, the more isolated they were the more worries they had. The stereotypical sadomasochist had turned out to be anything but stereotypical.

The American SM scene

The German study was soon followed by several conducted by American sociologists. One group, Weinberg, Falk, Lee and Kamel (1983), quickly discovered that American devotees did not match the psychologists' stereotypes either; and their observations of the San Francisco and New York scenes, over a seven-year period beginning in 1976, offered a completely different interpretation of what was going on.

The sociologists discovered that self-identified SM devotees tended to keep themselves to themselves, rather than attempt to involve non-devotees in their sexual interests. This was decidedly uncool. While the devotees clearly enjoyed defying contemporary sexual taboos themselves, their SM acts were deliberately undertaken in private, precisely because they wished to avoid giving any offence to 'straights' who, it was believed, would never understand the pleasures SM had to offer. The SM community which grew up around the devotees' clubs, meetings, organizations, contact sheets, magazines and stores not only generated a set of SM social values which rationalized and justified the devotees' interest in SM, it also went to great lengths to ensure the physical safety of its own members. Far from promoting pain, SM devotees had their own techniques, rules, beliefs and language to reduce the possibility of harm, promoted by their own organizations, facilities and experts, who helped new initiates to explore their feelings in safety.

Charles Moser and Eugene E. Levitt, sexologists at the Institute for the Advanced Study of Human Sexuality in San Francisco, confirmed (1987) that not all SM experiences involved pain: only certain types of pain in certain types of situations were arousing, and that the 'pain' was not experienced as pain anyway owing to its transformation into pleasure by the sexual arousal. In its stead, the typical SM experience, according to Weinberg, consisted of five features. First, dominance and submission: an appearance of rule by one partner over the appearance of obedience by the other. Second, role-playing: an exaggeration of the expectations that surround the particular dominant and submissive roles chosen. Third, consensuality: a voluntary agreement to enter into this 'play' and to honour certain 'limits.' Fourth, a sexual context: the presumption that the activities have a sexual meaning. And fifth, mutual definition: an assumption of a shared understanding by the participants that their activities are SM. If one of these features was missing, devotees would not define what was happening as an SM act; and the closer one looked, the more obvious it became that the very people who are supposed to be obsessed with painful acts did not even consider pain a necessary ingredient at all. In both fantasy and role-play, dominance and submission was the most common and important feature. The 'sadist' and the 'masochist' involved did not have fixed proclivities either; most participants had tried, or were interested in trying, both roles. Many devotees regularly switched roles depending upon particular partners, or along gender lines; so that, for example, a woman who liked being submissive with women might dominate men, with the exception of a particular one.

The sociologists discovered that SM fantasy-enactment involved a great deal of elaboration on top of the basic dominant and submissive roles adopted in what was called 'a scene'. The devotees seemed to utilize polarized roles, such as a mistress and servant, because this made it easier to sustain the fantasy situation when both partners knew they were really playing a game.

The specific SM acts used in each 'scene' could range from simple verbal humiliation, through a series of specific acts, right up to complete playscripts, some of which even included the intonation of the voice to be used. The extensive paraphernalia of hoods, corsets, chains, paddles, enema equipment, rubber panties, gas masks, scuba gear and restraints, were utilized for variety enhancement, rather than to induce pain, and also served to reinforce the sense of sexual adventure for the participants. Far from reflecting sinister connotations, the roles and paraphernalia to be used were always consensual and tended to be agreed amongst the participants beforehand; anyone who broke the agreement would quickly find themselves ostracized by other devotees as word travelled fast.

The sociologists quickly discovered what everyone on the scene would have already known: if forceful acts, such as caning, were to be used, the dominant participant was expected to have developed the skills required to make their use pleasurable; while each submissive would have his or her own established preferences and thresholds, known as their 'limit', beyond which the act would fail to effect the transfer, and become painful. Whatever else was going on, the 'scene' would then steadily work up to the limit; so that the acts remained pleasurable and never became painful. As an individual's general 'limit' is flexible, being determined by the amount of arousal experienced at the time, limit-setting methods such as stop-words or signals would be used, although many participants said that these were unnecessary in 'really good scenes', because an experienced dominant can easily tell when a submissive's limits are being approached. Indeed, the more experienced the partners are, the more possible it is to agree to a flexible, continuous process of consent because this makes possible the periodic experience of 'pushing the limits', whereby submissives steadily increase their general limit.

Naive outsiders constantly fail to appreciate that what may appear to them to be a particularly painful act is experienced as nothing of the kind by the submissive participant. The more painful the act appears to be, the more experienced the submissive will be. Painful acts are, however, relatively rare, and many devotees find they can experience similar forms of pleasure enhancement through bondage 'scenes', using chains, ropes, gags, suspensions, and lots of fantasy.

Like the Germans, the Americans in the sociological studies were not exclusively SM devotees, and enjoyed 'ordinary' sex more often than scenes. Even when in a scene, participants could alternate between being overwhelmed by their feelings and putting on a charade to maintain the fantasy. There was also a lively debate amongst the devotees over which practices should and should not be called SM.

Some participants, for example, did not think 'bondage and discipline', or B&D, was 'real' SM precisely because it did not involve extensive role elaboration. Others likely to find themselves excluded by most devotees' definitions were those utilizing SM type arousal to reach altered states of consciousness. The biggest debate at the time was whether or not the gay 'leather scene' formed part of the SM community.

These insights into SM activities, and the differentiation debates, reinforced the American researchers' general conclusion that the psychiatric models of sadomasochism were over-generalized, essentialist and atomistic. They were over-generalized in presupposing motives and meanings not shared by devotees, because they were more applicable to non-consensual sexual violence designed to hurt. While sexual criminals would run a mile before calling themselves sadomasochists, self-identified SM participants would run a mile from any real violent sexual crime. The psychiatric models were essentialistic in that they asserted that SM activities and interests were innate to an individual's 'nature', when SM devotees could take it or leave it. SM sex was really a set of social acts rather than a collection of 'sadistic' or 'masochistic' characters. The previous theories were atomistic in centring on an individual's alleged sexual 'drives', while completely ignoring the important role of the SM scene in constructing the meanings which devotees then drew upon both to define and to shape their sexual activities. Far from being an individual's 'problem', SM simply could not exist at the level of the individual; SM was a shared activity and a group phenomenon.

SM theatre

In order to try to explain what they saw, Weinberg and his colleagues made an analogy between SM fantasy role-play and the theatre, based upon 'frame analysis' devised by a sociologist called Erving Goffman, who drew attention to the way we all use 'frameworks', or particular perspectives, to understand social actions.

In order to grasp the essential sociological point about the way in which different people use different 'frameworks', based upon their beliefs about the world to produce a different interpretation about the same event, just consider the 'meaning' of smoking marijuana. What amounts to a religious act for a Rasta is a crime to

a policeman, a major means of demonic possession to a fundamentalist Christian deliverance minister, and a good excuse for a book by
a sociologist. The less intelligent people are, or the more committed
they are to a set of beliefs, the fewer frames they will have to draw
upon when trying to understand something. Some people can
readily pick up and understand others' frames; some people are
clueless. The most important thing to remember, however, is that a
social group's primary frameworks are also the central elements of
its culture. As Goffman explained in *Frame Analysis* (1974),

> Frames are central components of the culture of the group
> through which its members interpret the world . . . Frames
> tell people what is and what is not proper, acceptable and
> possible within their world. They define and categorize for
> their members, situations, settings, scenes, identities, roles
> and relationships.

In a modern society, numerous social groups share common frames,
and Weinberg and colleagues suggested that SM is best understood
by reference to the very common theatrical framework.

The participants know what is going on, and so do those 'in
the know'; but someone who does not know the conventions, by
which something with one meaning in one framework can be
transformed into something else based upon it in another framework, could easily become confused. Movie car chases, for example,
are not complete make-believe; they really do end up with several
cars being write-offs, but the risk of real injury is reduced by the
stunt stand-in's skill.

In SM the participants use various actions and devices to
transform what would normally be considered violence or dominance into make-believe. Some people cannot understand that real
violence does not occur, because they do not know all the
conventions of the theatrical frame, especially one of its major
features whereby

> unlike the everyday world where a degree of uncertainty
> obtains, participants in this activity have the opportunity
> to 'play the world backwards' i.e. to arrange now for some
> things to work out later that ordinarily would be out of
> anyone's control and a matter of fate or chance . . .

The uncertainty of real life does not occur. This is why in the SM world the submissive really takes control, and why professional dominants obtain an indication of their clients' limits in advance.

The sociologists then attempted to illustrate the point by drawing attention to the over-representation of 'dominant' women and 'submissive' men in the SM world, which is contrary to our society's social conventions. Within the SM fantasy scene, however, the roles taken are reversed only in the sense that an individual who is 'really' dominant and male makes himself 'subservient' to another who is 'really' a subservient female. While some roles adopted may be taken from real social relations, such as 'governess/child', 'mistress/slave' and 'teacher/pupil', other men need to dress as women or take the roles of animals in order to be submissive, owing to their social beliefs and associations. What goes for a professional scene also applies to non-professionals.

But while this reference to frame analysis can help to put SM 'pain' into its true perspective, the most significant revelation in this sociological attempt to explain what is happening is the incredible commonality of the roles adopted by devotees.

Even allowing for the fact that most devotees would not have personally experienced such roles during their lifetimes, SM fantasies and scenes are clearly not unique to individuals, private or idiosyncratic, but are obviously drawn from the numerous culturally generated symbols involving stereotypical figures, situations and actions which are then codified and re-shaped by those on the SM scene to become the means to facilitate fantasies about dominance and submission. In taking a role which is not 'really' their 'own', the participants are obviously defining and making the scene an act of 'play', 'make-believe', 'fantasy' and so on. It could hardly be otherwise, given the distance between the roles adopted and the participants everyday life; how else, for example, could a man who might feel a 'need' to be occasionally submissive separate the role he performs in SM from his diametrically opposite social identity?

This explanation could and should, however, be taken further. Theatre audiences simultaneously know that the actors playing Romeo and Juliet do not really die, but suspend their disbelief and pretend that they do die in order to enjoy the play. While SM is similar, the sociologists would be much better off comparing it to a movie. Some of the actions in SM are 'real'; just as the cars in movie chases really crash, people really get spanked in SM. The real point to grasp is that just as the stunt stand-ins do not get hurt but actors play dead, and the audience pretends they are dead, in SM the participants, who also play the actors, stunt stand-ins, and audience at one and the same time, are not damaged either, owing to their skills and 'limits'. Likewise, one of the major reasons why people do not 'understand' the role of the 'theatrical' frame in SM is not that they cannot do so but that they simply do not want to. They would, and do, object to SM whether or not any real pain is involved, either because the idea of an 'effeminate' male's crawling round on his hands and knees barking at his mistress's beck and call makes them feel very uncomfortable when confronted with the proof that the social conventions they live by are pretty flimsy things, or because they oppose the use of hedonistic arousal – transforming 'dominance' into pleasure.

These two points need to be spelt out, because while the element of make-believe is obvious in the case of professional services offered in contact magazines, it is easy to forget make-believe when non-professionals are involved, as the contrast between a couple of advertisements offered by Weinberg, complete with their allusions to particular scenes, props and costumes, demonstrate. The two professionals are obviously offering a temporary service:

> Blonde dominatrix dressed in rubber or leather costume. Seeks experienced or novice slaves who believe in dominant female superiority. I'm well qualified in B&D, water sports, humiliation, petticoat training and have equipment built by slaves.

> Tall, cruel, Creole Beauty seeks Dominant Male partner to assist her in controlling; disciplining her many slaves. Come be my King so we can play King & Queen. Do not answer if you are not sincere and generous. Letter, photo & phone gets you a surprisingly quick reply. This is for dominants only, have too many slaves now.

And a non-professional's offer to be submissive maintains this impression:

> Very pretty 30 yr old female has fantasies about receiving hand-spankings on bare behind. I've never allowed myself to act out any of the fantasies. Is there anyone out there who'd like to correspond with me about their fantasies or experiences with spankings?

Yet it is easy to see how people may not be able to suspend their disbelief when confronted with an advert like this one:

> Cruel husband seeking experienced dominant man to assist in training petite, shy, young wife. Eager to watch her transform from shy, personal, sex slave to slut. Presently serving me and a friend in humiliation, verbal abuse, deep throat, GR, golden shower, lewd dancing, nude posing, public display. Prefer man with extensive movie/erotica collection, over 50, obese with a fetish for petite, young girls or hung Black.

In reality the husband could be very kind while the wife could be the dominant partner; and the acts might simply allude to the particular fantasies the couple enjoy together. Judging by the wording, this couple may have been into 'humiliation' games for some time, and are now seeking someone else 'in the know' to play particular roles. Any idiot thinking that this 'white-slavery' scenario was for 'real' would be weeded out at the initial reply stage.

The political opponents of SM not only draw upon people's ignorance to cover up this fantasy factor when pointing the finger at SM devotees, they deliberately promote this kind of misconception in order to gain support for their own frames for interpreting the world. The staff members on the American Meese Commission into Pornography, for example, put on slide shows of decontextualized SM imagery in their public sessions in the hope that this would convince people that all pornography was violent. Unfortunately for them, the media saw through this systematic suspension of the common conventions one uses to analyse any images. As Carol Vance explained:

> When we see science-fiction movies, for example, we do not leave the theatre believing that the special effects were

real or that the performers were injured making the films. But the commissioners assumed that images of domination and submission were both real and coerced.

The supreme irony, however, is that many contemporary acts of SM 'humiliation' are borrowed from the moral crusaders' frame of reference. While the SM participants would not believe the likes of oral sex or posing are really humiliating, they temporarily pretend to accept the moral standards which make them so, because the idea that one is being 'humiliated' can be transferred into sexual arousal just as easily as any physical sensation.

Learning the ropes

Having provided a complementary means to understand the SM acts which help to effect excitation transfer, the sociologists then sought to demonstrate how SM was an acquired rather than innate taste.

Although entrance to the SM community could either be fortuitous, by meeting another participant and discussing the subject, or a deliberate decision to attend a group, contacting an organization, or using contact magazines, once initiates are inside the SM world, any preconceptions they held would quickly be altered through their education in the techniques, rules, motives, rationalizations and attitudes promoted by the community. Indeed, during the late 1970s, Weinberg found that 'The development of apologias, attitudes and ideologies, supportive of SM appears to be more important than the dissemination of specific techniques for restraining people and inducing pain and discomfort.'

While not being so naive as to believe that all rationales are necessarily viable, the sociologists realized that whatever one thought of sadomasochism before entering the subculture, its theories would eventually be worked out in practice. By having to make social choices, individuals would not only find their previous beliefs being tested against the views of others, they would have to learn the rules of behaviour promoted by the group. Though social groups' 'reconstructed logic' and *post facto* idealizations do not always provide a true description of their participants' motives, when SM devotees' activities were compared to the alternative explanations offered by opponents, it quickly became clear which group was offering the more accurate description.

Weinberg and his colleagues came across four kinds of SM group: 'consciousness raising' groups, publishing organizations, sex clubs and a theatrical company. Though their primary purpose varied, they all provided similar functions, including opportunities for participation, and disseminating both information and rationales about SM which enabled participants to separate their SM behaviour from the other areas of their lives.

The New York Eulenspiegel Society, named after a German folklore character who carried heavy loads up a hill because it felt so good when he put the load down, held weekly meetings to discuss SM and sponsored lectures and demonstrations by SM experts. The House of Milan, based in Los Angeles, published several contact magazines, including *Latent Image*, *Aggressive Gals* and *Bitch Goddesses*, involving female domination, spanking, transvestism and rubber fetishes, and organized occasional parties. Chateaux 19, a New York SM club, offered facilities like the straight sex club Plato's Retreat. The Project, founded in the early 1970s, brought SM fantasies out of the closet, by performing their fans' fantasy scenarios for churches, colleges, singles groups and private parties. Their programme *Another Way to Love*, for example, included:

1 The Beauty of Looking Beastly: a psycho-sexual fairy tale, wherein the 'ugliest man in the world' lives his most beautiful moment – a scene in which a man is publicly humiliated by a beautiful woman who forces him to wear a collar and leash and a mask hiding his face.

2 I'm The Haughtiest Girl in the Whole USA: a fetishistic 'Judge' who specializes in 'justice' for pretty girls convicted of pretty-girl crimes liquifies his toughest prisoner into a splash-pool of humiliation by getting to the bottom of her evil – A man dressed as a man puts a woman into stocks, forcing her to publicly confess her crimes of 'haughtiness', and then tortures her by tickling her bare feet.

3 Bottoms Up!: a peek into the bedroom of an earnest young wife who endeavours to redesign her colour scheme

by pestering, plaguing and provoking her posterior
decorator – a spanking fantasy.

4 Paul(a): the fantasist awakens her husband to a galaxy
of life changes most profound – a woman dressed up in a
translucent black body-suit, high heeled boots, and armed
with a whip, forces her husband to dress in a French
Maid's uniform complete with underwear and a wig.

If ever one needed proof of the social as opposed to private nature of
SM, this was it. SM was a recreational as well as a sexual interest,
and had become an economic industry too. One had only to look at
the publications filled with advertisements for expensive clothing
and equipment, as well as the lucrative magazines, movies, sex clubs
and prostitution services, to see that.

The social process through which individuals learn about
SM, as opposed to simply acting out a pathological urge, was then
illustrated by Weinberg and Kamel's (1983) accounts of SM
participants' life-histories. These also serve to highlight the importance of mutual respect and affection involved, the norms adhered
to, and how control is shared in SM relationships.

There was the couple where the wife, Jeanie, had first felt
uncomfortable about being asked to dominate Daniel who was
initially motivated by his previous masochist fantasies about being
bullied by girls; but once he switched, following an experience with
a female co-worker whose domineering attitude at work belied her
own submissive fantasies, Jeanie quickly took to the SM scenes,
involving extensions of the stereotypical patriarchal heterosexual
relationship, which then followed. So much for childhood fixations.

Gay Glen's experiences were a perfect example of how an
individual's perceptions and goals could change as a result of
learning experiences. An early childhood sense of isolation in his
family, induced by a bullying father's habit of calling Glen the
'family faggot', inevitably led the youngster to believe he really
might be 'a homosexual'. Desperate to prove the family wrong, he
got married; but once he 'came out' at twenty-five, Glen was able to
experiment with some old adolescent homoerotic fantasies involving restraint and bondage with the help of some new friends
involved in the gay leather scene. Having initially gone into leather

bars looking for 'masculine' men, Glen's curiosity about SM was enhanced by these diverse experiences before he found his perfect partner, who despite being extremely dominant in the bedroom was extremely loving and caring. As the domestic decisions, chores and responsibilities were also shared equally, the differentiation between his fantasy and real life suited Glen perfectly.

Vito, a college student, certainly did not have a fixed sexual identity, and when interviewed was still trying to make sense of his feelings through sexual experimentation. This conventionally masculine young man had been confused by his masochistic desires, which flitted between homosexual and heterosexual interests. The large number of psychology texts which he read to find out what was going on served only to invoke a deep sense of inferiority which seriously undermined his relationships with girls during his high school years; which, in turn, served to convince Vito that he was definitely a 'submissive' person and possibly a 'real' homosexual too. Having tried out professional dominatrixes, because that's what the books said people like him do, he went through a short homosexual SM relationship, before attending a mixed-sex SM group, which served to re-orientate his interests. While his SM fantasises still involved male partners, Vito began to look for the 'right' woman, though he was still wary of risking a heterosexual relationship. Unfortunately, his attempt to seek psychiatric help had left him with a lack of self-confidence and insecurity.

These observations were complemented by considering the role of professional female dominants, who at the time seemed to be the major source of sexual contact for submissively orientated men. One could select a service from hundreds in both SM and 'ordinary' contact magazines or papers, with fees ranging from $50 to $100 for an hour's session, depending upon the extra and special skills required to create one's perfect fantasy scenario. Apart from magazines, gays could make contact in special bars by displaying symbols such as coloured hankies or the position of their key rings which allowed others to know at a glance what their preferences were. Heterosexual couples used contact magazines and SM organizations.

To some extent the prevalence of professionals and gays in these early studies detracts from the lessons to be drawn about the subculture's role and promotion of rules about conduct, because many heterosexual couples never used the subculture and kept their interests behind closed curtains. However, as we saw, meeting other SM participants can be important when it comes to making sense of one's 'feelings', which despite reflecting one's childhood experiences are in no way fixed. Yet, while experimentation can change people's perceptions, nothing is straightforward either; people's understanding and subsequent actions are primarily determined by the limited range of interpretations of sexual tendencies that are available to them. The more interpretations people come across the more they can choose what they want to be.

Pain

When Kamel toured the leather bars in the United States and Europe posing as a potential participant, he discovered the way in which certain fetish items transcend the need for pain within SM.

In the gay community, use of leather apparently helped to establish masculinity and role definitions. Articles like cock rings (straps that in some way constrain the genitals), whips and restraint devices were designed to maintain roles and control sexual reactions, thereby depriving 'the slave' of choice and directing power to 'the master'. Most of the equipment used symbolized this act of yielding of freedom from one to another; though yielding without physical bondage could represent even greater submission and compliance.

The acts of humiliation which then followed provided the means by which the 'slaves' then prove they are actively giving themselves to their partner, a key ingredient of this type of SM scene. Whatever detractors may like to think, the most common form of 'humiliation' was simply verbal: in gay interactions, for example, degrading name-calling such as 'cock-sucker', or 'punk' (meaning a weak person), or 'worthless slut' (the equivalent of a British 'slag'; as opposed to 'slut', the female equivalent of a slob). Harsh-sounding commands and 'threats' are also employed. A more active alternative could consist of something like 'kennel discipline': the demasculinization and dehumanization of 'the slave' by treating him literally as one may treat a dog, so that 'the slave' might have to lick the master's boots, be led around on a leash wearing a dog collar, have to eat from a dog bowl, and even spend the occasional night at the foot of the master's bed.

While specific actions like being urinated on are often sexual variants in their own right, in SM sex they serve to 'degrade' the slave rather than enhance sexual excitement, being symbolically used to donate worthlessness. Discovering what degrading terms or acts 'a slave' finds erotic can be difficult, though Kamel did not appear to consider its importance. British equivalents in heterosexual relationships could, for example, include 'filthy slag', 'whore', and 'dog'. Since the participants are sexually enlightened, their pleasure derives from the meaning such terms hold in wider society, as they are unlikely to accept the connotations and use such pejorative terms themselves.

Kamel's close contact studies led him to suggest that 'fear', rather than 'pain', was the essence of role maintenance; though, given his descriptions, 'anticipation' would probably have been a better word.

Amongst gay leather sex relationships, pain was rarely a feature despite the equipment used:

> The whip, for example, takes on a threatening meaning for the masochist, and when in the possession of the master, it signifies who is boss. Even if used only lightly, the feel of the whip verifies or maintains their respective roles. The administration of pain is not defined as doing harm to another, but as dominating another. How much pain is desirable or tolerable is a highly individual matter, but it seems to be far less than is commonly supposed.

Indeed, the most common form of physical 'domination' was spanking; and many of the activities which could be associated with pain were not actually painful, as anyone who has accidentally spilled candle wax on their hand can tell you. Participants were extremely cautious of anyone who indulged in painful acts, and the possibility of an unwelcome act was drastically reduced by the vast array of norms which controlled activities. In the gay SM clubs, even a rumour about one extreme activity by a 'leatherman' could ruin his reputation citywide. In any event, the best 'masters', whatever their sexual orientation, had often served as a 'slave' or a tutee of another master; and when John Alan Lee (see Weinberg and Kamel, 1983) interviewed hundreds of gay SM participants, between 1975 and 1977, to test the theory against practice, he found only eleven examples where some form of physical harm had occurred, which is an extremely small rate of injury compared to 'normal' heterosexual activities.

Slaves and masters

Meanwhile, Dale Patrias, then a Ph.D. student at New York University, who had explored the local world of social sadomasochism, was able to supply a considerable amount of detail about the average devotee and their activities, and to offer another sociological definition of SM, which far surpassed those based around psychiatry.

When Patrias (1978) sampled the community by inviting contact column advertisers from *Screw* magazine, *Village Voice*, *The Advocate* and *Fetish Times* to answer a questionnaire about their experiences and definitions, he received over two thousand initial replies, many of whom were seeking partners. Patrias was immediately struck by the fact that many potential devotees were in a similar position to homosexuals and lesbians ten years before: they were extremely reluctant to declare their proclivity openly because they would be condemned. As a result, Patrias only found 108 current active participants who were willing to be interviewed.

Be that as it may, there were 26 heterosexual males, including 6 self-identified dominants; 63 homosexual males, 17 of whom were dominants; 17 heterosexual women, 2 of whom were dominant; and 2 lesbians, one of whom was dominant. This made the dominant to submissive ratio 1:3, although the majority of submissives had played the dominant role at least once. Of the sample 42 per cent were under twenty-nine and 40 per cent between thirty and thirty-nine; half were university graduates; 16 per cent higher executives and professionals; 28 per cent business managers and lesser professionals; 30 per cent administrative, small businessmen and minor professionals; 11 per cent clerical sales and technicians;

5 per cent skilled workers; 8 per cent semi- and unskilled. Their occupations included physicians, college professors, school teachers, writers, clinical psychologists, attorneys, actors, taxi drivers, a news stand operator and a priest. As all respondents were white, Patrias's sample reinforced the idea that SM is the prerogative of high status, educated, middle-class people.

Like the other sociological researchers, Patrias also discovered that SM sex resembled a game with specific rules and roles, in which the decisive factor was the fiction of complete submission or domination rather than the administration or suffering of physical pain.

Most of the interviewees were not interested in pain at all; and those who were insisted that the word 'pain' was redundant, given that their activities were geared towards creating pleasurable rather than unpleasurable 'sensations'. They also preferred the terms 'master' and 'slave' to 'sadist' and 'masochist', because these better described the motives and nature of the sex games they played. As a consequence, Patrias suggested that sadomasochism would be more appropriately defined as 'a sexual encounter between voluntary participants involving role playing at being dominant and submissive, which the partners have mutually defined as sadomasochism (S and M)'. Even when excitation transfer featured, the power within the relationship was still shared, as one respondent explained: 'the Sadist runs the scene; the Masochist sets the limits. The Masochist says what you can't use and how far you can go. But within that, the Sadist can do anything.' The interviewees' natural answers also highlighted the fantastic rather than real nature of the activities. Asked to define what SM was for him, one representative interviewee explained:

> A: To me it means dominating somebody and having total control over somebody else. Or being dominated.
>
> Q: Would the person who is being totally controlled have any influence over the course of the scene?
>
> A: In your head or in reality?
>
> Q: Both.
>
> A: In my head, I've got complete control over – No, I take that back. In my head, I have no control. In my

> fantasy I have no control. I am at the whim of this
> other person. In reality, I am in complete control. I
> have set up the guidelines before we started, . . . I'm
> calling the shots because they would be doing what
> I want them to do.

As for the role of the 'sadist', an explanation by a 'master'
completely debunked the stereotype of a whip-wielding maniac who
was out of control:

> A: . . . When I am involved in sex, I'm generally
>   concerned about the other person and how they're
>   enjoying it, but I want to be in control.
> Q: Does the M[asochist] have any control over the
>   scene at all?
> A: It may sound kind of ironic, but I think in some
>   ways maybe the M has total control. You sound out
>   – as the S[adist] you sound out what the M wants
>   but the M directs what is going to happen . . . The
>   M's decision is whether or not to become involved
>   in it and it is the M's decision how deeply involved
>   to get. The M really says yes or no. If the M says
>   no, there is no scene. If the M says yes, the S tends
>   to be guided by the kinds of things the M wants
>   done. And if the M is putting conditions on it, then
>   the M is really in some kind of control.

Within these limits the master has to choose from among the
alternatives open to him, and what happens then depends upon his
imagination and creativity. The control of the sadist and the
submission of the masochist promoted by the Spanner judges, is,
therefore, a fiction.

When collating devotees' stated SM preferences, Patrias
found that they fell into several major types. There were the master/
slave relationships which he quantified as centring on specific
activities within an atmosphere or mood of inequality, complemented by tones of voice or facial expression and the means of
address. As expected, the 'humiliations' then imposed upon the
'slave' consisted of various acts that would be generally considered
degrading, embarrassing or demeaning. These could be replaced
with, or enhanced by, numerous forms of restriction from simple

hand binding to complete immobility, with the aid of special equipment; and some devotees collected a large amount of this equipment, including racks and hoists, to create special 'play-rooms' complete with necessary chains, leather straps and belts, ankle and wrist bracelets, harnesses, leg irons, tape, blindfolds, gags, hoods, masks, from stores and catalogues catering for SM devotees. Sensation-generating physical acts ranged from spanking and caning to the use of body clamps to which weights could be attached, though acts which left marks on the body were rare. There were fantasy role-playing games centred on social relationships from master/mistress and servant to psychiatrist and client. Others liked sex involving 'watersports' and 'wet sex' which consisted of any kind of activity that got the body wet or dirty by utilizing enemas, mud, ice cubes, snow, baby oil, eggs, body rub creams, and grease amongst others. And, finally, there was fist fucking which involves the insertion of a hand and sometimes the forearm into the anus or vagina.

How these seven activities are actually carried out depended upon several variables: the particular participants, the extent of their knowledge about SM, their experience, imagination, interests, or willingness to explore new situations, as well as the intimacy between the partners and their personal preferences and limits. The majority of interviewees also expressed interest in the use of various kinds of clothing in fabrics from black leather and rubber to silk or fur. Serious devotees had whole wardrobes full of their favourite styles and materials, which could further enhance their sexual arousal.

Whilst this description still reflected the greater number of gays amongst the sample, the results were somewhat similar to another study conducted by Moser and Levitt in 1987, based on 47 females and 178 males, 85 per cent of whom were heterosexual and members of the Eulenspiegel Society, the Society of Janus in San Francisco, or readers of SM Express, a restricted-circulation devotees' magazine.

These participants' median age was in their thirties and they enjoyed high educational and income levels. Only 8.6 and 7.5 per cent respectively were exclusively dominant and submissive. Over 40 per cent indicated that they liked to switch by inclination.

Although 26 per cent reported a first SM experience by the age of sixteen, 43 per cent were twenty-five or older before they had theirs. Table 1 shows the SM activities they had tried.

Moser's survey confirmed what one would expect from previous sociological accounts: the more 'painful' the activity the

Table 1: Percentage of SM devotees participating in various sexually orientated behaviours

Behaviour	Tried	Enjoyed
Spanking	82	66
Bondage	77	65
Humiliation	67	56
Rope	69	54
Fetish behaviour	60	51
Whipping	65	50*
Dildos	57	48
Kissing ass	59	48
Handcuffs	54	47
Leather	49	42
Blindfold	53	42
Chains	53	41
Cock binding	46	36
Gag	49	36
Watersports	45	33
Biting	40	32
Face slapping	36	31
Group sex	40	30
Enemas	42	30
Ice	41	27
Hot wax	37	24
Hoods	27	20
Mask	28	20
Rubber	31	20
Swinging	22	18
Pins	18	14
Piercing	15	11
Burns	18	9
Scat	13	9
Branding	10	7
Tattoos	7	5

N.B.: The difference between those who have tried and enjoyed behaviours does not necessarily mean that the behaviours were disliked. It could have just as easily been a neutral experience.

* Whippings refer to continuous blows with an implement not necessarily a whip.

less often it was practised; and because those trying out the less popular activities are hardly likely to engage in them every time, there being a limit, for example, to the number of nipple rings one can have, the figures are no guide to frequency.

On the other hand, as the most popular activities are spanking, role-play humiliation, bondage, and use of fetish clothing, most SM sex really consists of B&D; all other SM activities had been enjoyed by less than half of the devotees. After spanking and whipping, which would obviously involve excitation transfer, the most common 'painful' activities such as biting and face slapping, are not necessarily painful at all. Consequently, those activities which could move from the potentially painful to the definitely painful, such as piercing, use of pins, tattoos, branding and burns, are not only minority interests; their frequency is unlikely to be high. Likewise, the more specific roles available were far less popular than simply following commands (Table 2).

Table 2: *Percentage of SM devotees participating in various role plays*

Role play	Tried	Enjoyed
Master/slave (mental)	68	58
Master/slave (physical)	61	52
Master/slave (both	46	38
Teacher/pupil	32	25
House/servant	31	26
Guardian/child	20	16

Taken together, the tables, based upon Moser's research, clearly show that the most common forms of SM activities involve no more than bondage, spanking and mental subservence. Most active 'sadomasochists'' activities, contrary to what we are constantly being told, have nothing to do with physical pain at all. And given that all these activities were restricted to private consensual sexual contacts, those who practise them are harmless rather than dangerous, be they heterosexual, professional or gay. While 30 per cent reported that SM was essential for a gratifying sexual experience, 70 per cent did not; so devotees can hardly be called compulsive either.

Consequently, Patrias and Moser have demonstrated that the standard SM stereotypes regarding polarization, psychological dependency, single orientation and a tendency towards ever more extreme and harmful practices cannot be justified at all.

Becoming a sadomasochist

When it came to the relationship between the devotee and the subculture, Patrias suggested that there were several degrees of involvement along a continuum, with core devotees (with distinctive styles of dress and a special jargon) at one end and prostitutes who may engage in sadomasochistic activities only for money at the other. Between these two extremes there were discernible levels of interest. The development of an individual's SM career was a simple process: Patrias's respondents' socialization into sexual SM almost always began as a result of some kind of contact with an existing devotee, leading to the novice's first scene. If they enjoy themselves, novices then gain sexual partners who are already involved, or take their own initiative and seek one; but if the original contact was not experienced and defined as pleasurable and sexually exciting, or retrospectively interpreted as pleasurable, the individuals' SM conduct will not continue. One cannot be 'corrupted' by SM.

If novices progress further, they will quickly discover that there are things they must learn, like techniques, which are vital for success and that there are attitudes and postures to assume if one is being dominant or subservient. As one interviewee put it, SM is an art, especially when it involves physical acts:

> Bumbling to me is not being able to handle it . . . The skill comes in *how* you do it . . . the whole thing is so that both people get turned on. The S brings the M up a little bit, and then the M brings the S up a little bit by the way he reacts. And these things are very, very subtle. Anybody can swing a belt, anybody can swing a whip, but to swing that belt and swing that whip to turn the other person on and to turn you on, whether you know that person or not, it has to be a very subtle kind of thing.

Patrias discovered that failing to learn the norms, and develop a minimum proficiency, 'culminates in unhappy, unsatisfactory sexual encounters, probably a lack of partners, a definition of sadomasochism as not being pleasurable, and eventually withdrawal from the scene'.

To ensure that potential partners are proficient, participants can spend a lot of time initially sizing each other up, much like other 'swingers', or attending groups which organize meetings for new members. Given what is to follow, these meetings can be crucial, because only when potential participants feel confident with each other can a 'scene' take place. As Weinberg had found, in order to assess one another:

> the participants . . . discuss their needs, fantasies, fears, and what they are and are not willing to do. What ultimately occurs during a scene is the outcome of this discussion, in which the original thoughts are somewhat modified, then subjected to a bargaining process by which the verbalized desires of the partner are accommodated.

As contact with clubs can be limited by geography, many make use of contact magazines like *Fetish Times*, *Latent Image*, *Aggressive Gals* and *SM Ads*.

By the 1970s, few respondents had the same difficulties that North's sample had, or assumed that they would have, with their wives. One of Patrias's respondents, for example, a twenty-four-year-old male masochist, had not mentioned his proclivity or fetish for silk and leather prior to marriage, but once he had suggested to his wife that some aspects of life might be more exciting if she wore silky clothes, one thing led to another, and she became more than happily adept at SM. Many couples were so happy with their particular partners that they found no need to involve others; and when couples did 'swing', they tended to restrict their activities to a small number of people with whom they were acquainted. Some submissive males continued to use professional dominants precisely so that they did not have to be concerned with their partners' reactions or wishes. Women also seemed to be more active in Patrias's sample. Those who gained a reputation for their skills, like a thirty-two-year-old female dominant, gained slaves through word of mouth.

Despite this increasing opportunity, SM devotees could have even more difficulties than other sexual minorities when it came to openly admitting their sexual preferences; as a forty-year-old female masochist explained to Patrias:

> I did summon up enough courage to bring it up two times with people I was dating, but it didn't work out either time. The first man thought it was really sick and depraved, so I dropped the matter very quickly . . . The second time, the man was really willing to spank me, but he thought it was kind of silly. Now, if the other person just laughs and thinks it's funny, it's not going to work at all. He would have done it, but he wouldn't have received any enjoyment of it whatsoever. He would just have done it to please me. So I told him to forget all about it.

Given this kind of reaction, which somewhat belies the fallacious assumptions of the separatist feminists, it is hardly surprising that the number of potential female devotees is grossly under-estimated. Yet an ever-growing number of women were willing to persevere, despite initially accepting this odious kind of negative stereotyping, as a twenty-eight-year-old female heterosexual masochist explained:

> I thought it was something unusual about me; that it was forbidden to think about things like that. I felt I would be criticized. I considered it abnormal, and I denied that I would be interested in it until quite recently. But it was always a psychological condition in me that I couldn't act out. It seemed unusual for a person to want to hurt you and for you to admit that you enjoyed it. I was brought up to want nice things and not want to be hurt and not to introduce a new emotion you didn't realize you had is very traumatic. I never rebelled against anything when I was growing up. I was a model person. I think just not pursuing it was a way of denying it. I put it out of my mind because I didn't think I should be thinking about it, which is probably why it took so long. I recently started an SM relationship and now I admit what I want, and it's

much nicer. It's the one thing sexually which really turns me on. At the beginning, my fascination was more vague, but it's becoming more specific now.

Ironically, individuals' potential fear of denunciation, rejection or feeling that they must be 'sick' is frequently accompanied by the complementary fear that, unlike themselves, all other devotees are likely to be dangerous. Whether this is due to the prevalent social stereotypes or, as Patrias frequently discovered, because those who exhibited apprehension also tended to feel guilty about their own desires, is not clear. Yet, like Spengler and Moser before him, Patrias suspected that potential devotees' somewhat hesitant and sporadic ventures into SM often detracted from the enjoyment available, and maintained their confusion about their desires. In contrast, respondents who were seriously involved and participated more or less regularly exhibited no guilt or condemnatory attitudes. Patrias was particularly impressed with the Eulenspiegel Society, whose philosophy was that SM was far more satisfactory when practised by those in a dedicated marriage or partnership, where the couple had a sincere desire to please one another, and were honest and open; and that SM could encourage these features, frequently lacking in normal sexual relations. Those who were happy with their proclivity were far from happy with society's reaction, and were indignant that they were singled out while society ignored many more serious forms of 'sadism' including the suppression of minorities, rape, war and police brutality.

Despite these problems, the increasing number of non-professional women who appear in Patrias's and Moser's samples demonstrates that as time was passing more and more women were willing to 'come out' and seek partners if they were unattached. Those in Moser's sample tended to be more inclined to bisexuality and were generally more submissive than the men. On the other hand, they were more experimental, having tried more of both SM and 'straight' activities; though only 9 per cent thought SM was required for a truly satisfactory sexual response.

Today, it is common for heterosexual SM social groups to cater for both couples and single women. Ironically, much of the credit for this must go to lesbian women. Pat Califia's outspoken views concerning lesbian sexuality in general, and SM in particular, radically changed the gender balance within the subculture, by bringing women's SM out of the closet. Battling first against conservative gay attitudes and then against fundamentalist feminists, Califia made use of taboo social symbols as a means to commit 'deliberate, premeditated, erotic blasphemy', and in doing so did much to give women 'permission' to admit their true sexual preferences.

The sociology of SM

The sociologists' excursions into the emerging SM scene during the 1970s revealed not only how SM devotees had absolutely nothing in common with pathological 'sadistic' serial killers but also how every single assumption behind the psychiatric definitions could be challenged and then dismissed with real evidence. Even if SM desires were the result of some infantile experience, psychiatry was clearly clueless when it came to the devotees behaviour or anything else which followed.

The diversity exhibited by devotees, their lack of exclusive role orientation, the absence of violent attitudes or activities, and the elaborate preparations involving role-playing and scene-setting, along with an aversion to real pain, raised a series of new questions about motivation. As one had to learn a range of techniques in order to engage in a co-operative venture, one is made rather than born an active devotee; and these socially acquired skills become a means to distinguish between the socially harmless devotee and other people with violent criminal intent. Without mutual consent and agreement neither side in an SM scene could enjoy the power plays.

Yet, for all its insights and answers, the sociological alternative still leaves an essential question unanswered. While the role of excitation transfer easily explains why supposedly painful acts are sometimes incorporated into SM acts, we still do not know why devotees do it, or why SM should have taken the form it has.

Over the last decade, dozens of individual devotees have gone into print, TV or video to offer their own reasons. Pat Califia, the apologist for lesbian SM, for example, delights in undermining her own socialization, and justifies doing so by emphasizing how exciting SM is for women who were socialized to dread sex or fight it off, or provide it under duress or as part-exchange for romance and security. No doubt SM can appear liberating for any woman who has found herself taking responsibility for other people's gratification and feigning pleasure for those who pretend to have her pleasure in mind; but no one, not even Califia, has ever clearly stated the obvious, for devotees still tend to be apologetic and defensive.

If SM scenes are deliberately organized in order to avoid 'pain' and effect excitation transfer, SM sex is essentially organizing and controlling the enhancement of sexual pleasure at the same time. Far from administering pain, the so called 'sadist' is actually a technician of pleasure; and far from getting their kicks from painful stimulation, 'masochists' crave nothing but pleasure.

For all the 'subcultural' data offered up by sociologists, we have still heard far too little about the pleasure afforded by SM. Being dependent upon the nature of gay and professional–client SM interactions, and having failed to make inroads into the lesbian network which has existed since the early 1970s or to consider thousands of 'off-scene' happy SM couples, sociology failed to explore the importance of pleasurable mutual fantasies at all.

Given that it was inevitable that the growth of the SM subculture would lead women of independent means and couples seeking to increase their range of activities to become more open about their sexual preferences, the sociologists could and should have spent more time considering the nature of couple's and female desires. It is more than likely, for example, that the real reason why many of the sociological surveys' male devotees thought their wives would not be interested in SM was because the devotee was a 'masochist' and would require his wife to act in a dominant manner. Far from demonstrating that wives, or women generally, were not interested in, or were horrified at the idea of, SM *per se*, these devotees may merely be proving that their wives may simply have felt uncomfortable about acting out of character. Long before the SM community sought to accommodate couples, the sociologists could have found numerous clues as to what invisible SM couples were doing by making more use of the contact advertisements to estimate numbers and codify their fantasy worlds.

I could say a lot more about Weinberg's use of Goffman's 'frame analysis' and the theatrical analogy, which I had to simplify for the purpose of this volume; but, rather than boring the reader with an obscure sociological debate, I will say only that a more systematic use of Goffman's theory would have necessitated far greater attention to the role of fantasy and the participants' own views rather than the imposition of a sociological analogy upon events. When asked, the sociologists' informants invariably placed a greater emphasis upon their fantasies than upon the overt role-play activity the researchers were interested in. I suspect that this failing followed from the early studies' reliance upon examples taken from professional dominatrixes, whose services involve offering role-sets to accommodate their clients. Yet the reason why clients request one role rather than another is not even considered.

Consequently, it would be foolish to allow all this talk of technique and symbolic acts to detract from the fact that the role-sets adopted, despite being somewhat stereotypical to facilitate role-play, reflect real power relationships, and could indicate a desire to execute that role in real life. Opponents of SM like to imply that this is the case, and the authorities, by playing up some of the one-off extreme acts, do so too. Devotees, like Califia, are aware of this charge, and have attempted to rebut it by alluding to an obvious alternative explanation. She has suggested that SM's threat to the 'established order' which persecutes devotees follows from the fact that the roles adopted poke fun both at the stereotypical sexual norms covering orientation, gender and class, and at the political system which cannot handle a concept of power unconnected to a real form of privilege; for the role-sets parody the repressed sexuality to be found in most forms of authority, be it the priest's robe, the cop's uniform, the president's business suit and the soldier's khaki.

While I suspect that Califia has identified one aspect of authority's fear of SM, sociological explanation will remain incomplete until we know more about participants' preference for particular roles. Apart from raising questions about the nature of sexual pleasure in general, the devotees' common fantasy pathway from real life to role-play and back again raises intriguing questions about the origin and nature of SM desires. Where do these stereotypical fantasies come from? How far are they shaped by the role stock of the SM community as opposed to the wider society? Are they fixations or are they 'reversible' too? In order even to begin to answer those kinds of questions, we need to look at this issue of fantasy in more detail.

Chapter six

The Fantasy Factory

THE psychobabblers' century-old obsession with pain has blinded almost everyone to the obvious fact that the real essence of SM is to create, maintain, and then intensify sexual arousal for the purpose of pleasure. Even when so-called painful acts are involved, their purpose is to create sensations which, with the aid of excitation transfer, enhance the arousal and increase pleasure.

In this way, SM sex is not really much different from 'normal' sex, which is frequently preceded and enhanced by a lot of talk about love and devotion, buying of chocolates and flowers, wearing special clothes, listening to music or watching movies, tickling and licking, talking 'dirty', moving in and out of bedrooms, changing positions, adding sex toys, and so on. All that SM really does is to add a few more garments, some equipment, a fair amount of sophistication and a phenomenal amount of fantasy.

Whether or not the SM proclivity derives from a biological drive, an unconscious interaction between the ego and the id in the pre-Oedipal child or a single seminal experience at a public school is for all practical purposes irrelevant. As the SM 'potential' created by such events could and would become reality only when one began to fantasize about doing things, the real 'mystery' of SM lies in the fact that some people turn their potential into *conscious* fantasies about various forms of domination and submission, and others do not appear to do so; at least, they are not admitting it. Yet, there cannot be so many men who have not dreamed of controlling other people in one way or another, and there can not be so many women who have not wished to devote themselves to another person in one way or another. What bemuses me is why sections of society deem those who then act out their fantasies in a sexually playful way as far more dangerous than those who do so in either anti-social or self-destructive ways.

Intellectualizing sex

Incredible as it seems, despite the millions of words in print, and billions more on silly chat shows, we still shy away from discussing what we really *think* about sex. We spend a lot of time reading and talking about what other people *do*, and moralize in one way or another about why they might do it; but owing to the Christian tradition of sexual privacy and the Freudian imperative to sublimate one's desires for civilization's sake we are not supposed to intellectualize about so base an instinct as sex. Psychobabble has also reinforced the Christians' traditional worries about polluting the spiritual mind with lustful thoughts about flesh, by denouncing any form of sexual diversity or difference as a 'perversion' and denying it any intellectual properties. No wonder the babblers kept on insisting that SM had to be related to pain. For pain, being a simple physical sensation, could then be simply associated with another physical 'urge' called 'lust' which, because of its supposed property of always destroying the object of attention, made it very easy to denounce and condemn those who knew differently. Trying to restrict SM to the status of a mere impulse, however, makes no sense at all. Without recourse to fantasy, or what the early definers called the 'power of the imagination', active sexual sadomasochism simply could and would not exist.

Krafft-Ebing's first two categories of SM, the mental and symbolic, clearly depended upon subjective or fantasy elements to make the acts of dominance or submission, associated with status, humiliation and degradation, effective. Likewise, Ellis's theory was dependent upon intense mental activity. While he also realized that some form of excitation transformation was taking place, Ellis was convinced that the 'principal enjoyment is in the imagination' and that a 'vivid imagination' was vital, not least when switching preferred roles, because 'it is the realisation of the imagined situation that gives the pleasure'. Even when they referred to physical pain, the early theorists all thought that the *mental* representation of pain was *the* powerful sexual stimulant, owing to some process of 'emotional intoxication'. Bloch had even suggested that it was the mental rather than the physical intensification of pleasure that separated sadomasochism from ordinary sexual instincts. But once Freud effectively buried this line of inquiry in a metaphorical minefield of mythology, despite his clients' constant references to books and other fantasy fodder in their 'beating fantasies', psychologists relegated the role of fantasy to a mere mechanism of compulsion.

The power of the imagination, however, could not be buried for long; and once the sociologists unveiled the importance of consensual fantasy role-playing in the contemporary SM identity, the necessity of reconsidering the importance of sexual fantasy within SM should have been obvious to all. The 'scenes' and role-sets of the 1970s SM community merely enabled devotees to slip in and out of their own sexual fantasies in a controllable setting; the props and equipment made possible role-play and suspension of disbelief in the service of fantasy-realization, and the historical role-sets delineated the boundary between fantasy and reality. Fantasy rather than technique was the beginning, middle and end of all activities.

Ironically, popular criticisms of sadomasochism have always alluded to the importance of fantasy in SM. Despite invoking fears about sex murderers like Ian Brady, who actually drew his inspiration from crime and spy films, morality groups oppose media representation of sex, let alone SM, precisely because of its alleged effect upon people's imagination. They believe that the intellectualization of sex removes the guilt which Mary Whitehouse once admitted was 'a necessary form of control' in society. The politically correct crowd are no different. While the weekend therapists agonize over how they can blame their clients' personal failings upon an incarcerated libido, fundamentalist feminists denounce contemporary media and advertising as a sadomasochistic fantasy promoting eroticized violence. The common fallacy shared by all three groups, of course, is the simultaneous but contradictory belief that while everyone's fantasy life must be restricted in order to inhibit 'immoral' acts, everyone supposedly automatically copies

153: The Fantasy Factory

what they see in whatever media, which implies that no one has an imagination of their own! While this nonsense sometimes alludes to the sensible idea of innate human weaknesses, it always raises the question of original sin. Yet while the detractors think that involves avoiding sex, the tree bearing the forbidden fruit was labelled 'knowledge', and some 'moral' people would rather not know the truth about themselves or their own bizarre fantasies, which they then try to exorcize by projecting them on to SM devotees, who do not actually share them. Therefore, those who wish to know what is really happening have to consider where SM fantasies come from.

Fantasy

The task of uncovering the origin of SM fantasy is not aided by the nonsense that passes for knowledge about sexual fantasies in general. Our lack of honesty about this subject, due mainly to embarrassment, is compounded by our failure to record our fantasy histories. By the time any of us bother to get round to seriously thinking about our own fantasies, our memory about how they began and what was added where, when and why will often be so hazy that we frequently compensate for our lack of precision by guessing, and that serves only to keep the nonsense coming.

When Eysenck and Wilson tried to cover the subject in *The Psychology of Sex*, the only thing they were sure of was that our highly developed representational processes which internalize images such as memories and hopes, are pooled and refined over time in such a way that the fantasies which follow not only provide powerful sources of sexual excitement, they are often more arousing than direct sensations, because the latter can also arouse self-consciousness.

It has been suggested that fantasies tend to reflect our outlook on life. Back in 1974, for example, Barbara Hariton and Jerome Singer discovered that women's fantasies could be divided into four types which reflected their personalities. Those with frequent and varied fantasies also tended towards a high degree of interest in nonconformist, exploratory, sex; and they also tended to be engaged in other creative activities. Women who hardly fantasized at all were the opposite in all respects. The third type, whose fantasies tended to centre on specific lovers, places and times, were like the first group, but also tended to be dissatisfied with the sexual side of their marriage. And those who dwelt upon fantasies of forced compliance, domination, rape, seduction, humiliation and abduction for enforced prostitution appeared, on the surface, to conform to the traditional, archetypal female. In short, women's fantasies tended to reflect their social outlook or extend it. What intrigued Eysenck, however, was that 'A striking thing about many of the fantasies . . . that occurs so frequently among normal people is that they correspond to some of the more common sexual deviations.'

Apparently, the more often one has sex, the more varied one's fantasies can become, but around 25 per cent of them revolve around sadomasochistic themes, if we include the images of any form of dominance, spanking and so on. While those who are shy or socially withdrawn tend to have stronger 'ideal' fantasies which can become fixations if one is self-indulgent because there is no direct link between fantasy type and fantasy enactment; and those with a lot of sexual experience tend to have a greater number of more varied fantasies; what is really interesting is that thoughts as well as physical sensations can effect excitation transfer too. Far from simply depending upon which feeling is dominant in a situation, transfer can be conscious, and one's fantasy could deliberately direct any thought or feeling towards sexual arousal. And so the mystery of our fantasy history is open to view.

Whenever they start, during childhood or puberty, sexual fantasies consist of core elements shaped by any emotionally arousing experience with sexual connotations, around which we then weave other ideas and experiences. The interesting point here is that the more self-determined the fantasies are, the more they will take on an 'ideal' form; and the longer it takes to come anywhere near realizing these fantasies, the more fixated they can become. In contrast, sexually active people are less likely to become fixated. Either way, our sexual fantasies become some of our favourite short stories, differing from the others only in their sexual content; and all SM devotees are really doing is enacting some of their fantasies, in temporary settings, in order to experiment with their arousal properties in real life.

While no one has yet discovered a correlation between people's fantasy preference and actual sexual experience, many people assume that there is one. An American sexologist, the late Robert Stoller (1975), thought that in the case of SM there was a link. He argued that enacted fantasies were an 'erotic form of hatred', whereby the pleasure derived from acting-out came from ridding oneself of a fear of repeating the trauma or frustration which led to the fantasy in the first place by 'avenging' oneself upon those who caused the trauma. In contrast P. Dally's *The Fantasy Game* (1977) argued that as our early childhood fantasies with their sadistic or masochistic tendencies – fuelled by the frustration, anger and anxiety caused by those holding power over us – were not generally realized or satisfied, they sought indirect expression through work or psychosexual difficulties, or anti-social acts like witch-hunts and war. In order to avoid such problems, he recommended that couples should act out their fantasies in some socially acceptable way.

What is obviously wrong with these kinds of theories is that they are premised upon the negative psychiatric assumption that fantasies are solely derived from adverse circumstances and never from pleasurable events. This also implies that most of our sexual fantasies are 'unnatural' and would not occur in 'ideal' circumstances; yet it is far more likely that, as we are dealing with pleasure promotion rather than some kind of 'erotic form of hatred' the lessons to be culled from self-reported fantasies, like those in Nancy Friday's *My Secret Garden* (1976), are going to be far less painful than many assume.

Friday's examples strongly suggest that most of our fantasies tend to consist of all the things and situations that social conventions would frown upon. In the case of women, fantasies break a double taboo. In general, they offer women a means to transcend social norms which restrict their behaviour, within the safety of fantasy, because real life exploration, given the continual existence of sexual double standards, could be somewhat risky. In particular, they enable women to experience everything that patriarchal society and fundamentalist feminists insist that a women should not do. Yet very few of Friday's respondents mentioned any kind of traumatic childhood, even though many found SM-type activities, from being exhibited to being sexually used, very pleasurable. Most had not acted out their fantasies or even wanted to risk doing so unless they were shared with a 'stable' partner. This suggests that the only danger in having certain fantasies is that they offend people of various religious or ideological persuasions who may then take action against you. This, of course, does not explain where such desires come from, and what it is that leads people either to keep such fantasies to themselves, act them out with 'stable' partners or become anti-social as a result. Thankfully, Maria Marcus's account of how her SM desires developed can offer numerous clues.

A taste for pain?

Marcus's journey of discovery and search for an explanation for her masochistic desires recorded in *A Taste for Pain* (1981) should be read in full to appreciate its value; but what one can immediately point to is that, as far as she can remember, her 'masochism' appeared first through a series of activities rather than fantasies. Like many other children, Marcus did not link her 'punishment games' with other children and her self-testing trials to anything connected with sex. Even when she developed a crush on the male teacher, who, despite never actually punishing her, was to become the central figure in a complicated fantasy world in which he 'did things' to her, she still did not realize that sex was involved. The 'things' simply became more and more elaborate, drastic and ritualistic, including at one point being hung up in a tree and beaten.

While some people may like to pretend that Marcus must have been 'sick' to think about such things, and suggest that such fantasies are 'abnormal', what she experienced is far from unusual. If everyone was honest, these kinds of acts and fantasies would be recognized as being extremely common, at least in western societies. Though they may not be inevitable, these fantasies appear to be directly linked to western societies' inability to accommodate young people's innate desire to experience 'something' emotionally powerful with sexual knowledge and experimentation. When these feelings begin to occur, many children, just like Marcus, have no understanding of sex at all. At first, they are completely bemused, and have no idea that lots of other children feel exactly the same way. For those children who do experience what can amount to an overwhelming 'feeling', the extent to which their sexual socialization and general emotionality is controlled and curtailed by adults will then help to determine the way in which they begin to link these feelings to any and every phenomenon that they think could or would produce a similar effect. I suspect that the longer the period between the onset of these feelings and some effective understanding of what sexuality is all about, the more bizarre the scenarios can become, and more likely they will be introduced into the child's masturbatory history. Consequently, those who go through this phase can then spend the rest of their lives trying to accommodate or control what follows in their fantasies. Incredibly, we have yet to work out and agree upon the best way to handle this facet of western society, because those who remember going through this phase rarely admit to it, and no one else does either. Having failed to find this recorded in any standard text on sexuality, despite frequent passing references to it in psychological literature, I suspect that people are afraid to discuss it, whether or not it causes them any problems, precisely because they see that those who cannot successfully deal with the consequences, or are 'exposed' even if they do, become labelled 'perverts'. If one or other facet emerges during a child's development, we write the child off as odd or dangerous, talk a lot of tangential nonsense and pretend we know nothing about it, because we do not want to be labelled perverts either. Psychiatry certainly does not want to admit that such a phase exists, because it could completely negate any need for Oedipal and other ridiculous theories which offer a rationale for its existence. Consequently, a very common experience is completely written out of accounts of human intellectual development.

Be that as it may, while still completely 'naive' about this missing piece of the human physical and emotional jigsaw, Maria Marcus had progressed to tying herself up in various positions, pretending that she could not escape, while fuelling her imagination with the nearest social phenomena she believed would produce an overwhelming emotional and physical response. Her head became full of scenes from well-known boarding-school story books, the initiation rites of exotic tribes and barrack rooms, episodes from the history of slavery and details of Chinese, Japanese and Indian systems of torture, supplemented with Greek myths and historical novels, especially those about ancient Rome. Consequently, like millions before her, Marcus began to create her masochistic 'character'. Over time, her delight in these historical footnotes led to concentrating upon descriptions of torture and punishment, which she firmly linked with fulfilment of her desire for strong emotional experiences; and she used the powerful imagery of such scenes to effect some form of excitation transfer. Not that Marcus wanted to experience such situations for real:

> Everything is relative. I cannot use reality until it is
> sufficiently distant from me to no longer appear as a
> reality, and I can persuade myself that it is fantasy. Then I
> can prostitute it instead, buy it like goods to be used as
> sexual stimulants. Then I can devote myself to its
> pornographic worth.

Growing older, and keeping these interests a secret, Marcus eventually found herself being drawn to physically strong men; and the more forceful her sexual encounters were the more she liked it, for they approached the level of feeling she had come to regard as pleasurable. Yet, because the experiences did not correspond to her now complicated and specific fantasies, the effects always wore off quickly, and she even began to find herself provoking her partners into being 'rough' with her.

Having eventually decided to find an explanation for her experiences, Marcus came to the conclusion that she must be a 'masochist', and labelled herself as such, even though nothing she read really seemed to describe her particular experience. Then:

> one day he was there, my Black Prince – my dream lover,
> the sadist, just like in fairy tales when someone waves a
> wand. Everything went of its own accord. I didn't even
> have to provoke him. He did everything I had hoped for in
> my fantasies. He spoke quietly and menacingly and he beat
> me, and while in bed forced me to do humiliating things. I
> was taken up as high as never before.

What really surprised Marcus, however, was that it could hurt! Whether or not the Black Prince was poorly skilled in the art of SM, at some point Marcus would inevitably have discovered that, whatever existed in one's fantasies, physical stimulation had to be strictly limited, because, as Zillmann pointed out, real pain inhibits rather than enhancing pleasure. However, she discovered that the experience could always be used for later fantasies: 'There has to be a moment when I hate and loathe the pain, and only wish I could get away from it. But once you have been on the pain-level, it can be used sexually at another moment in time.'

Having finally worked out that it was the psychic rather than the physical side of the experiences which was decisive, Marcus began to bypass experiences of physical pain completely and replaced them with various symbolic acts of humiliation. Whether it took the form of invoked fear, feelings of shame, powerlessness, dependency or 'nothingness' or being actively submissive did not matter; they all achieved the same effect. She even ended up being able to pretend convincingly that a man's perfectly innocent act was 'really' a conscious act of 'sadism'; but she simultaneously discovered that being an 'instrument' or an 'object' of her 'master' would provide pleasure for herself only if she was in control of her 'subjection'. Marcus had finally discovered the existence, and meaning, of SM.

Whilst only one experience amongst millions, Marcus's history clearly demonstrates that fantasy is far more important to SM than the acting-out of any painful experience, and reveals how one's imagination is vital in setting up, controlling and determining the reaction to events. As the Greenes suggested, SM is an extensive mental representation of sexual response.

For many participants, thoughts of painful acts could be the legacy of early non-sexually-orientated attempts to maximize the intensity of that early emotional experience. The pleasure this brings then leads to the devotees' desire to replicate the experience. This is then controlled and manipulated through fantasy and fantasy role-play in order to avoid real harm as one learns to harness the ability to intensify one's feelings through substituting imaginative symbolic humiliations for real acts of power. As the sense of 'nothingness' felt in submitting oneself to the whim of others appears to have the same effect, physical pain can even be abandoned altogether. Meanwhile, those who have discovered the excitation transfer can, of course, always explore the various sensation-inducing equipment that has become part of the stock of SM paraphernalia.

Whatever the final outcome, the SM experience is an adult solution to filling in the gap between desire and fulfilment experienced by millions of older children and adolescents, by marrying one's subsequent fantasies with the strong emotional response gained by having sex with a partner who understands the need and has the means to enhance pleasure. No wonder SM exhibits a high degree of theatricality; which belies the simplistic assertion that no one is able to control their desires. On the contrary, active SM is the perfect means by which one learns to do just that. It is those who avoid learning how to control their feelings and desires, and often become fixated with seeing or doing particular acts without learning the harm it can cause, who present a danger to individuals and society. Moralists' assertions that one can always achieve the same effect by repressing all desires are belied by their obsessive judgmental crusades against those who choose the SM path. Yes, people can repress and deflect their desires into alternative and constructive channels. But in order to do so, one needs an incredible strength of will, clearly not possessed by most, as the vast numbers of vindictive or self-destructive people in society demonstrate. What I find very interesting is that the 'moralists' I have met who exhibit that strength of character share one thing in common with SM devotees: they are both self-effacing and non-judgmental.

Given this pivotal role of fantasy, it would have made far more sense to use fantasies as the means to study the origin and nature of SM and 'sadomasochism' all along, rather than speculate on other factors. Apart from linking the individuals' initial desires for an overwhelming emotional experience with their move into symbolic power or submission, drawing upon the wider culture and the potential influences of the SM community, the way in which fantasy is organized, and then realized, or not, can provide clues to the difference between harmless active sexual SM devotees and those who promote or invoke real violence or domination.

It may also make sense to explore the possibility that the compulsive moralists' real hatred of SM sex is related to the way that it exposes how the likes of authority figures from mistresses to magistrates, and from slave owners to school teachers, have used their positions to enforce real vicarious pain upon others, by parodying their sexless sadism and 'tropical frenzy'. Califia may well have hit the penis on the head, as it were, by insisting that there are enormous hard-ons behind the uniforms and façades of authority and power: a power that can exist only as long as the penis remains concealed and elevated to the level of a symbol.

Goodbye de Sade

The importance of fantasy for active devotees permeated Patrias's study. Some informants had vivid memories of their earliest SM-like feelings, recalling being 'sexually aroused' as children by horror films or pirate scenes; three mentioned the same corset scene, featuring Vivien Leigh and Hattie McDaniel, in *Gone with the Wind*. For others *The Lone Ranger*, with its masks and frequent bondage scenes, was remembered with affection. Spanking scenes, of course, used to feature regularly in popular films like *Kiss Me Kate*. Most, however, remembered fantasizing about submitting in some way to an adult in an authority position, such as a parent, school teacher or summer camp counsellor. On the other hand, it was only later as adults that they were aware that an SM community existed and began to seek out partners in order to see if they could help to realize some of their fantasies. By this time, of course, most of their fantasies had crystallized into variations on standard themes. The personal fantasy histories of SM devotees, therefore, conflict with the standard assumptions about their content.

Dally, for example, like many other commentators, believed that most male masochistic fantasies involved submission to someone else, usually a powerful being, while female fantasies consisted of being physically overpowered, taken into slavery, being impregnated by an animal, rape, abduction or seduction, or being controlled by another woman. He then suggested that various forms of social conditioning or experience were evident as previously vague fantasies took their final form; so that oral fantasies, for example, would usually arise only after reading about or experiencing cunnilingus or fellatio; whereas religious symbolism would be most prevalent amongst those educated by a religious order.

But SM fantasies involve far more than Dally's stereotypical representations of first masochistic, and then sadistic, content:

> Rougher, tougher, masochistic fantasies may consist of being tied up, handcuffed, chained to a bed, hooded or blindfolded, beaten up and tortured in various ways and degrees of severity. . . . In a typical sadistic fantasy the man imagines himself in a position of power (e.g. a headmaster or a school prefect) and lashes the naked bottoms of the four hundred girls (or boys) under his control, in turn, for some offence they have committed.

On the contrary, SM fantasies can begin and end with simply being told what to do, or giving orders. From being carried away by a sheik to licking boots, most masochistic fantasies actually amount to being placed in a position where one is not responsible for one's fate, so that one cannot be held responsible for enjoying oneself. Some 'masochists' merely like the effect of excitation transfer. 'Masters', 'tops' or 'sadists', whatever they are called, appear, contrary to popular belief, to have far fewer fantasies, and do not imagine themselves as SS officers running a concentration camp; they are far too busy working out how to handle their masochistic charges, and reflecting upon past achievements in manipulating arousal. In any event, to concentrate simply upon particular roles and acts is to miss the essence of SM fantasy, as a quick dip into SM pornography reveals.

Numerous forms of domination–submission and role-play SM literature existed long before de Sade and Sacher-Masoch turned up, and the history of SM fantasy demonstrates that this pair have very little to do with it. This truth has been lost to history, because, as yet, no one has taken the time to analyse what was going on in an extensive genre too readily dismissed as simply 'flagellation'. Even the greatest of the nineteenth-century erotic bibliographers, Henry Spencer Ashbee, who should have known better, scathingly insisted that SM books '[from] a literary point of view . . . are generally worthless, and are insufferably dull and tedious – one idea – one only – is harped upon throughout all of them and this is not true to nature'.

What Ashbee and many others since have missed was that all this dull and tedious detail was precisely what ensures that writing about SM is far from mere harping on about another manifestation of *le vice anglais*. It actually provides a sensible historian with the ability to trace the predominant overt fantasies in each generation used by new devotees to learn the symbolic language and meaning of SM from their predecessors, in order to explore and explain their feelings.

Apart from the inevitable references to various 'painful' acts, from the mid-eighteenth century to the present day, domination literature has tended to consist of variations upon five major themes, which have more than a passing similarity to the sociological findings.

First, there are numerous references to dominant and submissive relationships, which involve various forms of restriction, humiliation or powerlessness. A lot of attention is paid to the indignity, shame, or outrage supposedly felt by the submissive participant, before they succumb to their 'instincts', and find themselves enjoying the experience. Second, the stories are full of 'theatricality', which extends far beyond styles of dress. A considerable amount of the text is devoted to the 'masters" planning and then enactment of events, with detailed descriptions of the rooms and equipment utilized. Likewise, the text will dwell upon the overall presentation of the scene produced, including the specific role-sets and role-plays. Third, the themes of pleasure and enjoyment will be presented either directly through the dialogue concerning the promise of rewards to come or in the detailed descriptions of the joy experienced by the now enlightened individuals, who may or may not then utilize their new found knowledge to initiate someone else. Fourth, all acts of 'violation' or humiliation will involve a direct rationale or justification; for, in one way or another, the 'victims' will have transgressed some norm and 'deserve' their punishment. Fifth, the action will take place within some kind of 'super-setting'. This facet is distinguished from the second theme in that it provides the boundary between the action and everyday reality. It can take an overt form, such as references to vast wealth, chateaux or country houses and so on, which obviously distances the action from the everyday experience of the reader; or it can simply sexualize a normally non-sexual situation, in which the restrictions that would be present in real life are, for some reason, absent.

Each and every one of these themes enables a devotee to soak in the atmosphere created and empathize with the characters' situation, share in the excitement and anticipation, and learn about the postures and attitudes they could, if they wished, utilize for themselves in their SM experiences.

When we then look at the way in which the interrelationships between these themes have varied over the last two hundred and fifty years we can also see how SM has developed through time from what was a simple fascination with flagellation to high-tech sex in the service of excitation transfer.

Before 1780, for example, most flagellation material did place an emphasis upon the anticipation or nature of the physical activity, in which men were invariably beaten by women. Between 1780 and 1820, however, one begins to see far more use being made of the notion of humiliation, as male devotees also begin to consider the delight of flagellating women. Incredible as it seems, most of this redirection occurred in public through the letter columns of respectable national journals discussing the lively issue of corporal punishment in girls' schools. Historians seeking evidence of sexual trends who have dismissed these letters as fiction masquerading as true accounts, as Ian Gibson does in *The English Vice* (1979), have missed the point, especially when complaining that many of the letters draw upon their predecessors, and that 'the same expressions, images, and turns of phrase recur endlessly'. Of course they did: the letters' authors were devotees penning their fantasy scenarios, and dreaming of a woman who would share their interest.

Although de Sade's work was available, as the six-month sentence handed down to George Cannon in 1830 for publishing *Juliette* demonstrates, he had little influence upon the genre between 1820 and 1880. While some flagellants were still filling the letter columns of *The Englishwoman's Domestic Journal*, other devotees were reading the elaborate details of ritualized initiation ceremonies in novels like *The Merry Order of St Bridget* (1870), or following the role-sets in the *Fashionable Lectures* (1872), where a specific scene is presented in each chapter with titles like 'Kept Mistress whipping her Keeper's Son'. In contrast to de Sade's own work, British material in this period was beginning to include considerable detail about equipment, costumes and the anticipation felt by participants.

References to de Sade and Sacher-Masoch turn up only around 1880–1910, when several stories also refer to the new 'scientific' theories about sadomasochism. Not surprisingly, they readily opt for the idea of 'innate propensities'. Yet the theme of 'humiliation' rather than 'pain' rules the submission and domination matrix, as the text crosses over from the flagellation-style ceremonies of the earlier material to more subtle, but elongated, descriptions of dress, feelings and equipment. It is in this period that the genre becomes almost completely meaningless to non-devotees, as a comparison between the earlier *The Merry Order of St Bridget* and *The Yellow Room* (1891) demonstrates. When acts are described, the equipment and how it is used is far more important than an account of the physical effect.

Between 1920 and 1960, the roles and rituals of the past are somewhat subsumed within an ever-increasing emphasis upon the types of clothes, equipment and other activities which take place. Former justifications are now superseded by references to the latest medical authorities, and in the case of *Straps: The Artful Tricks of a Female Flagellant* (c. 1935) we are even offered a psycho-sexual life history of a 'masochist'. Submissive initiates no longer experience a 'conversion' experience, whereby they initiate others, but serve the fixed role of their 'instincts'. 'Masochistic' characters, for example, are often seen deliberately provoking the 'sadistic' reactions of others in order to satisfy their supposedly innate passion. We also see the rise of numerous sub-genres, especially a return to male humiliation through enforced cross-dressing. Exactly why transvestism became as popular and as widespread in Britain as America I cannot say; but at this point it was more often than not related to SM, because cross-dressing was seen as a form of humiliation. Stories like *Miss High Heels* (1931), concerning a 'rich young gentleman under the control of his pretty stepsister and her aunt, written by himself at his stepsister's order', simply reversed the submissives gender in what would otherwise be a typical SM story. Towards the end of the period, however, a clear division emerges between novels which deliberately return to historical super-settings and specific role-sets like 'masters' and 'French maids' and those which concentrate upon the technological advances in equipment and clothes within contemporary settings. In the latter, ritualization declines to some extent, because the detailed descriptions of the subjects' interaction with the equipment and costumes can serve to symbolize power relationships and can carry connotations of roles without further elaboration.

Consequently, long before the 1960s any readers of SM fantasy literature would have to be schooled in the traditions, symbols and the connotations of other elements like settings, costumes and roles before they could make any real sense of what was going on. As this is a somewhat time-consuming job, it remained much easier to parrot the standard nonsense about pain, though lack of interest in making such an effort probably explains why SM tends to provoke laughter or boredom rather than disgust in most non-devotees. Be that as it may, it is this dull and tedious detail about who does what, where, when and why, rather than specific acts of pain which constitute the real SM or 'sadomasochistic' tradition. The same holds true from the 1960s to the present day.

John Willie's classic SM comic books, like the *Adventures of Sweet Gwendoline*, which enjoyed huge popularity in the 1970s, despite their earlier origins, consist of a series of witty, implausible adventures with exaggerated characterizations, not unlike comics in general; and which have been copied in other media. Good SM videos invariably pay far more attention to the clothing, equipment, props and scene setting than the normal hard-core counterparts, and strive to capture the essence of the roles and rituals involved, as the catalogue description of *Adventure in Bondage* suggests:

> Rachel, disappointed that her husband isn't coming home as early as planned, accepts a last minute invitation from her friend, Diana, for an evening of girl talk. Little does she know she is about to be thrust into the world of Bondage and Domination. Shocked, but curious, Rachel watches the sensual and erotic interplay between Mistress and Slave. Wanting to join in but hesitant, Diana offers to tutor her in the role of Dominant. Quickly she becomes aroused and tries her hand as a Dominant . . . but her real pleasure comes when she finds herself in the role of slave, totally helpless and at the mercy of her friend.

> Lots of leather bondage items . . . Armbinders, Mittens, Leg Spreaders, Restraints, Helmets, Straitjackets, just to name a few.

Non-devotees would find the time then spent homing in on these features of the video as boring as they would find an SM novel. It is precisely this feature which ensures that one will never 'catch' SM from watching a video, and then, as detractors would have us believe, demand more and more SM material to satisfy one's lust for violence: lovers of violence are far too busy watching kick-boxing movies. This truism still holds even when the fantasy motifs of country mansions and French chateau locations are replaced by the inside of a mock dungeon or play-room, where the location is left to the imagination.

This fantasy world is a secret one only in the sense that it does not seek to proselytize. If at times SM 'dramarama' appears to invade an art college diploma show, or a TV advertisement, any appeal it may have is solely dependent upon the existing susceptibility of the audience. The meaning of SM is open for all to see, and one can easily take it or leave it. Far from reflecting any spirit of our own age, contemporary SM is the latest phase in the devotees' attempt to understand themselves. In each historical period, devotees have simultaneously attempted to utilize the current state of knowledge about sexuality in general to understand their desires and utilized technology to extend the limits of sexual arousal. The only thing that has really changed is that as a greater percentage of the population become more affluent they have more time to consider the meaning and nature of SM. This trend can be clearly seen in the rapidly expanding world of rubber fetishism since the 1960s.

Rubberists have gone to extensive lengths to marry new technology with neo-Gothic SM imagery, as demonstrated by *Harrowing Plight in Rubber Land* (*c.* 1960) released by Nutrix, which produced dozens of novelettes and photo-story books. Anita, a buyer for a mid-western store, pays a weekend-long visit to her old college friend, Mabel, who shared her interest in bondage games; and then discovers why Mabel's house is called 'Rubberland' when she is taken to the basement, which:

had been fitted with a lot of unusual and mysterious apparatus strewn about the room. Anita stretched her legs and inspected the surroundings. Her eyes caught the shiny metal ring laying [*sic*] on the edge of the table which stood to one side. 'A thigh band,' she asked, holding it aloft.

'Nope. That's your waistlet.' 'You're kidding, I hope' said Anita. Mabel laughed and said, 'Just what everyone says. But the other victim got into hers all right so let's see how we can do with you.' . . .

[After Anita has started dressing in a costume] Her hostess walked over the machinery lined wall and stopped before an arrangement of multiple L-shaped arms that extended horizontally from the mechanism, the legs of the Ls pointing downwards to the floor. There were six of these arms and they were so arranged that the legs formed a tight circle. Mabel lifted free the wide rubber circlet which hung loosely from one of the arms just as Anita completed her dressing and strode over to watch interestedly. The rubber band was about a foot wide and tapered toward the centre so that each end was a slightly larger diameter than the middle. Anita took the nipper (i.e. the rubber band) and tried to stretch it between her hand, without success. 'Whew Mabel! This is rugged stuff!'

Mabel smiled. 'Here, you might as well help me. Take it and hold it open. That's it. Now slip it over those metal fingers as far as it will go. Now hold it there but don't get your own fingers between the metal and the rubber.' She walked over to the wall and threw a lever. As she did so there was a hum of machinery and, as Anita watched excitedly, the metal fingers spread outwards until they had partially stretched the rubber. The nipper was now held in position by the metal fingers and Anita stepped back. The length of the fingers was such that about three inches of rubber circlet protruded beneath their ends towards the floor.

Mabel moved the lever further until the rubber was stretched to more than twice its original dimensions. 'Now to get you into it,' said Mabel as she threw another lever.

Anita looked upwards and noted a set of shackles descending from the ceiling. They dropped to about waist height before stopping. Mabel stepped forward and clamped them about the girl's wrists, positioning them in front of her, then returned to the switch and started the shackles back towards the ceiling, lifting the girl high off the floor. A quick turn of another control knob and the overhead mechanism positioned the girl directly over the stretched rubber band.

Mabel then lowered the girl slowly, directing her feet through the circlet until they were just touching the floor, the stretched rubber being at her waist level. Mabel locked the mechanism so that the girl's arms were held high above her head. Then she put a rubber gag between Anita's teeth.

Similar themes existed too in the more overt Fem-Dom rubberist paperbacks of the period, whether they were professionally produced or like the amateur *Male Slaves in Rubber*, a 96-page duplicated volume with eight photocopied drawings which North found sold in Soho bookshops during the 1960s. This kind of material, written and produced by devotees themselves, was still turning up when I did a tour of the stores during the early 1980s. In *Male Slaves* young men were enticed from restaurants, nightclubs or the tube by a Baroness's beauty and rubber dress to her town flat. Once there, the young men are drugged, and, when they come to, find themselves bound prisoners in the Baroness's remote castle, guarded over and punished by her beautiful female servants. Their task is to serve the Baroness sexually. Raymond, a handsome and effeminate young man, failed in his task, and is therefore to be punished. He is dragged naked to the torture chamber by two females dressed in black leather bikinis and thigh boots. There they shave his head and genital regions. He is then encased in a black skin-tight rubber one-piece suit, a rubber headmask and gagged, before being suspended by his thumbs from a gibbet. He is then subject to a series of tortures; including having his testicles and penis caned. Needless to say the amount of detail devoted to the various tortures is surpassed by that covering Raymond's reactions and the clothing of his torturers. While one can muse upon what de Sade may have made of latex rubber, the unfolding historical process which merges history with technology and fantasy clearly demonstrates that it is SM's detractors rather than its devotees who are obsessed with de Sade.

In order to understand contemporary SM, therefore, one would have to explore the devotees' literature, beliefs and practices to see how they are simultaneously drawing upon and reshaping the SM tradition. While that task is beyond the space of this volume, it is, thanks to a bizarre historical irony, not very difficult to undertake the task yourself.

Owing to the vagaries of the Obscene Publications Act, a large number of SM publications have managed to avoid prosecution because they did not exhibit genitalia or sex acts. North, for example, tells an interesting story about one 1960s rubberwear manufacturer who received a visit from the police when he began offering photographs for sale in his newsletter to customers. Being aware of the boundaries which then existed between the 'pornographic' and 'non-pornographic', he produced a set of typical photographs which would never be prosecuted for obscenity in a court: models posing in the open air in rubber mackintoshes, sweatsuits, leotards, capes and boots. There were no masks, gags, straitjackets or bondage; not even any underwear. His 'Damsels in Distress' photographs, while showing girls with their hands behind their backs or leaning against trees or posts, only implied that their wrists were tied together. The police informed him that he had better not go any further. Though 'things' have gone a lot further since, the fact that SM imagery still concentrates upon the costumes and scene setting means that it can survive; and since the early 1970s, when it became almost impossible to convict any written text for obscenity, many of the Victorian classics can even be purchased in high-street stores. Convictions of imported material, however, were common, and still are. The main reason for this is that the legal test for indecency is lower than for obscenity, and stipendiary magistrates, once they've had a good look at the material, invariably decide that anything to do with sex is indecent.

Consequently contemporary SM material can be found on many newsagents' top shelves. It ranges from the *Sadie Stern* magazine, which would be avoided by a real devotee, to the glossy magazines like *Skin Two* and *Janus*. The first covers rubber, 'PVC', and leather fashion 'scenes' for couples, while *Janus*, with its stories and pictures about corporal punishment fantasies, is more likely to appeal to solitary devotees, who may or may not get the opportunity to put their fantasies into practice. The same applies to other titles like *Dear Mistress, Smooth, Scorpion* and *Pleasure Bound*, which cater for male 'submissives', rubberists, spanking and bondage enthusiasts respectively; though more and more couples also appear to be consuming this kind of material, for want of something better. Once one progresses into the community, however, the amount of material available, obtained through mail order, rapidly expands and becomes more diverse. It is also probably significant that *Fetish Times*, probably the best national guide available, and an excellent introductory publication for couples, is run by a woman, Niki Wolf.

Fantasy in practice

Contrary to the impression offered by North, Britain's devotees have been fairly well served with SM clubs and organizations of one kind or another, from the overt to the not so obvious.

Back in the 1960s, the failure of the isolated rubberists to organize themselves encouraged, according to North, a persistent rumour that a secret rubber-lovers' club existed. One version of the mythical club referred to a group of fourteen, all highly educated, well-respected people, meeting once a month in a private house. Elaborate precautions were taken to prevent the members knowing each other's names or recognizing one another. A special maid in a rubber uniform was employed to take the members on their arrival straight to a changing room where they were fitted with black rubber head masks with just eye and mouth holes which were padlocked at the neck band to prevent unauthorized disclosure. The member's club number was on the mask in white. Though the rest of the costumes were of the members' own choice, the men had to wear black rubber gloves and the women white ones; in addition, the latter also wore leg-fetters, consisting of a lockable steel ankle cuff joined by a twelve-inch steel chain. Men also could wear fetters if they wished. Meetings apparently consisted of lectures, not on rubber themes, followed by a cold buffet without alcohol, and the infliction of punishments for breaches of the club rules.

The reality was somewhat different. Early attempts to set up clubs in London did not meet with much success. In 1967, for example, when rubberists were given the opportunity to join a club based on the mailing lists of rubber suppliers and fetish magazines, only half a dozen of the 250 male rubber fetishists brought their wives or girlfriends along. North's attempt to use this as proof that women were not into fetishism generally and rubber in particular is belied by the incredible success that contemporary high fashion fetish clothing companies enjoy. The real problem that the 1960s rubberists faced, and many still face, is their own compulsions and fixations. They have still to learn the art of compromise, and how to play with others. The younger generation have learnt this and during the late 1970s and 1980s several national and local clubs and organizations were established to cater for the growing number of honest devotees.

DSSM International, for example, based in London, organized get-togethers, 'training sessions', fashion shows at various discotheques, and helped in 1985 to organize 'The Great International Leather Ball' which was attended by four hundred people dressed up as masters or mistresses complete with their slaves or French maids. The Maitresse Club, which met in a well-known London discotheque once a week, was once described by a reviewer as

> a place for all sadomasochists, leather, rubber and other
> fetishists. In reality it is basically straight, with a
> reasonable sprinkling of gay men (but no dykes so far),
> and very into fantasy, but not fantasy fulfilment – most
> people just stand around instead of 'doing things'; some
> get down to some action but make it all show and
> dramarama.

Women were particularly inventive in this period. The Artemis Club was based around a journal of the same name catering for 'Ladies and Gentlemaids'. The journal included a 'thriving contact service', stories, articles, letters, cartoons, book reviews and a serial, centred on the common fantasies of life in girls' boarding schools, and the middle-class mistresses' household 'serving maids' between 1900 and 1930. It came as no surprise, therefore, to find the club recommending readers to attend the London production of *Daisy Pulls It Off*, in which Daisy outsmarts two cads, discovers a lost family fortune hidden in the school, and scores the all-important goal in a vital hockey match.

The Wildfire Club produced a newsletter, *Mistress – for the Modern Mistress and Her Household*, catering for the 'upsurge in the number of girls wanting to give themselves in voluntary service to dominant ladies, and of ladies wishing to receive such service'. The first issue included articles on training and discipline for servants, fashion items and tips, corsetry and music, along with a fantasy discussion on the merits of employing butlers, and testimonials from satisfied mistresses and their maidservants. If one then wanted to explore the merits and methods of the 'modern Olympian household' a little further, numerous supplementary publications obtained through the club's 'employment bureau' were available. One, *When the Wind Is Free*, a handbook for the bonded maidservant and her mistress, asked prospective readers:

> Have you ever wanted a mistress? Or wanted to be a mistress? Have you ever wanted to be utterly owned by another? Or to own another? If you have, you are not alone. You are certainly not strange, sick or silly. You simply feel called to one of the most ancient and noble vocations in the world: that of a bonded maidservant or mistress.
>
> Dozens of girls today live in voluntary bonded service relationships. But would such a life suit you? What would it be like? And how could you go about entering one?
>
> This book looks at all these questions and many more. It is a sound, sensible, no-nonsense introduction to the subject designed to help you decide whether a bonded relationship is what you want, and if so, how to go about it. It covers subjects ranging from contracts and the organization of a bonded household to practical home discipline.
>
> Even if you are not considering such a life for yourself this book will open your eyes to a whole rich, warm and varied world which is thriving in Britain today.

The ultimate experience for women, however, had to be a week at St Bride's School, on the coast of Ireland. Anyone who fancied the idea of role-playing an Edwardian schoolgirl would be sent a prospectus, which emphasized that:

> While the academic progress made during such a short stay must necessarily be limited (though certainly by no means negligible), we believe that girls may derive considerable benefit in character, poise, health and happiness . . .

The subjects offered for the all-inclusive weekly fee of £90 included Maths, Elementary Latin, Grammar and Literature. A bell would wake the boarders at half-past seven, and the 'girls' would have to be ready for breakfast at eight-fifteen. Lessons began at nine o'clock, continuing till three o'clock, with a mid-morning break and luncheon provided.

> The remainder of the afternoon is usually free for the children to enjoy themselves, only providing that they do any preparation and other work which may have been given them. The amount of unsupervised recreation allowed depends upon the age and behaviour of the children concerned, but a great deal of freedom is granted in after-school hours to all girls who can be trusted not to abuse it.

Responsible girls could explore the grounds and even venture 'out of bounds' if permission was granted. The indoor activities after high tea included reading, games and even a 'modern gramophone', 'which may sometimes be used by an unsupervised group of girls, provided that great care is taken to avoid overwinding'. Any 'girl' who gave the appearance of being bored or 'listless' would be quickly organized by a mistress to undertake some definite activity. Bedtime was at nine-thirty, when the 'girls' could have a story read to them.

Serious scholars, however, had other options.

> Most girls come to *St. Bride's* ready to take the experience just as it comes. But if you have any special requirements to make or would like to discuss anything before you

arrive you will find *St. Bride's* very flexible to individual
needs . . . if there is any special way you would like to be
treated, any way you would like *St. Bride's* to take account
of your own imaginative world, you are welcome to
discuss it with us.

But remember that you must discuss such things by letter
(or by telephone) before you arrive.

For those with no imagination, the London *Standard* alleged that the
St Bride's system of discipline sometimes went beyond the warning
in the prospectus that 'naughtiness and mischief would be dealt with
in the ordinary school ways'.

Like the many contemporary SM organizations which adver-
tise their services in publications like *Forum* and *Fetish Times*, these
1980s clubs sought only to cater for those who were interested and
knew what they were looking for; and as one would now expect, this
revolved around fantasy enactment rather than painful sex. A group
called Motivation, for example, saw itself as 'an association of
people interested in SM *in all its many variations and to all degrees
of intensity*, whether as an interested student or as a practitioner'.
Anyone making contact would be supplied with a newsletter
containing offers of discounts on clothes and equipment, notifica-
tion of meetings, details of the 'scene' both in Britain and in Europe,
short stories, educational material and explanations for one's sexual
proclivities. Motivation went to some length to explain the various
forms of physical and psychological stimulation and fantasy play to
its members, as an extract from an article on restraint demonstrates:

Bondage is the restraint of one partner by another through
the use of such paraphernalia as chains, ropes, gags and
suspensions. Sometimes bondage and discipline – referred
to as B&D – is distinguished from S/M or is a milder form
of S/M. This is because 'pain' and/or the exaggeration of
dom or sub roles need not be the major element of
bondage. It is noted that struggling and being tied up can
be physically arousing regardless of any symbolic meaning.
The constricting feeling of tight clothing such as rubber
body suits or leather pants etc., can be physically
stimulating themselves.

Bondage can fit well into a framework of dominance and submission. It can provide a sense of being physically and sexually at the mercy of another, and thus produce psychological stimulation.

When it came to the 'gentle art' of domination, Motivation explained that outsiders always misunderstood what was going on because they knew little about the nature of 'pain':

Much is made by opponents of the scene of the 'pain' aspect but those who gain enjoyment and satisfaction accept this in just the same way as a long distance runner or mountaineer. How often have you seen on television the agony of a runner suffering from cramp but despite all the pain carries on till the end of the race. They cannot in a literal sense 'enjoy' those last moments but they accept the pain as part of their activity to ensure the satisfaction of completing the race just as a submissive accepts, in all probability far less pain, as part of the ultimate satisfaction of our scene.

Likewise, detractors invariably misrepresented the meaning of SM power relationships:

The scene is very much a fantasy world and allows the participants to enact out feelings that otherwise could build into frustrations which may well effect the health of those persons. The human mind has limitless expanse and it would be very interesting to be able to know exactly how many people had at some time or another not experienced the feeling of either wanting to dominate or submit themselves to another. It would be a very, very large percentage of the population.

Since to a very large extent it is a fantasy world, the dominant must ensure that they do not completely enact that fantasy since once fulfilled the submissive could find their mind has nothing to imagine and evolve.

A true dominant need not require any form of restraint at all but some is normally used since from the submissive's enjoyment the symbolic point of being physically unable to control what happens is a vital ingredient of their satisfaction.

Being a national club, Motivation's contact service section revealed the kind of roles British SM devotees wished to experiment with. A couple from Birmingham wanted to meet submissive males and females for 'training, bondage, spanking, CP, maid duties etc.' A London 'Gentleman' required a second 'Slave' as companion for his first. Another couple were setting up a series of 'fantasy' evenings and invited participants and ideas. One member simply listed an 'Excerpt from School rules' which included '24. You will send photograph and 100 lines to the Headmaster immediately'; followed by the contact number! Members could also hire equipment from others, and one dominant 'mistress' opened her 'correction chamber' to other devotees in the organization.

Nothing in Britain, however, comes anywhere near the SM devotees' ultimate fantasy: Club Doma, based at Asterstraat 107, Den Haag, Netherlands. The Doma-SM Society, founded by male and female devotees, seeks to gain social recognition for SM as a legitimate form of sexual activity by various means. Apart from legal lobbying, it publishes a couple of magazines, *Doma Magazine* and *Slavegirl Magazine*, makes videos, runs a contact service, and opens the doors of Club Doma to anyone who wishes to join. Offering visitors privacy and anonymity, the Dutch, as ever, have a sensible way of organizing their activities. Members of any sex or sexual orientation can utilize the bar and watch videos. An *à la carte* menu is offered in the Club room overlooking a small stage decked out with every SM requisite imaginable, where live shows are offered on Club nights. These consist of voluntary participants, carefully guided by a couple of resident dominants and their contemporary submissives. Non-exhibitionists can alternatively hire the cellar, playroom or rubber-chamber, located downstairs. New initiates can, if they wish, be carefully trained by the resident dominants there as well.

Similar permanent clubs exist all over continental Europe; and no one turns a hair. After all, those who attend such clubs are merely acting out their own sexual fantasies, which, whatever reason one chooses to explain the origin of one's SM desires, obviously draw upon a wide variety of sources throughout history completely independent of de Sade or Sacher-Masoch.

Play it again

Given that all sexual fantasies involve some form of role-play, the only real difference between SM devotees and the rest of the population is that the formers' fantasies involve overt elements of power relationships. In many cases, knowing that the imagination is often more stimulating and satisfying than reality, SM devotees would not attempt to realize them; but when they do enact fantasy role-play the imagination is still the most important feature. It is this feature which helps to distinguish SM devotees from those who promote violent sexual crimes against unwilling victims, and ensures that devotees are perfectly harmless.

The fact that Freudianism tried to bury this feature of SM, far from lending any weight to the gross misrepresentations promoted by psychiatrists, fundamentalist feminists and some Christian moral reformers, seriously undermines the detractors' ideological concerns. As the controlled and often innocuous activities of SM devotees belies the stereotypes of compulsive 'sadists' and 'masochists', the major rationale for outlawing SM – the suggestion that enactment of fantasies is socially harmful – is bogus. As the SM community also clearly demonstrates a very rational and sensible approach to its proclivities, I can only conclude that detractors' fears are either ultimately based upon their own fantasies or an ideological opposition to the attempt to intellectualize, and develop skills in enhancing, sexual arousal. After all, without exception the detractors all allude to the SM potential that resides in all of us. While it is easy to see why Christians may consider a preoccupation with such skills a distraction from holy worship, like everyone else they have to realize that the interests of society are best served by understanding our sexual selves and the origins of our proclivities; and that when it comes to sadomasochism, SM devotees, by exploring their fantasies in a sensible way, are far closer to a real understanding of SM than any psychobabbler or ideologue.

Far from engaging in an act of 'regression', SM devotees would appear to have found a very civilized means to deal with what are allegedly bestial desires. The paucity of that allegation, however, can be easily seen in the way in which it rests upon a series of theological and ideological assumptions rather than any knowledge of the SM community, its techniques, beliefs and motivations, which ensure that the boundary of fantasy is maintained. If some of those within the SM community wish to take advantage of their excitation transfer threshold, I have yet to come across any viable reason why anyone else should attempt to stop them. This is hardly surprising given that no useful purpose could be served by outlawing a wish to enhance one's sexual arousal; and that the 'shock-horror' brigade who are appalled by SM never seem to have a problem finding justifications for enacting real violence in everything from corporal punishment to war.

Chapter seven

Criminalizing SM

HAVING identified the misleading nature of the term 'sadomasochism', and some of the reasons why perfectly harmless people are attracted to the potential pleasures of SM sex, we can now consider the way in which SM sex was criminalized and assess the viability of the judgments which made it so. As we do so, there are two major questions to consider: first, should SM have been criminalized at all; and second, did the legal rationales used to do so justify the judgments made?

Posing a problem

Back in 1976, L.H. Leigh, a Reader in Law at the LSE, having noted that 'sadomasochistic' acts were hardly in the same league as compulsive murders and sexual assaults on women, suggested that it was about time the law came to terms with, and defined the legal status of, stylized SM practice. Although there was no law forbidding the practice, it could be subject to a charge of assault, and the current legal precedent, the *Donovan* case, was unsatisfactory because, in allowing a discretionary application of the law, it enabled any judge so inclined to outlaw all but the mildest of SM practices. In 1934, Donovan had lost an appeal against a conviction for assault, for strapping a girl of seventeen in a garage in Morden, because he had done so for the purpose of his own sexual gratification, even though the girl had consented.

Leigh thought this unreasonable. As SM practised by married couples, gays and professional women seldom led to any kind of permanent physical harm, and as the participants' involvement was a deliberate choice, there were three issues the law needed to consider in order to clarify SM's legal status in relation to existing statutes and case law. First, how could one assess what degree of 'harm' was tolerable; i.e. how forceful did a blow have to be before it was necessary for the law to intervene? Second, how one could distinguish between, and establish a defence for, a normal case of violence as compared to a ritual flagellation, within the limit for blows set? Third came the somewhat bizarre question as to whether or not the law should make any special provision for cases in which the consent given followed from an act of exploitation, such as a threat of real violence, or where one participant was of a subnormal intellect. That should have been obvious.

In his own answers to these questions, Leigh insisted that one would have to determine what 'harms' were tolerable in law before anything else, and that there should be a stipulated ceiling specifying the acceptable degree of harm as closely as possible, because the current standard, appreciable bodily harm, could be too restrictively applied. He then suggested that the line could, and should, be drawn at any form of mutilation, defined in law as 'deprivation of a limb or some principal organ of the body, disfigurement, be it permanently or for an extended period and requiring surgery, and any serious impairment of mental or physical powers, be it permanent or for a protracted period'. Wherever one drew a clear standard separating sexual role-play from serious harm, Leigh's suggestion was important, because both statute and case law were extremely imprecise and full of arbitrary definitions; a conviction of unlawful wounding bore a heavier penalty than causing someone grievous bodily harm, but where the distinction between the two offences falls has nothing to do with the nature and extent of the harm involved.

Leigh then recommended that, even if the ceiling was not drawn as high as he had suggested, the consent of all parties to the SM act could and should be a defence to any charges arising, as long as the consent included prior knowledge of SM's general characteristics, and consent to each and every one of the particular acts undertaken. If a charge then followed from the fact that one party had consented to a set of sadomasochistic activities, but not necessarily to the type or degree of harm which had then been inflicted, Leigh suggested that the problem could be dealt with by using some guidelines. First, the person inflicting the blows would not be liable unless they had deliberately intended to apply greater harm than that consented to, or had been reckless as to the result of their actions. Second, as long as the person receiving the effect of the act had been made aware of the general nature of the act to be performed, the defence of consent should still apply even if it transpired that the 'victim' was unaware how far, precisely, the 'aggressor' would go, as long as that ignorance could not be attributed to a deliberate deception on the part of the 'aggressor'. Third, a defence of consent would obviously not apply where one party had not given their consent and the other was aware of the fact; and the same rule should also apply to actions which continued after consent was withdrawn. Fourth, given that sexual arousal enables people to enjoy what would be 'painful' in a non-aroused state, disputes that arise about consent to an increase in the use of force could be solved by a jury deciding whether or not the person charged had been reckless and failed to secure consent to the increase in force which had occurred.

Although Leigh realized that this could mean that a considerable amount of bodily harm could be inflicted without either party incurring criminal liability, he thought this both acceptable and appropriate in law given the nature of the act being considered.

Leigh's proposals made a lot of sense, even though they were obviously based upon the misguided idea that SM sex concerned the application and reception of painful blows, and clearly envisaged a client–prostitute flagellation scenario rather than a sophisticated role-playing couple. His second test, for example, was designed to cover the potential circumstance in which a man who desired some form of flagellation ritual inadvertently picked a professional woman who specialized in severe whippings. Leigh suggested that the woman should not be liable to an assault charge either because she had not reached the law's new designated ceiling for such a charge or because she believed that she had the 'victim's' consent to strike him harder than he really wished.

The proposals still made sense, not only because client–prostitute agreements would have to be covered in order to protect professional women from vindictive clients or police harassment, but because the extent of harm and nature of consent are the central issues. The effects would be to prevent anyone using SM sex as an excuse for deliberately inflicting a violent injury upon someone else, to offer legal protection to professional SM practitioners, and to inhibit anyone taking advantage of the ignorant rather than finding a consenting partner for their own gratification.

Unfortunately, as nothing had been done by the time the law lords had to hear the appeal against the Spanner convictions, on 11 March 1993, the justices had to decide for themselves, without benefit of wider discussion. To make matters worse, British legal practice would ensure that any decision made would be with reference to the particular technicalities of the appeal, rather than the issue as a whole.

The issue of assault

In law, there are three types of assault, supposedly determined by their order of gravity: common assault; assault which occasions actual bodily harm; and assault which inflicts grievous bodily harm. Despite the problems identified by Leigh, it was widely believed, until Judge Rant's ruling in the Spanner trial, that consent was a defence to a charge of common assault, but not to serious injury, such as maiming, implied by a charge of grievous bodily harm. The Spanner defendants had thought that consent would protect them, but they were convicted both of assaults occasioning actual bodily harm contrary to Section 47 of the Offences Against the Person Act 1861 and of wounding contrary to Section 20. Consequently, the law lords had to decide whether or not Judge Rant's ruling was correct, and whether or not consent was also a defence to a charge of 'actual bodily harm' and 'wounding'. Even if they preferred not to decide whether or not SM was immune from assault charges like popular violent sports or clarify the ceiling on the level of force permissible before the law intervened, in order to make their judgement they would have to define what 'actual bodily harm' was, and in doing so effectively set the ceiling.

The law lords, therefore, had to make two sets of questions. First, they had to determine whether or not the SM acts that the Spanner defendants had used constituted an assault in law, and, if so, in what way. In order to do this they had to overcome the imprecise nature of existing legal definitions, negotiate their way through various precedents by considering the questions of intent and recklessness, and, whether they wanted to or not, address the question of the ceiling for levels of force. Second, they had to determine whether or not SM could and should be made an exception to the laws of assault as are many contact sports. This was well within their power; and whatever they decided they would have to consider the issue of consent, the nature of the acts and the possibility of physical injury.

Definitions

In order to clarify the defence of consent, the law lords had to refer to various precedents and legal opinions about assault and consent, which the reader needs to appreciate contain various legal definitions of words and acts that may not coincide with common usage.

The first definition of assault to consider came from the Criminal Law Revision Committee, 1980, and was being considered for adoption by the Law Commission:

> At common law, an assault is an act by which a person *intentionally or recklessly* causes another to apprehend immediate and unlawful personal violence and a battery is an act by which a person intentionally or recklessly inflicts personal violence upon another. However, the term 'assault' is now in both legal usage and in statute regularly used to cover both assault and battery.

To make any sense of this one would have to have a definition of 'unlawful personal injury', and consider what precisely constitutes both intent or reckless behaviour; so this did not really help.

The second set of definitions related to the catch-22 mentioned in the Introduction, whereby one had to decide whether an act was *de facto* unlawful, preventing a defence of consent, but where it was frequently impossible to make a decision about lawfulness without considering the nature of the consent first.

Once Judge Rant had declared that consent was not applicable because of the charges, the defendants had to plead guilty to acts contrary to Section 20 of the 1861 Act, which states:

> Who so ever shall *unlawfully and maliciously wound* or inflict any *grievous bodily harm* upon any other person, either with or without any weapon or instrument, shall be guilty of [an offence], . . . and shall be liable . . . [to a maximum penalty of five years imprisonment.]

These definitions are extremely vague, and depend upon several others determined in case law. A 'wound', for example, after *J.J.C.* v. *Eisenhower*, 1983, required that 'The whole skin must be broken and not merely the outer layer called the epidermis and the cuticus'. Since the *DPP* v. *Smith* case in 1961, 'grievous bodily harm' had also meant that the 'harm' involved had to be 'really serious'. The term 'unlawful', after *R.* v. *Mowatt*, 1968, meant that the accused had no lawful excuse, such as self-defence. And the word 'maliciously' in law means no more than intentional.

On the face of it, the nature of the wound would not determine anything; for as long as serious harm had not been intended, which is unlikely in an SM act, everything would depend upon whether or not SM was going to be regarded as a 'lawful' act.

The third set of definitions addressed that question, and required their lordships to review several major legal precedents which covered the lawful exceptions to charges of assault, whereby even serious bodily harm is deemed acceptable because the injury is a *foreseeable* part of a lawful activity, such as surgery, ritual circumcision, tattooing, ear piercing or violent sports. This review was supposed to help determine whether or not SM acts amounted to more than a common assault but less than actual bodily harm, because, although the letter of the law is vague, it was assumed that there was no logical reason why SM should not be exempt from a defence of consent when extremely violent sports like boxing, which are inevitably far more harmful than SM acts, are granted automatic immunity from prosecution and so never even have their right to consent tested in the courts.

The major precedents to be considered were the 1882 *R. v. Coney* case, the 1980 *Attorney-General's Reference*, No. 6, and, of course, *R. v. Donovan*. The importance of *R. v. Coney* was that amongst other decisions it attempted to lay down the difference between blows struck in lawful and in unlawful circumstances. Unfortunately, at first sight, the justices' ruling did not concur exactly. Justice Cave, for example, had determined that

> A blow struck in anger, or which is likely or intended to do corporal hurt, is an assault, but that a blow struck in sport, and not likely nor intended to cause bodily harm, is not an assault, and that an assault being a breach of the peace and unlawful, the consent of the person struck is immaterial.

But, whereas Justice Cave had placed the emphasis upon the role of anger, the possibility of harm and the context when considering a defence of consent, Justice Stephen's judgment in the same case had concentrated upon establishing a ceiling of harm and injury in lawful sporting events, and this could be seen as an alternative:

> In cases where life and limb are exposed to no serious danger in the common course of things, I think that consent is a defence to a charge of assault even when considerable force is used, as for instance, in cases of wrestling, single-stick, sparring with gloves, football and the like . . .

Why people who are regarded as having Britain's best legal minds continue to believe that these two rulings are contradictory, when simply to contextualize them reveals their complementary nature, I do not know. It is not difficult to see that intent is all important.

Where the problem really begins, therefore, is with the *Attorney-General's Reference*, No. 6, 1980, which followed a case of assault involving actual bodily harm. The two men concerned had quarrelled in a public street and had then fought with bare fists. On appeal against a conviction for assault, Lord Lane had emphasized that the concept of 'the public interest' was all-important when deciding whether or not consent would be allowed as a defence. This idea had been purloined from Kenny's *Outlines of Criminal Law*, which argued that even complete consent could not legalize an assault where there were public grounds for prohibiting certain acts. Consequently, Lane insisted that

> It is not in the public interest that people should try to cause, or should cause, each other bodily harm for *no good reason*. Minor struggles are another matter. So, in our judgment, *it is immaterial whether the acts occurred in private or in public; it is an assault if actual bodily harm is intended and/or caused.* This means that most *fights* will be unlawful regardless of consent. Nothing which we have said is intended to cast doubt upon the accepted legality of properly conducted games and sports, lawful chastisement or correction, reasonable surgical interference, dangerous exhibitions, etc. These apparent exceptions can be justified as involving the exercise of a legal right, in the case of chastisement or correction, or as needed in the public interest, in the other cases.

This ruling seriously qualified both *Coney* judgments, which decided that the blows in that case were *de facto* unlawful and therefore not entitled to a consent defence because the prize-fight concerned took place in public, and as such fights involve intentional harm a breach of the peace could follow. Although the two young men in the *Attorney-General's Reference* case had fought in a 'public' street, as no one else was present their Counsel had argued that it was a private fight between individuals and so could not possibly cause a breach of the peace. Lane's decision had made the threat of a breach of the peace irrelevant; and in its stead created a new core justification for declaring an activity unlawful. By placing the emphasis upon the completely subjective concept of 'no good reason' judges could decide everything upon their own whims and fancies, for it also negated the importance of the role of intent to cause injury, and enabled Lane to by-pass the apparently crucial issue of exactly what constituted an 'actual bodily harm'.

The final precedent considered was ultimately to prove the most important; for Justice Swift's ruling in *R. v. Donovan* was used to justify the belief that sadomasochism could not be considered a sport, and was erroneously seen as reinforcing Cave's judgment by determining that 'It is an unlawful act to beat another person with such a degree of violence that the infliction of bodily harm is a probable consequence and when such an act is proved, consent is immaterial.' This is obviously absurd, because it merely reinforces the need to consider the intent involved, and again raises the question: what sensible reason, as opposed to the excuse of the defendants' enforced 'guilty' plea, is there for making boxing an exception to assault charges, while denying the same lawful status to sex?

The defence

The defence, both at the Court of Appeal and before the law lords, employed various strategies; the two major arguments can, however, be summarized as follows:

1 The defence of consent should be extended to that of occasioning actual bodily harm under Section 47 of the 1861 Act, because the actions that had taken place were not the serious wounding or the infliction of serious bodily harm implied under Section 20.

2 Consent should provide a defence for charges under both Sections 20 and 47 because everybody has the right to deal with his or her own body as he or she pleases. And in doing so, everyone had the right to consent to the infliction upon himself or herself of bodily harm not amounting to serious harm or maiming, at which point public interest intervenes.

These two lines of defence addressed the issues of the ceiling and the vague legal definitions; and, given the circumstances, were a fairly good strategy. The same could not be said for the first of the three supplementary submissions made to suggest that SM was not harmful.

3 The sexual appetites of sadists and masochists could be satisfied only by the infliction of bodily harm, and that the

law should not punish the consensual achievement of sexual satisfaction.

4 Each submissive would have, and utilize, a code word if they found the activities taking place beyond their personal limits, and thereby no pain or harm could have been inflicted.

5 Any instruments employed were always clean and sterile thereby avoiding the possibility of permanent injury and infection.

In playing up to the stereotypical image of SM and trying to negate the inferences in particular statutes concerning assault, the defence were laying themselves open to manipulation. They then threw in a wild card, submitting that

6 Some of the group's activities, while technically involving 'offences of gross indecency', were time barred, and thereby negated the police's ability to charge them with offences under the 1861 Act. In any event, the Act of 1861 was an inappropriate means to charge homosexuals with committing such acts, when they could have been charged under the Sexual Offences Act of 1956 to 1976, and the common law offence of keeping a disorderly house.

This was then followed by a long shot, but one which raised extremely pertinent questions about modern society.

7 A reference was made to the principles contained within Articles 7 and 8 of the European Convention of Human Rights:

7 No one shall be held guilty of any criminal offence on account of any act or omission which did not constitute a criminal offence under National or International law at the time that it was committed . . .

8 (1) Everyone has the right to respect for his private and family life, his home and his correspondence. (2) There shall be no interference by a public authority with the exercise of this right except such as is in accordance with the law and is necessary in a democratic society in the interests of national security, public safety or the

economic well-being of the country, for the prevention of disorder or crime, for the protection of health or morals, or for the protection of the rights and freedoms of others.

In other words: as the defendants thought that their consent was a defence against a charge of assault, and that the issue of consent was being decided by their court case, they could not commit and had not committed a crime; and, as SM proclivities were an aspect of a person's private life which had not placed the defendants at risk, they should not be subject to any interference by the authorities.

Just in case this failed, the defence addressed the *Attorney-General's Reference*, by submitting that:

8 The appellants' consent to their activities was not injurious to the public interest.

Finally, if all else failed, they sought to suggest that the ceiling should be raised:

9 If SM activities constituted assault, a distinction should be made between 'serious' and 'non-serious' bodily harm. Only acts of grievous bodily harm should be prosecuted.

The Court of Appeal judgement

Despite the judges having been offered even greater discretionary powers than those that had worried Leigh, when Lord Lane heard the first appeal he added to the confusion surrounding the legal situation. Like many others in the legal profession, Lord Lane believed that Judge Rant had been wrong to dismiss out of hand the idea that a prosecutor had to prove absence of consent in order to secure a conviction for assault. Unfortunately for the defendants, Lord Lane let Judge Rant off the hook. He referred to their 'guilty' pleas to a charge of wounding, then belaboured the extreme but rarely used practices undertaken, and finally added his own insistence that satisfying the 'sadomasochistic libido did not constitute a good reason' to deny the defendants the right to a consent defence. As far as Lane was concerned, the law was not there to offer protection to people who 'willingly and enthusiastically participated in the commission of acts of violence *against each other* for the sexual pleasure it engendered *in the giving and receiving of pain*'. By defining SM acts in this way, Lane was also able to reject the submission that there could be no assault without a hostile act, by arguing that the *intention* 'to inflict *pain and suffering* constituted an assault'.

On the other hand, Lane then admitted that, because 'the victims' were not only consenting parties but seemed to derive pleasure from the assault, the private nature of the acts and the defendants' belief that they were not criminal acts 'puts these offences into a different category from the type of assault with which this court is ordinarily concerned'.

But rather than use the fact that the trial judge had erred, and the categorical difference, to dismiss the case, Lane merely reduced the sentences, and then took the opportunity to warn the public that:

> We take the view that the function of the Court is to mark its disapproval of these activities by imposing short terms of immediate imprisonment. We are prepared to accept that the Appellants did not appreciate that their actions in inflicting injury were criminal and that the sentences upon them therefore should be lenient. In future, however, that argument will not be open to a Defendant in circumstances such as these.

The law lords' judgment

While Lord Lane's warning did not bode well for the appeal to the House of Lords, the continuing confusion surrounding the law meant that there was more than just hope. As long as the law lords made more sense of the existing precedents by carefully considering their context, there was no reason why they could not raise the ceiling or declare that in this modern day and age SM sex should become one of the exceptions immune from charges of assault. Many people, including myself, expected that the Lords might produce some form of compromise to let everyone off the hook. So what came as a shock was not that the law lords upheld the conviction or even that henceforth SM sex became *de facto* an 'unlawful activity', but just how bizarre the Lords' justifications and rationales were. The decision was such a blatant fix that it should be considered a scandal.

Rather than approach the subject in the same way as Leigh had done, three of the five law lords appeared to have already made up their minds that any form of SM sex was unacceptable and that the consent defence should not be allowed even in the case of common assault, and spent most of their written judgments trying to justify their decision.

Far from considering the issues of consent or the ceiling, the three law lords offered a series of tautologies and made numerous inconsistent, mutually exclusive, assertions to shore up the gaping holes in the law's theory and practice. Lord Jauncey, for example, used the appellants' lack of medical qualifications and failure to use a referee to imply that there were 'obvious' differences between bodily harm caused by surgical operations or 'a properly conducted sport' and SM sex, which he then made directly analogous to an illegal prize-fight by asserting that life and limb were inevitably endangered by SM sex.

Despite the fact that Spanner was supposed to be a test case, the law lords' discussion of the *Donovan* and *Coney* precedents, which being subject to numerous contextual caveats could easily have led to the upholding of the appeal, amounted to a raid for selective quotations to justify what began to look more and more like a predetermined decision. They even rewrote one of the precedents.

The more closely one follows the arguments advanced by each law lord the more difficult it becomes to avoid the conclusion that other, non-legal, considerations were also involved, including the law lords' attitude to homosexuality in general, and SM sex in particular.

Although Judge Rant had claimed that he was not concerned with the fact the men were homosexuals, most of their lordships appeared to be obsessed with the subject; and their interest went far beyond the problems caused by the Sexual Offences Act 1967, which restricted a homosexual gathering for the purpose of sex to two people.

Their lordships were also quite blasé in throwing around erroneous assertions concerning the nature and meanings of the activities that took place; but there was nothing slipshod about the purpose for doing so. Each 'submissive', even when he had clearly demonstrated his switchability, was assumed and asserted to be a 'victim' of a 'sadist', and by repeatedly using the word 'victim' their lordships could deliberately avoid addressing, let alone admitting, the obvious fact that the 'submissives' were 'masochists' enjoying what was happening; because, as we shall see, to have done so would have had vital implications when considering the precedent set in the *Donovan* case.

Likewise, every SM act was automatically considered to be an act of 'violence', and anything which could help effect excitation transfer was denounced as 'torture' and 'cruelty', in order to secure the definitions needed to bolster their lordships' shaky legal arguments. Lord Templeman, for example, by insisting that all sadomasochistic encounters were violent and involved a 'sadist' indulging his cruel impulses by causing the degradation of his victims, was clearly implying that submissives could only ever be passive, which conveniently justifies using the 1861 Act, and helped to distance SM from friendly two-sided sporting contests because 'the violence of sadists and the degradation of their victims have sexual motivations, but sex is no excuse for violence'. Without these kinds of definitions, the judgment would have had to go the other way.

By any other name

Of the three judges denying the appeal, Templeman's role appeared to be to lay down the definitions of SM needed to apply the law in an adverse way. At least that is what he did, when zipping through the defence's submissions; but in doing so, all he really demonstrated was his complete ignorance of, and prejudice against, SM sex.

The appellants' argument that the defence of consent should be extended to cover 'actual bodily harm' was dismissed by Lord Templeman on the grounds that any new exceptions should be decided by Parliament, which could call upon the advice of doctors, psychologists, criminologists, sociologists and other experts, and also sound out and take into account public opinion. While this may have been an excuse for their lordships to ignore the current state of academic knowledge, it certainly presupposed that consent was not and could not be a defence as the law stood and implied that SM encounters were already covered by existing law and precedents. Both assumptions were groundless; after all, if the legal position was so obvious, the case would not have reached the House of Lords.

He then argued that consent could not apply in this case, because, as sadomasochistic participants had no way of foretelling the degree of bodily harm which would result from their encounters, it would be impossible for juries to distinguish between actual and serious bodily harms. This is an odd thing to say. First, it completely ignores the safety record of SM sex compared to other sports and 'dangerous exhibitions' in favour of stressing the unsubstantiated and anachronistic belief that 'sadists' can not stop themselves getting carried away. Second, it ignores the necessity of 'masters' to pay very careful attention to their partners' arousal in order to be effective. Third, it establishes a very good reason for outlawing most contact sports because their participants, referees, and ruling bodies likewise cannot guarantee the level of bodily harm that could occur. By accident or design far more people are so seriously injured in sporting contests that they cannot participate again without lengthy surgery, and sometimes not even then.

Rather than addressing the issue of consent in the second defence submission – which drew upon Justice Stephen's ruling to argue that 'submissives' had a right to consent to bodily harm up to a ceiling of maiming, or serious harm, or where public interest intervenes – Templeman sidestepped the issue completely, by asserting that the appellants did not 'mutilate' their own bodies but inflicted 'bodily harm' upon willing victims. In doing so Lord Templeman obviously implied that if they had inflicted 'bodily harm' upon themselves this would be acceptable; but offered no reason whatsoever why someone who asked another to accomplish such a task on their behalf should be considered a 'victim'. This raised another legal question not covered by any adverse judgment. If a 'masochist' asks a 'sadist' to spank him, for example, the 'masochist' does not consent to an act: the 'sadist' does. As the 'masochist' initiates the act and sets the limits, Templeman was deliberately and grossly misrepresenting what happened, and was asking us to accept something akin to blaming the American fleet for the actions of a kamikaze pilot.

Lord Templeman seemed so determined to maintain his fictions about SM sex that, when he dismissed the third (erroneous) defence submission – that SM devotees required forceful sex to achieve sexual satisfaction – he promptly contradicted himself. While he was correct to assert that there was no evidence to prove that sadomasochistic activities were essential to the happiness of the appellants, saying so somewhat undermined his, Rant's and Lane's assertions that there was a 'sadomasochistic' libido upon which so much else rested. In typical Templeman fashion, he attempted to hide this embarrassing contradiction behind another outburst that, because sadomasochism was concerned with 'violence' and was 'unpredictable', 'dangerous', 'degrading to body and mind', 'developed with increasing barbarity' and 'taught to persons whose consent was worthless', he would not accept the proposition that SM promoted sexual satisfaction. Apart from simply making the contradiction more obvious, it also did not square with his complementary assertions that a 'sadist' draws pleasure from inflicting or watching cruelty, whereas a 'masochist' derives pleasure from his or her own pain or humiliation. While judges like to think they are smarter than the rest of us, the fact that Lord Templeman was well aware that someone was likely to spot this glaring inconsistency and selectivity is strongly implied by his use of a supplementary but desperate rationale.

Throwing any last cell of reason to the wind, and completely ignoring the issue of switchability, he implied that recreational drugs and alcohol were deliberately employed by the 'sadists' 'to obtain consent and increase enthusiasm'; and then sought to reinforce the inference that there was no consent by also arguing that 'because the victim was usually manacled so that they could enjoy the thrill of helplessness, they had no control over the harm which the sadist, likewise stimulated by drink and drugs, might inflict'.

There was, of course, no truth in this at all. The consent of all parties was informed; and the presupposition that 'stimulated' persons are never able to control themselves is a legal fiction based upon the Judeo-Christian dislike of stimulants. While heavy use of stimulants can often impair judgment, such claims are usually advanced by defence lawyers in an attempt to imply that their clients are not fully responsible for their actions; yet this myth is frequently dismissed by juries, prosecution and judges alike precisely because it does not reduce culpability. To then turn this reasoning on its head and insist that it always reduces consent is typical of how British law is applied in practice: any argument will do. In this instance, Lord Templeman was using it to imply that a single incident of 'blood letting' proved not only that 'things' had recklessly got out of hand, and that there was a threat of serious bodily harm through HIV transmission, but that SM also inevitably led to 'blood lust'.

This answer was pathetic. While cutting is an extremely rare occurrence in SM sex, any 'excitement' caused, as any expert in this extremely minority interest will tell you, is in the nature of the cutting, really no more than a nick, that leads to arousal enhancement, and not the sight of blood. Not that this would interest Lord Templeman, because he was simply grasping at straws to get over the awkward fact that none of the group had sustained any injury at all. The introduction of HIV and the notion of recklessness were simply his means of insisting that the 'sadists' were reckless as to causing 'serious bodily harm' in order to justify using a charge of assault. While he admitted that nothing of the kind could be proved in this case, he reasoned that his argument was viable because the defendants' actions *might* have injured someone in *another case*, which we had not heard about because this 'victim' would 'obviously' not have complained to the police for fear of implicating himself and because his doctor, bound by the confidentiality code, would have said nothing either. Why this hypothetical 'victim' would have failed to speak to the police when participation in SM sex was not yet a criminal act, Lord Templeman declined to tell us.

To undermine the fourth defence – that the use of code words and signs maintained continual consent in acts of SM sex – Templeman did a Lord Lane, and avoided this tricky one by simply harping on and on about the 'extent' of some of the acts which occasionally took place, as if the nature of any act freely undertaken somehow negated consent.

In keeping with his power to be completely inconsistent, Lord Templeman then cited both the practice of 'stop' words and the 'care taken with the instruments used' to suggest that the appellants were aware of the obvious danger of personal injury to undermine the fifth defence; even though in doing so he promptly destroyed his justification for dismissing the third defence submission.

The appellants' attempts to cite the European Convention on Human Rights was then dismissed with the standard Catch-22. While Lord Templeman's contention was that the Convention could not absolve one from a criminal offence under English law, the charge of inflicting actual bodily harm or worse obviously required the acts concerned to have been defined as assault *prior* to considering a defence's argument that would question one's ability to define them in this way. Until the law lords' judgment had been heard, SM was not *de facto* a criminal offence in British law. Article 8, the right to privacy, was then dismissed on the grounds that it could not invalidate a law which forbids 'violence which is intentionally harmful to body and mind': this again rests upon the false premise that SM sex is intentionally 'harmful', whereas its clear aim is to promote sexual pleasure through excitation transfer.

The suggestion that Lord Templeman may have been well aware of this fact, but was personally opposed to its truth, can be found in his ultimate justification for dismissing the appeal: 'Society is entitled and bound to protect itself against *a cult of violence*. Pleasure derived from the infliction of pain is an evil thing. Cruelty is uncivilised.' This makes no sense, either in its own terms or objectively. Apart from Lord Templeman having no justification for calling SM a 'cult of violence', he admitted as much when he then attacked the possibility of people deriving pleasure from pain as 'an evil thing'. Why excitation transfer is 'evil' or an act of 'cruelty' he did not tell us; and he never will. For while cruelty may be uncivilized, SM excitation transfer could only be cruel or evil if the enhancement of pleasure is cruel and evil; and not even a law lord would dare risk looking that foolish.

Such an argument might just make some sense if Lord Templeman believed that the 'cruelty' derived from a 'sadist's' deliberate act of taking advantage of a pathetic 'masochist's' weakness in body and mind; but, apart from this being a patronizing view of submissives' motivations, Lord Templeman never even hinted at such a view in his judgment.

As a result, it is impossible to come to any other conclusion than that Lord Templeman found the Spanner defendants guilty either because he was completely ignorant of the nature of SM sex, which would make him unfit to judge such a case, or because he was deliberately manipulating the evidence to justify a personal preference, which would make him unfit to judge any case.

Ignoring precedent

The major reason for their lordships' rejection of the first two defences was provided by Lord Jauncey, who justified not granting SM sex the same immunity that violent sports and dangerous exhibitions enjoyed from the charges of assault on the ground that the consent defence was 'so broad a proposition [that it] could not stand up and that there must be some limitation upon the harm which an individual could consent to receive at the hand of another'. I could not agree more. There should be a limit to consent; but one would need a very good reason for completely outlawing sexual practices which are far less injurious than the many legal sports and dangerous exhibitions which have no ceiling whatsoever, making it perfectly acceptable to kill yourself or another with impunity. Likewise, if there are to be limitations to fully consensual activities, not only should they be clearly stated, but, as Leigh argued, there would also have to be compelling reasons why the ceiling should not be universally applied in all lawful activities. Here was the law lords' chance to do just that; but they did not.

Rather than even attempt to lay down a definition of the rather nebulous concept of 'the public interest' established by the *Attorney-General's Reference*, Lord Jauncey assumed that it was self-evident, and, as a result, the more he referred to the previous precedents and then attempted to by-pass their embarrassing rationales, the more mess he made. Making complete sense of the previous precedents would have been a near-impossible task in the best of circumstances, given that 'the line' is drawn according to the alleged purpose of the activity, rather than the many different kinds of injuries that are possible, but Lord Jauncey appeared determined to add some new complications of his own.

Before considering three major precedents, Lord Jauncey thought it 'interesting' to consider the meaning and definitions of 'maim', 'assault', and 'battery'. Referring to Hawkins's *Pleas of the Crown*, which was published back in 1824, he defined 'maiming' as 'such a hurt of any part of a man's body whereby he is rendered less able in fighting, either to defend himself or annoy his adversary'; 'assault' as 'an attempt to offer, with force and violence, to do a corporal hurt to another'; and 'battery' as 'any injury whatsoever beit never so small, being actually done to the person of a man in *an angry, revengeful, rude, or insolent* manner'. He then emphasized that a lack of consent was not necessary to constitute an assault or a battery.

This introduction was somewhat pointless as everyone already knew that the definition of 'assault' was the only one that could really apply in this case, and that, while a lack of consent was not required for a prosecution, the existence of consent was all important. But what made the exercise ridiculous was that, as the case would effectively rest upon the concept of 'bodily harm', Lord Jauncey was ignoring the real issue.

When he finally got round to addressing the first precedent, despite noting in passing that the *Coney* judgment's rationale rested upon the fact that 'the appellants were spectators at an organised fight between two men at a public road', Lord Jauncey ignored this aspect completely and merely concentrated upon the issue of intent. Consequently, he ensured that every point of law he addressed thereafter was decontextualized and could be manipulated at will.

Lord Jauncey began by quoting the section in Justice Cave's *Coney* decision which determined when a consent defence could be used and when it could not. Justice Cave had declared that 'the consent of a person is immaterial' when a blow is 'struck in anger, or which is likely or is intended to do corporal hurt'. Such a blow constituted an assault because it was unlike a blow struck in sport which was 'not likely, nor intended to cause bodily harm'. As Lord Templeman had defined SM sex as 'violence', Lord Jauncey was obviously trying to imply that precedent demanded that SM sex was analogous to blows struck in anger or with the intent to do corporal hurt, and so was not entitled to the consent defence. Yet the *Coney* precedent could not really be used in that way.

Apart from the fact that SM sex 'blows' are neither struck in anger nor necessarily intended to do corporal hurt, it is highly debatable that Justice Cave's distinction is generally viable. A blow struck in a sport like soccer can be just as angry, likely, or intended to cause harm to an opponent as a blow struck in anger, as many players can testify. Yet, even if we ignore their lordships' subscription to this anachronistic fallacy, since Lord Jauncey, like Lord Templeman before him, quoted only a third of Justice Cave's rationale, he completely missed the specific reason why Justice Cave could make such a distinction in the Coney case. And the moment one recontextualizes Justice Cave's rationale, it becomes obvious why their lordships were being very selective.

As well as the blow having to be struck in anger, Justice Cave clearly stated that he believed that it also had to have the potential to cause a breach of the peace; and that is why Justice Stephen, who laid down the extremely high ceiling for lawful activities, deliberately reinforced that very point when ruling that

> consent of the person who sustains the injury is not a defence to the person who inflicts the injury, if the injury is of such a nature, or is inflicted under such circumstances that its infliction is *injurious to the public as well* as to the person injured.

In other words, far from disagreeing about the ceiling, Justices Cave and Stephen were in complete agreement that the consent defence could not be used when the act was injurious to the public interest; and that this yardstick should also be used to determine whether or not the act committed constituted an assault in the first place. Once this is understood, it is easy to see how Justice Stephen's high ceiling clearly complements Justice Cave's demarcation between lawful sports and lawful acts: as long as the act was lawful and did not involve anger or injurious intent, 'considerable force' could be used. Consequently, far from having anything to do with the kind of blow struck, which so preoccupied Lord Templeman, the two quoted *Coney* judgments tied lawfulness and intent to a 'public interest' rationale. Indeed, it would have been impossible to justify making violent sports legal without it; and, when it came to prize-fighting,

Justice Stephen had a particular reason for believing that it would be inevitably injurious to the public interest:

> the injuries given and received in prize-fights are injurious to the public, both because it is against the public interest that the lives and the health of the combatants should be endangered by blows, and because prize-fights are disorderly exhibitions, mischievous on many obvious grounds. Therefore the consent of the parties to the blows which they mutually receive does not prevent those blows from being assaults.

The reason Justice Cave did not mention the issue, and Justice Stephen did not spell out exactly what these mischievous facets were, was that a third judge, Justice Mathew, had already done it for them. Prize-fighting was subject to a charge of assault, but not to a defence of consent, because the combatants would, for the gratification of those present, have incentive to fight on and on until their lives were endangered.

To compare private SM acts like spanking to public prize-fighting, irrespective of a third party's presence, is absurd for three reasons. First, the blows in *Coney* were against the 'public interest' because there was a serious likelihood that the activity would lead to loss of life or limb, and because such spectacles involved disorderly and mischievous conduct by the public who attended. Second, prize-fighters slogged it out until one was completely incapacitated, whereas SM devotees, even when using one of the minority techniques, are enhancing pleasure. Third, as SM acts actually become more skilfully controlled when minority techniques are used, they can hardly be disorderly.

In short, there was a very specific reason for declaring prize-fighting unlawful; and, when that is taken into account, SM sex is clearly more analogous to lawful sporting exceptions. Consequently, neither Jauncey nor Templeman before him was using the *Coney* precedent at all. By ignoring the logic behind it, they were quoting Justice Cave's rationale completely out of context. There are, however, even more compelling reasons for not automatically comparing SM sex to an unlawful act.

In his short review of the *Coney* case during his judgment, Lord Jauncey completely glossed over the fact that the justices involved went to great lengths to lay down rationales for principles that should be used in similar cases; and it is these that constituted the real *Coney* precedent for Spanner-type cases, as opposed to clearly illegal acts like fist-fights.

Justice Stephen's rationales for denying consent defences for 'unlawful' acts like prize-fighting were bolstered by two principles which were deliberately designed to help judges distinguish the exceptions to assault charges. As we have seen, the first was that consent was a defence 'where life and limb are exposed to no serious danger *in the common course of things*'. The second was that in '*all cases* the question whether consent does or does not take from the application of force to another its illegal character, is *a question of degree depending upon circumstances*'. In other words, Justice Stephen was clearly saying that there was *no set list of acceptable and unacceptable activities*, and that where life and limb were not inevitably endangered by an activity, that activity would qualify for a defence of consent: the complete opposite of how the law lords were trying to use the *Coney* precedent.

In order to extricate himself from the compelling logic of this aspect of the *Coney* decision, Lord Jauncey made a feeble attempt to re-write Justice Stephen's principles, by asserting, with no supporting evidence, that what Justice Stephen really meant to say was that sporting activities were exceptions to prosecutions for assault, because the danger to life and limb was merely incidental to the main purpose of the activity. But Justice Stephen was not just referring to 'sporting' activities; and even if he had been, Lord Jauncey's re-write would not have made one iota of difference anyway, because Justice Stephen's ruling that 'in all cases' the decisions concerning consent were a 'question of degree depending upon circumstances' meant that he clearly also wanted to allow for the possibility of prosecuting a specific act in a generally excluded 'sport' if such a need arose.

Thankfully, you do not have to take my word against Lord Jauncey's, for, in order to justify his reading of Justice Stephen, Lord Jauncey referred to select passages from Justice Hawkins, another *Coney* judge who did allude to organized sports. The problem for Lord Jauncey is that the moment one goes back to *Coney* and considers Justice Hawkins's judgment, principles and rationales in full, not only do they fail to support a rewriting of Justice Stephen's, they completely, in every way, undermine the way in which *Coney* was raided by their lordships in Spanner.

Justice Hawkins was even more demonstrative than Justices Cave and Stephen about the role of the potential breach of the peace in determining whether or not a consent defence could be used. In order to explain why, Hawkins summarized the existing legal approach to assaults:

> As a general proposition it is undoubtedly true that there can be no assault unless the act charged as such be done without the consent of the person alleged to be assaulted, for want of consent is an essential element in *every* assault, and *that which is done by consent is no assault at all.*

Lord Jauncey tried to dismiss the obvious interpretation in the same way as he had Justice Stephen's; asserting that, in his opinion, as if a clearly worded judgment was open to an opinion, Justice Hawkins did not intend to lay down a general principle applicable to Sections 20 and 47 of the 1861 Act. But if Justice Hawkins was not laying down a general principle, why on earth would he use the word 'every', and call it a general proposition? The answer is simple, but highly embarrassing for the law lords. Given his belief in this contemporary legal principle, Justice Hawkins was going to be very explicit as to why he considered prize-fighting an assault rather than a sport: 'It is not in the power of any man to give an effectual consent to that which amounts to, or has a direct tendency to create, a *Breach of the Peace*; so as to bar a criminal prosecution.' For Justice Hawkins a breach of the peace was also the major means by which one could distinguish between a lawful activity and those which were not when they both involved physical blows and consent:

> The cases in which it has been held that persons may lawfully engage in friendly encounters not calculated to produce real injury to, or to rouse angry passions in either, do not in the least mitigate against the view I have expressed; *for such encounters are neither Breaches of the Peace nor are they calculated to be productive thereof.*

In other words, activities like wresting, single-stick, sparring with gloves and football were considered 'legal' exceptions not simply because they were 'friendly' and unlikely to cause 'real injury' or rouse 'angry passions', but because they were unlikely to cause a breach of the peace.

In order to justify denying the Spanner defendants a consent defence, their lordships would have to be satisfied that SM sex was likely to cause real injury in the common course of events, which it is not; or rouse angry passions, when it does the opposite; and Justice Hawkins's reasoning concerning the necessity of 'calculated' acts strongly suggests that Lord Templeman's reliance upon the assumption that SM *might* have led to serious injury is not good enough. While they no longer had to consider the issue of a breach of the peace since the *Attorney-General's Reference* ruled that judges could make up their own minds about what was in the public interest, it is still impossible to ignore the importance of the threat of a breach of the peace when weighing up the logic of the *Coney* judges' interpretation of what was against the public interest and constituted an assault.

To put the *Coney* rulings about illegal blows in their complete context, it should be understood that prize-fights were illegal and the two participants, Burke and Mitchell, had attempted to oppose a charge of common assault on the grounds that they had consented to the fight. Their argument was dismissed because they attracted a crowd of some one hundred people, and could have invoked a breach of the peace; this had little to do with Mr Coney. What made the case really interesting was that several other people were also charged with assault by virtue of their presence at the fight, but three of them, including Mr Coney, had argued that they were not aware, until they had become trapped in the crowd which gathered, that they would be witnessing an illegal prize-fight; and there was a compelling reason why the *Coney* judges made the detailed judgments they did, and why we should pay particular attention to them.

The legal predicament this group faced was remarkably similar to that of the Spanner defendants. Just as Judge Rant had denied the defendants a consent defence on the grounds that they were being charged with an assault, Mr Coney and his two friends found themselves convicted of an assault, by virtue of their presence at the fight, because the Chairman of the Quarter Sessions had directed the jury that as prize fights were *de facto* illegal, Mr Coney and friends had committed an offence whether they thought so or not. Consequently, the important point to realize about Justice Cave's distinction, between 'blows' which would constitute an assault and those in sport which would not, is that he made them precisely because prize-fighting was still considered a sport by many, and this problematic issue had to be dealt with once and for all. Far from establishing a simple distinction between sport and non-sport, Justice Cave and the others were trying to establish the existence of three categories of blow. First, blows struck in anger, such as when one person attacks another, which would constitute an assault because there would be no consent on the part of the victim. Second, blows intended to or likely to cause an injury which *even if consensual* were liable to prosecution, because the intent and consequences made them illegal. Third, blows which could have the same effect, but were not intended to do so, because of the consensual nature of the act such as a sporting contest, but which, depending upon degree and circumstance, could still be prosecuted. As everyone agreed that the first type of blow was illegal and constituted an assault, the major purpose behind the *Coney* judgments was to spell out clearly why, *despite clear consent*, the participants in a prize-fight could not use consent as a defence against the illegal aspects of the activity. It was ruled that its illegality followed from the intent of the participants; and it fell to Justice Mathew to spell out the difference between sporting and non-sporting intent. Prize fighters were to be denied a consent defence, because

> the chief incentive to the wretched combatants to fight on until [as happens too often] *dreadful injuries have been inflicted and life endangered or sacrificed*, is the presence of spectators watching with keen interest every incident of the fight. The jurors would also know that money is usually staked upon the result by the combatants and by the spectators.

In other words, the blows in prize-fighting were illegal and constituted an assault because the intent and actuality was inevitably maiming and grievous bodily harm, or death. That was why Justice Stephen reinforced the point by spelling out that the difference between a legal and illegal activity was that in the latter the combatants' lives and limbs were exposed to serious danger in 'the common course of things'. What is even more interesting to note, given Lord Jauncey's emphasis upon intent, is that it was Justice Hawkins in his general proposition, rather than Justices Cave and Stephen, who gave the most specific rationale.

Contrary to Lord Jauncey's assertion that he was not establishing a general principle, Justice Hawkins spelt out that he was making a general proposition, in order to clarify why, although consent might debar participants from civil liability, that same consent could not be used to negate any proceedings instituted by the Crown 'in the interests of the public for the maintenance of good order'. He then spelt out why prize-fighting was not in the interests of the public for the maintenance of good order; and it becomes instantly obvious why their lordships Jauncey and Templeman did not want to dwell on the issue.

> Nothing can be clearer to my mind than that every fight in which the object and intent of each of the cohabitants is to subdue the other by violent blows, is, or has a direct tendency to, a Breach of the Peace, and it matters not, in my opinion, whether such fight be a hostile fight begun and continued in anger, or a prize fight for money or other advantage. In each case the object is the same, and in each case some amount of personal injury to one or both of the combatants is a probable consequence, and, although a prize fight may not commence in anger, it is unquestionably calculated to rouse the angry feelings of both before its conclusion. I have no doubt then, that every such fight is illegal, and the parties to it may be prosecuted for assaults upon each other. Many authorities support this view.

Not content with that clarity of mind, which obviously belies any inference that he could have meant anything else, Justice Hawkins then expanded upon *lawful activities* which would not constitute an assault:

> The cases in which it has been held that persons may lawfully engage in friendly encounters not calculated to produce real injury to or to rouse angry passions in either, do not in the least mitigate in the last against the view I have expressed. For such encounters are neither Breaches of the Peace nor are they calculated to be productive thereof, but if under colour of a friendly encounter, the parties enter upon it with, or in the course of it form the intention to conquer each other by violence calculated to produce mischief, regardless whether hurt may be occasioned or not, as, for instance if two men pretending to engage in an amicable spar with gloves, really have for their object the intention to beat each other until one of them be exhausted and subdued by force, and so engage in a conflict likely to end in the Breach of the Peace each is liable to be prosecuted for an assault: *Reg.* v. *Orton.* Whether an encounter be of the character I have just referred to, or a mere friendly game, having no tendency, if fairly played, to produce any Breach of the Peace, is always a question for the Jury in case of an indictment, or the magistrates in the case of a Summary proceedings.

In short, the blows struck in the *Coney* case were illegal because the aim of the conflict was to conquer or subdue the other participant by violence through the blows calculated to produce serious bodily injury, regardless of their actual effect. Whatever the original intent, a prize-fight would inevitably become like a fight begun in anger. And that is why prize-fights would constitute a breach of the peace and were *de facto* illegal.

Consequently, if the *Coney* precedent's rationales, quoted by their lordships, were followed to the letter, let alone the spirit, of the law, SM sex would be perfectly entitled to use a consent defence; because it is a friendly, consensual 'encounter', calculated to avoid real injury or angry passions by arousing sexual passions through the use of role-play and careful techniques. There is no intention to force any party to do anything, let alone cause permanent injury or death, in the normal course of SM sex. Moreover, since Justice

Hawkins was quite adamant that the friendly or hostile nature of an indicted 'encounter' must be decided by a jury and not a judge, the *Coney* precedent clearly calls into question Judge Rant's original direction in the first Spanner trial; Justice Hawkins's ruling also stresses that the motivation of the participants and the extent of *intended* injury are all-important.

No wonder Jauncey side-stepped all these issues by asserting that the *Coney* decisions did not give him 'any great assistance . . . towards the immediate resolution of the questions raised [in Spanner] where the offences charged were statutory and where no question of the Breach of the Peace arose'. Of course they wouldn't; unless one had an open mind, and wished to use directly analogous precedents to guide a judgment. On the other hand, *if* one wanted to deny the Spanner appeal, one dare not follow *Coney*; the charges' statutory status made no difference at all. For *Coney* is quite clear, whichever judge you quote: consent is a defence not only 'when considerable force is used', it is a defence because 'want of consent is an essential element in every assault and that which is done by consent is no assault at all', unless it is against the public interest. The decision made in *Coney* rested upon the various reasons why the blows struck and the intent of the combatants would cause a breach of the peace. Although a breach of the peace need not be caused or be likely since the *Attorney-General's Reference*, according to *Coney* the decision concerning motive and intent was supposed to be up to the jury to decide.

In order to get Judge Rant off the hook, and justify upholding the appeal, Lord Jauncey was, therefore, forced to fall back on *Donovan* and the *Attorney-General's Reference*; but this led to even more problems with his justifications.

Bodily harm

Given the way *Coney* was clearly working against them, it was not surprising that Lord Jauncey grabbed at Justice Swift's judgment in the *Donovan* case; for, after a selective citing of Justice Cave, Justice Swift continued:

> If an act is unlawful in the sense of being in itself a
> criminal act, it is plain that it cannot be rendered lawful
> because the person to whose detriment it is done consents
> to it. No person can license another to commit a crime so
> far as the criminal law is concerned, therefore, where the
> act charged is in itself unlawful, it can never be necessary
> to prove absence of consent on the part of the person
> wronged in order to obtain the conviction of the
> wrongdoer.

The obvious problem with quoting from Justice Swift is that he had,
by accident or design, also ignored the contextual nature of the
decisions of Justices Cave, Stephen and Hawkins. Perhaps that is
why Lord Jauncey thought it important to bolster his own with this
one; but two illogical judgments do not make one logical one. But
the endearing feature of Justice Swift, however, is that he provides
numerous decontextualized rationales for turning a judgment your
way; and not without good reason. According to Justice Swift:

> There are . . . many acts in themselves harmless and lawful
> which become unlawful only if they are done without the
> consent of the person affected. What is, in one case, an
> innocent act of familiarity or affection, may, in another, be
> an assault, for no other reason than that, in one case there
> is consent and in the other consent is absent.

In other words, while no amount of consent could make an unlawful
act legal, consent was a core situational consideration in deciding
when an otherwise legal act was unlawful. But when it comes to an
act of forceful blows:

> As a general rule, although it is a rule to which there are
> well established exceptions, it is an unlawful act to beat
> another person with such a degree of violence that the
> infliction of bodily harm is a probable consequence and
> when such an act is proved consent is immaterial.

In short, Justice Swift had potentially reversed the *Coney* precedent
by making the effect of the blow more important than the issue of
consent, irrespective of the public interest. But just as a closer look at

the contextualized *Coney* judgments exposed the weaknesses of their lordships' use of that precedent, a review of what really happened in *Donovan* makes the Spanner judgment a travesty.

Justice Swift, like Justice Stephen before him, had considered the exceptions to the general rule; and claimed that there were well-established exceptions by quoting from the list of hypothetical examples contained in Sir Michael Foster's *Pleas to the Crown*, which had, as far as I know, not then been tested in law. Amongst those listed, which were obviously capable of causing bodily harm, Justice Swift referred to friendly bouts of wrestling, foils and the use of cudgels. Apart from 'reasonable chastisement' by a parent or a person *in loco parentis*, he also included 'rough and undisciplined sport or play where there was no anger and no intention to cause bodily harm'. This unidentified category, which owed its origin to Foster's paraphrase of Justice Hawkins, could, of course, easily be extended to include consensual SM sex, with or without Lord Templeman's asinine reference to referees; but there were two reasons why this privilege was not granted to Mr Donovan.

Justice Swift insisted that, because the blows struck by Donovan were *de facto* an unlawful act in which a defence of consent would not apply, and Donovan's defence counsel had not offered any facts which enabled the case to be considered an established exception, the blows struck constituted a 'bodily harm', which Justice Swift defined as 'any hurt or injury calculated to interfere with the health or *comfort* of the prosecutor'. In order to quantify the nature of 'hurt' and 'injury' Justice Swift then laid down his often-quoted determining definition: 'Such hurt or injury need not to be permanent, *but must, no doubt be more than merely transient or trifling.*' Yet none of this makes any sense outside the specific context of the case, in which the young woman involved was supposedly 'severely' thrashed by Mr Donovan and, consequently, by any legal definition had suffered actual bodily harm. As it was also widely believed that Mr Donovan's actions were *intended* to cause such an effect, it made sense to consider Mr Donovan's actions within the illegal category demarcated by the three major *Coney* justices.

On the other hand, this does not allow Lord Jauncey to assume automatically that Mr Donovan's intent was present in the Spanner defendants' minds, let alone in all other SM activities. On the contrary, that would only apply if we accepted Lord Templeman's erroneous assertions about SM sex, based solely upon his fanciful claims about 'sadists' and 'victims', rather than the reality of switchability and excitation transfer.

In terms of Lord Jauncey's justification, these references to Justice Swift were almost irrelevant anyway. By themselves they added nothing and took nothing away from his line of reasoning; their value existed in his extremely weak progression from *Coney*, through Justice Swift's reference to bodily harm, to the fist-fight which resulted in actual bodily harm referred to in the *Attorney-General's Reference*.

Lord Jauncey was clearly impressed by Lord Lane's assertion that 'the public interest' required that the consent defence should be denied when any 'assault' occasioned actual bodily harm, whatever the intent, be it in public or private, unless it was a recognized exception; for it enabled him to suggest that, even though Lord Lane's and Justice Swift's reasoning 'differs somewhat', he could draw a clear conclusion: that the inflicting of bodily harm '*without good reason* is unlawful and that the consent of the victim is irrelevant'.

This was more than judicial licence on Lord Jauncey's part. Apart from ignoring the contextual judgment in *Coney* and the extraordinary decision concerning motive in *Donovan*, which we will examine in a moment, Lord Lane was clearly referring to fist-fights in which people were trying to 'cause each other bodily harm *for no good reason*'. The fact that Lord Lane did not include SM sex in his list of exclusions in the *Attorney-General's Reference* does not, however, mean that SM sex could or should be automatically considered analogous to a bare-knuckle fight in a public street. But in order to suggest that it was, Lord Jauncey referred to two other cases.

The first was *R. v. Boyea*, 1992, in which Lord Justice Glidewell had referred to *Donovan* in dismissing the appeal by asserting that 'An assault intended or which is likely to cause bodily harm, accompanied by indecency is an offence irrespective of consent, provided the injury is not "transient or trifling".' This was a good try, but completely undermined any logic Lord Jauncey may have possessed for three reasons. First, the case concerned an indecent assault upon a woman whose consent was in doubt, and who had in any event clearly suffered from an unwelcome injury that was more than minor. The legal dispute concerned whether or not Boyea had intended or was likely to cause the woman an injury by twisting his fingers in her vagina; and (following the 1991 *Savage* case), given the fact that actual bodily harm could be proved, his intent was irrelevant. In short, no one was disputing that harm had been inflicted. Second, Glidewell's definition of 'transient and trifling' in this case was based upon the premise that the level of vigour in sexual acts was higher now than back in 1934 when the *Donovan* case was heard, which meant that the voluntarily accepted risk of incurring some injury in the normal course of events was higher too. Consequently, Lord Jauncey was quoting a decision that would require him to raise the ceiling of bodily harm in sex acts, making them immune from prosecutions for assault. Third, the actual judgment was regarded as 'very questionable' by the *Criminal Law Review*, and is subject to controversy in legal circles:

> assault and battery require proof of *mens rea*, namely intent or recklessness . . . generally a person who intends to make some impact on the body of another, believing that the other consents to him doing so, does not intend to commit, nor is he reckless whether he commits, a battery. He has no *mens rea*,
>
> If, however, he intends to cause some injury (for which there is no social justification) or he is aware that he is likely to cause such an injury, then he does have *mens rea*, notwithstanding that he knows the other consents. He now intends to commit, or is reckless whether he commits a battery.
>
> What, however, if, though the act was likely to cause injury, he does not realise this? He does not intend to commit a battery, nor is he reckless whether he does so, because he cannot see that a battery may result. He foresees only consent to non-injurous impact; and that is not battery.

This not only raises numerous questions which were never considered let alone resolved by their lordships concerning the interrelation between intent, knowledge, assault, battery and so on that should be resolved before deciding any judgment; it raises the more important question why, if one was going to refer to sexual offences precedents, SM sex was being dealt with by precedents covering fistfights rather than sexual acts, which are completely different.

Be that as it may, Lord Jauncey moved straight on to the question of 'hostility', which the Spanner defendants insisted was a major determinate of an assault. To by-pass this issue, he referred to the 1987 *Wilson* v. *Pringle* case which had decided that 'hostility' could not be equated with 'ill will' or 'malevolence', as a simple unlawful act could also be considered a 'hostile' one. This was convenient for their lordships, but hardly reasonable given that this definition followed from the actions of the woman police constable in *Collins* v. *Wilcox*, 1984, who, in attempting to restrain the other woman when she had no right to do so, was thereby acting unlawfully, and so, the judges decided, with hostility too. To cite such a definition served merely to reinforce the catch-22 of consent, whereby if the appellants' activity was *a priori* unlawful, they were *de facto* being hostile.

Having selected all the definitions and precedents he wanted, and noted that SM sex was not a recognized exception, Lord Jauncey finally moved on to the nature of the bodily harm allegedly caused in Spanner. He promptly dismissed the major defence – that assault occasioning actual bodily harm should be below 'the line' – by prioritizing his interpretation of Justice Cave's ruling over that of Justice Stephen, by inferring that Justice Cave had decided that the infliction of actual bodily harm was enough to constitute an assault and negate consent, irrespective of the specific context.

Trying to agree

The third judge, Lord Lowry, readily agreed with Lord Jauncey's 'reasoning' on both *Coney* and *Donovan*; indeed, as he concurred with everything Lords Templeman and Jauncey had to say, Lord Lowry concentrated on how high the ceiling for consent defences should be, oblivious as to how it would lead them all to the time-bomb waiting in the *Donovan* judgment.

Lowry argued that although the definitions in the 1861 Act were not precise, the Act contained 'fairly clear signs' that an assault occasioning actual bodily harm, and wounding which results in actual bodily harm, were not common assaults but above the ceiling, being akin to inflicting grievous bodily harm. To support his interpretation, he quoted Sections 18, 20 and 47 of the Act; and drew attention to the fact that whereas the offences in Section 18 were felonies (discharging any kind of loaded arms at any person to maim, disfigure or disable a person), Sections 20 and 47 were misdemeanours, and that, although this difference had long since been lost in English law, there was a link between them. Having then tinkered around with several word associations, he finally reached the key point: the potential similarity between Sections 20 and 47. The former reads:

> Whosoever shall unlawfully and maliciously wound or inflict any grievous bodily harm upon another person, with or without any weapon or instrument, shall be guilty of a misdemeanour, and being convicted thereof shall be liable, at the discretion of the Court, to be kept in penal servitude for the term of three years, or to be imprisoned for any term not exceeding two years, with or without hard labour.

Section 47, effectively a guide to sentencing, reads:

> Whosoever shall be convicted upon an indictment of any assault occasioning actual bodily harm shall be liable at the discretion of the Court to be kept in penal servitude for the term of three years or to be imprisoned for any term not exceeding two years with or without hard labour; and whosoever shall be convicted on an indictment for common assault shall be liable, at the discretion of the Court to be imprisoned for any term not exceeding one year, with or without hard labour.

What impressed Lowry was that although Section 47 appeared to describe less serious offences than Section 20, the maximum penalty had been the same, and that this equality had been maintained with the maximum of five years' imprisonment when the distinction between felonies and misdemeanours was abolished.

He then argued that as the 'wounding' referred to in Sections 18 and 20 was regarded as grievous bodily harm it was therefore a serious offence, even though it might involve anything from a minor breaking or puncture of the skin to a near-fatal injury; and this meant that a 'wounding' could also occasion actual bodily harm as well as inflicting grievous bodily harm.

Consequently, the issue, as Lowry saw it, was that, to accept a consent defence of occasioning actual bodily harm, 'the line' would have to be drawn down the middle of Section 20; and he did not like that solution. Nor did he approve of the defence's submission that a consent defence should apply to a charge of wounding. Lord Lowry was concerned that this would mean juries having to consider whether anything more than actual bodily harm was occasioned, and he did not believe this was contemplated by Section 20; not that it prevents such a possibility. Given that the distinction between common assault and other attacks was that common assault did not necessarily involve *any* significant bodily injury, Lord Lowry thought it much easier to 'draw a line' between *no* significant injury and *some* injury, rather than trying to differentiate between degrees of injury. For Lord Lowry, this was more logical too, because to inflict an injury on another without 'good reason' would be an evil in itself.

In other words, having ignored the far easier, more logical and obvious solution of simply defining and raising the ceiling to a 'significant' injury, enabling a differentiation between degrees of injuries to be made, Lord Lowry left the ceiling and 'line' for consent defences where it was, with common assault, and at the complete discretion of the judges. This was then justified by arguing that Justice Stephen, alone amongst the 'inconclusive and sometimes conflicting statements' in *Coney*, supported the appellants' view, and that he had now been surpassed by *Donovan*.

This did not make any sense at all. Even if the *Coney* judgments were not complementary, which they were, *Donovan* could hardly have replaced *Coney*, when every decision after

Donovan, including the *Attorney-General's Reference*, looked to *Coney* rather than *Donovan* for guidance. The law was continually forced to do so for two reasons. The first real problem was the word 'assault'. Rather than define an assault by intent or recklessness, as opposed to the purpose of the activity, the law had messed around for two hundred years trying to make sense of a nonsense; and as *Coney* was the only case that had, for various reasons, covered, if not conclusively dealt with, all the issues involved, the law had no option but to go back to *Coney*. Unfortunately, the law, rather than apply the *Coney* judgments and definitions as they had been intended to be used, had tinkered around with them to suit itself, especially when following precedent was not convenient. The only difference with the *Attorney-General's Reference* was that, rather than tinker around with the definitions, Lord Lane had simply changed one. However undesirable it may be for two men to settle their differences in a deserted street in the early hours of the morning, as the law in all its statutes and precedents then stood they had not committed a crime, as a breach of the peace was impossible. But rather than accept that a very clever lawyer had found an obvious loophole, the law tried to cover its embarrassment by giving judges even more discretionary powers, ignoring the high ceiling set by Justice Stephen for lawful 'assaults', by denying their existence outside violent sports and dangerous exhibitions. The second reason was that the *Donovan* decision had not really superseded anything in *Coney* at all.

In *Donovan*, there was no disagreement about whether or not an indecent assault and a common assault had taken place. The issue in court had been whether or not the woman had consented. Mr Donovan said she did; she claimed she had not. The judge had told the jury that their decision should be based upon whom they had believed, and the jury ignored the evidence in Mr Donovan's favour and found him guilty. Mr Donovan's lawyers then appealed, pulling a fast one, arguing that the case should be dismissed because the judge had effectively misdirected the jury by telling them that the burden of proof relied upon consent. In the Court of Appeal Lord Hewitt, despite finding the case a 'revolting matter', and being extremely reluctant because of this, quashed the conviction. It fell to

Justice Swift, however, to provide the reason. The problem he really faced was that counsel for the Crown, both in the original case and at the appeal, insisted that it was unnecessary for the Crown to prove absence of consent, the same situation as the Spanner case. And this is where the fun began.

In the first trial, a doctor had given evidence for the Crown and had argued that the marks on the girl's buttocks, which he had seen two days after the event, indicated that she had suffered a 'fairly severe beating'. So that while 'actual bodily harm' had been caused, the injuries sustained were deemed to be more than actual bodily harm. Consequently, Justice Swift drew upon Justice Cave's reference to 'blows' struck in 'anger', to reason that

> So far as the Criminal law is concerned . . . where *the act charged* is in itself unlawful it can never be necessary to prove absence of consent on the part of the person wronged in order to obtain the conviction of the wrongdoer.

Justice Swift had then, however, continued, that:

> As a general rule, although it is a rule to which there are well established exceptions, it is an unlawful act to beat another person with such a degree of violence that the infliction of bodily harm is a probable consequence, *and when such an act is proved*, consent is immaterial.

The reason for saying this was that Justice Swift wished to make it very clear that he thought that Justice Stephen's belief that 'everyone has the right to consent to the infliction upon himself of bodily harm not amounting to maim', which reflected the law's leniency towards crimes of personal violence in the past, now had to be considerably qualified; but this had very little to do with Justice Swift's decision about the consent defence in the *Donovan* case.

The very specific circumstances in the *Donovan* case not only failed to alter *Coney*; they potentially opened the door of immunity from conviction for consenting SM sex, for if the *Donovan* precedent was followed to the letter, their lordships had no other option than to grant the Spanner defendants' appeal.

Donovan

If their lordships' use of *Coney* was dubious, their manipulation of the *Donovan* precedent has to be one of the biggest judicial sleights of hand this century; for the context and implications of Justice Swift's decision were totally ignored.

Mr Donovan liked the idea of caning women. This desire led him to have several telephone conversations with a Nora Eileen Harrison during February 1934, which led to both parties attending the pictures at Marble Arch on 8 March, before returning to Mr Donovan's Morden garage together; where, according to the record, he caned the seventeen-year-old's buttocks 'in circumstances of indecency'. Five days later, Mr Donovan received a visit from a detective inspector, who, when going through Mr Donovan's possessions, found 'a sealed envelope, the terms of which left no doubt as to the nature of the practices to which he was *addicted*'.

Mr Donovan was then charged with assault and indecent assault. Fortunately for him, one of Nora's friends, who had been present during the phone calls, placed the truth before her friendship, and testified that not only had Mr Donovan made no secret of his intention to cane Nora, but that Nora had 'expressed her willingness to submit herself to the kind of conduct to which he was *addicted*'. Indeed, Nora did not deny this until after the events of 8 March. Whether Miss Harrison had been misled by Mr Donovan as to the extent of the corporal punishment, or there was another reason for her complaint, the record does not say; but she now claimed that she had never consented to the act. Mr Donovan continued to insist that she had full knowledge of his intentions and consented, even during the act. Just before the summing-up, in the absence of a jury, the prosecution tried to convince the justices that it was unnecessary for them to prove absence of consent; which strongly implies that they feared the evidence against Miss Harrison was damning. The justices, however, turned down this submission, and when the jury returned informed them that they should carefully consider the issue of consent as it was the major factor in a case like this. The jury, having sought guidance as to whether or not a belief that consent had been given constituted consent and been told by the chairman, 'Definitely no', returned a verdict of guilty. We will never know whether this verdict meant that the jury believed Miss Harrison, against the evidence offered, or whether they decided that Mr Donovan should be punished for his sexual proclivities, irrespective of consent; but, whatever the reason for the verdict in court, Justice Swift held that two mistakes had been committed.

According to Justice Swift, the chairman should have gone further than leave no doubt in the jurors' minds that the onus of proving lack of consent lay with the prosecution; he should also have spelt out the steps by which the jury should reach their decision. By failing to spell out the legal Catch-22 in consent defence cases, the chairman had effectively ensured that

> in the absence of a finding by the Jury that the beating was likely or intended to do bodily harm the verdict could not stand.
>
> The Chairman ought first to have put to the Jury the question as to whether the beating was likely or intended to do bodily harm, and if the question had been answered in the negative, the issue of consent then becoming relevant, [the Chairman] ought to have directed the Jury that the burden of proof was on the prosecution to show absence of consent.

It was in reaching this decision that Justice Swift made his pertinent remarks. The first referred to a principle in *R. v. May* that if the facts are such that consent is a possibility, the jury ought to be directed by the judge on that question; and that the issue of consent can be proved or negatived 'only after a full and careful review of the behaviour of the person who is alleged to have consented'. If the jury is not convinced beyond reasonable doubt that the person did not consent, the person charged is entitled to be acquitted. In other words, if one was to follow Swift, as Lowry insisted we should, Judge Rant's court should have heard arguments concerning the nature and intent of the actions before considering the question of consent. If Justice Swift had heard the appeal against Judge Rant's direction that the issue of consent could not be heard at all, he would if he was consistent, have allowed the appeal.

It was only after making it very clear that the proper procedure had to be followed, and that as it had not been in the

Donovan case the appeal would be upheld, that Swift then moved on to *Coney*, and Cave's comments about blows in anger or sport.

The only reason he did so, however, was that the Crown were still claiming, as they had at the original trial, that they did not have to prove absence of a consent, and because both sets of barristers were citing Justice Cave while quibbling over the issue. Having reviewed the authorities upon which Justice Cave's decision was based, Justice Swift insisted that if an act was unlawful 'in the sense of being in itself a criminal act', it could not be rendered lawful by consent, especially when it concerned the beating of another person 'with such a degree of violence that the infliction of bodily harm is a probable consequence'. But Justice Swift also prefaced his decision by stating 'our opinion as to the law applicable in this case'. In short, Justice Swift's comments were highly contextual.

Justice Swift's aim was to strengthen Justice Cave's rationale regarding the distinction between illegal intentional blows struck in anger an unintentional sporting bodily harms, compared to Justice Stephen's high ceiling for non-sporting activities, which allowed consent as a defence all the way up to maiming. Justice Swift thought that the law should now have a right to intervene in non-sporting activities before that ceiling was reached. Ironically, in order to do so, he picked an even earlier authority, Sir Michael Foster, to emphasize that, if an act is *malum in se* (i.e. if itself it is unlawful), consent could not convert it into an innocent act. In saying this he laid a time-bomb for the Spanner judges.

Foster's distinction between lawful exceptions to a charge of assault and unlawful acts with no defence of consent, while resting upon a logical basis at the time, has now become a bizarre anachronism. Foster believed that persons who, in perfect friend-ship, engaged by mutual consent in contests including cudgels, foils and wrestling which were capable of causing bodily harm were lawful for two reasons. First, bodily harm was not the motive on either side. Second, the acts were '*manly* diversions, they intend to give strength, skill and activity, and may fit people for defence, public as well as personal, in time of need'. In other words, the justification for, if not necessarily the origin of, 'lawful' violent but friendly contests, which enjoy a defence of consent, was their usefulness for the defence of the realm. While I've no doubt there are other authorities I have yet to come across, one can easily see a purpose behind making some violent sports exceptions to a charge of assault and the reasons for allowing a defence of consent. What is mystifying, however, is why this rationale failed to feature in the *Coney* case. Its failure to do so strongly suggests that the rationale for the exceptions has changed over time, and that the law is nowhere near as consistent as it likes to pretend it is; and the implication of that for the *Attorney-General's Reference* is obvious: while there may be 'recognized' exceptions to assault charges, there is *no* rational reason for them, and to now make an undefined 'public interest' the test merely perpetuates a confidence trick. At the very least, if one is to bring the law up to date, one could hardly justify any exceptions by utilizing the ancient and anachronistic justification of the defence of the realm; so while this reason may have been good enough for Justice Swift, it is not now. What was even more enlightening, however, was Justice Swift's use of Foster to justify why he thought Mr Donovan guilty of committing an unlawful act.

Having briefly discussed the other exceptions to the rule, including 'rough and undisciplined sport or play where there is no anger and no intention to cause bodily harm', whereby such acts become unlawful 'only if the person affected by it is not a consenting party' (which completely negates Templeman's twaddle about SM sex's lack of a referee), Justice Swift returned to Mr Donovan's particular act. Carefully, and with great deliberation, he offered three very specific reasons why caning Miss Harrison constituted an assault, and *could not* be regarded as an exception, as opposed to *was not* an existing exception.

The first reason concerned Mr Donovan's motive, or intent:

> In the present case it was not in dispute that the motive of the appellant was to gratify *his own perverted desires*. If, in the course of doing so, he acted so as to cause bodily harm, he cannot plead his corrupt motive as an excuse, and it may truly be said of him in Sir Michael Foster's words that 'he certainly beat with an intention of doing some bodily harm, he had no other intent,' and that what he did was *malum in se*.

In other words, Mr Donovan, the caning 'addict', was guilty of an assault because he was solely motivated by the wish to gratify his own desires as opposed to those of Miss Harrison. Consequently, he could have no other intent than to cause her bodily harm, and that intent made his actions *malum in se*.

Second, Justice Swift explained why Mr Donovan's self-gratification could not be comparable to the exceptions accepted in law:

> Nothing could be more absurd or more repellent to the ordinary intelligence than to regard his conduct as comparable with that of a participant in one of those 'manly diversions' of which Sir Michael Foster wrote. Nor is his act to be compared with the rough but innocent horse-play in R. v. *Bruce*.

Justice Swift had obviously found the idea of a 'pervert' caning a seventeen-year-old for his own sexual enjoyment so distasteful that there was no way he was going to compare it to a 'manly sport', irrespective of the violence such sports might entail.

On the other hand, Justice Swift was not going to let his prejudice completely rule his sense of judgment, and so made it quite clear, thirdly, that despite this glaring contrast, the ruling that Donovan's caning was unlawful was also dependent upon both a presupposition and a caveat:

> *Always supposing*, therefore, that the blows which he struck were likely or intended to do bodily harm, we are of the opinion that he was doing an unlawful act, no evidence having been given of facts which would bring the case within any exceptions to the general rule. In our view, *on the evidence given at the trial*, the jury should have been directed that, if they were satisfied that the blows struck by the prisoner were likely or intended to do bodily *harm* to the prosecutrix, they ought to convict him, and that it was only if they were not so satisfied, that it became necessary to consider the further question whether the prosecution had negatived consent.

In other words, if there had been some evidence which could have led the jury to believe that blows like caning committed by people like Mr Donovan were *not* likely or intended to do bodily harm, and/or evidence had been offered that could have brought such acts into the category of an exception, then Justice Swift supposed, the jury could, *and by implication should*, have come to a different conclusion and then made acts like SM sex immune from prosecution.

Consequently, Justice Swift's three-stage judgment lays down clear guidelines for the Spanner judges. While there was a dispute about consent in *Donovan*, there was no dispute about consent in Spanner, and the jury rather than Judge Rant were supposed to make the decision about the assault charges. If Judge Rant had followed Justice Swift's directions on procedure in such cases, the defence were entitled to call any qualified person to explain to the jury that whoever was administering the cane or any other instrument was effecting excitation transfer primarily for the benefit of gratification of those on the receiving end. If such evidence had been heard, and the jury been directed along Justice Swift's guidelines, it is more than likely, given the changes in sexual attitudes, that the Spanner jury would have acquitted the defendants.

If their lordships had actually read Justice Swift's precedent guidelines, rather than simply pull out of the judgment what they found convenient for their own argument, they would have found the procedure almost identical to the one recommended in *Coney*, and should have been forced to think twice at appeal; especially when, even after all those carefully contextualized statements, Justice Swift was not yet finished. He first covered the standard by which one should make a decision concerning bodily harm, and then limited the powers of judges as opposed to juries:

> For this purpose we think that 'bodily harm' has its
> ordinary meaning and includes any hurt or injury
> calculated to interfere with the health or comfort of the
> prosecutor. Such an injury need not be permanent, but
> must, no doubt, be more than merely transient and trifling
> . . . There are many gradations between a slight tap and a
> severe blow, and the question whether particular blows
> were likely or intended to cause bodily harm is one
> eminently fitted for the decision of a jury upon evidence
> which they have heard. We may have little doubt what that

decision would have been [in the Donovan case], but we cannot, consistently with the practice of this court, substitute ourselves for the jury and decide a question of fact which was never left to them. *It is, therefore, impossible to say that facts have been proved which show the appellant's act to have been unlawful in itself. Without proof of such facts he could be convicted only if the prosecution negatived consent* . . .

This was a major embarrassment for their lordships; and Lord Lowry dismissed its relevance by implying it would make life too difficult for juries, and saying that he found 'this part of the judgment hard to follow'. On the contrary, it is very easy to follow. Justice Swift is saying that juries not judges should decide where the line is drawn in such cases, whether judges like it or not; and the implication is equally obvious.

Given that every single one of their lordships admitted that the Spanner 'masochists' were obtaining pleasure from the activities, it becomes difficult to see how any 'blows' struck by the 'sadists' were intended to cause hurt or injury interfering with the health or comfort of the 'masochists'. As Justice Swift's rationale for denying a consent defence was premised upon the fact that Mr Donovan's 'perverted desires' were not shared by his 'partner', who received no gratification from the act, it would logically follow that as the Spanner 'victims' were having their 'perverted desires' gratified by those carrying out the forceful acts, the circumstances in the Spanner case are the complete opposite of the *Donovan* case. As the blows made by Mr Donovan were defined as injurious *because* of his intent to pleasure himself, the 'blows' in the Spanner case were not; if the *Donovan* case is any kind of precedent, the Spanner ruling should have gone the other way.

Furthermore, whereas no psychologist would have appeared at Mr Donovan's trial to justify his actions, there are dozens of 'experts' who could have provided the 'other evidence' that Justice Swift would have been prepared to hear in order to change his mind: as most SM devotees, like the Spanner defendants, are not solely gratifying themselves, their actions cannot automatically be considered as intending or likely to cause bodily harm. On the contrary, in Spanner all parties agreed to, and welcomed, everything that took place, because the aim of all activities was to promote sexual pleasure.

Even without adding the rationales in the *Boyea* judgment about higher ceilings in sexual acts, it was impossible in strict legal terms for the Spanner defendants to be causing bodily harm; with one exception. The only act in Spanner that could in any way have constituted bodily harm was the single incident of branding. But, as Justice Swift made very clear, that was for the jury not for judges to decide.

Having carefully followed the *Coney* and *Donovan* precedents, in which the justices were adamant that the issue of intent and consent were interlinked, one is tempted to believe that the refusal of the modern judges to follow the procedure to determine such cases was a deliberate act. Although the *Coney* and *Donovan* judges clearly disliked the activities they were considering, and found reasons for excluding them from the list of 'recognized' exceptions, unlike the modern judges, Justices Cave, Stephen, Hawkins and Swift seriously considered whether or not the issues before them could constitute exceptions. Fortunately, their lordships could use the *Attorney-General's Reference* not to do so.

The Attorney-General's Reference

Having re-written the meaning of Swift, in an attempt to justify why *Donovan* over-ruled *Coney*, Lowry now had to explain why the *Attorney-General's Reference* did not over-rule *Donovan*.

This was tricky, for, whatever else he did, Lord Lane had clearly argued that an essential element of any assault was that it had to be done contrary to the will, and without the consent, of the alleged victim. Realizing, however, that people can consent to things which may not be in the public interest, Lord Lane had suggested that the essential question was: at what point do the courts draw the line? This implied that the issue of consent was alive and well, except when there was a particular reason making it detrimental to the public interest; and there were no obvious ways out of this fix. Legal authorities, like Professor Glanville Williams, author of the *Text-book of Criminal Law*, had already noted that recent rulings were effectively extending the law against assault, and leading to judicial paternalism; and Lord Lowry did not want to be seen doing this.

Lord Lowry perfected an escape by reviewing Lord Lane's suggestion that the law should adopt a 'partly new approach' to the question of consent, considering the viability of the new test of 'the public interest', to avoid the problems that *Coney* and *Donovan* presented to paternalistic judges.

Having noted Lord Lane's belief that the law should consider that it was not in the public interest for people to try to cause each other actual bodily harm for 'no good reason', irrespective of whether the act occurred in private or public, so that 'it is an assault if actual bodily "harm" is intended and/or caused', Lord Lowry made two simple deductions. First, as Lord Lane was not intending 'to cast doubt on the accepted legality of properly conducted games and sports, lawful chastisement, surgical interference, or dangerous exhibitions', it followed that Lord Lane's comments concerning fighting were not confined to fighting. Second, as Lord Lane had not specifically referred to SM sex in the list of exceptions, this meant that SM sex was comparable to fighting.

On the contrary, SM sex could easily be placed in either category. But, while it would just be possible to make SM sex comparable with fighting because some of the occasional actions involve 'blows' like spanking and strapping and more rarely piercing, the nearest analogies would be lawful chastisement and inserting ear-rings. To then declare that 'there was no good reason' for people to indulge in SM sex would require the law to declare that the enhancement of sexual arousal is not a 'good reason', and insist that sex should be reserved for procreation and excitement restricted to 'manly sports'. Lord Lowry did not dare to be so blatant, so he merely agreed with Lord Lane that

> What may be 'a good reason' it is not necessary for us to decide. It is sufficient to say, so far as the instant case is concerned, that we agree with the trial judge that the satisfying of the sado-masochistic libido does not come within the category of 'good reason' . . .

In other words: we don't have to justify why our personal dislike of SM devotees amounts to a lack of 'good reason'! This is a scandal. Judges have now given themselves the right to lock anyone up without saying why. Unfortunately, for them, by having a lot to say about homosexuality, their lordships gave the game away.

Gays, satanism and sex rings

Contrary to their assertions regarding the irrelevance of homosexuality, their lordships all felt compelled to comment upon this aspect of the Spanner case. Lord Templeman began with the observation that, while the attitude of the public to homosexual practices had changed, the Wolfenden Report, upon which the 1967 Sexual Offences Act was based, had declared that the function of criminal law in relation to homosexuality was

> To preserve public order and decency, to protect the citizen from what is offensive or injurious, and to provide sufficient safeguards against exploitation and corruption of others, particularly those who are especially vulnerable because they are young, weak in body or mind, inexperienced, or in a state of special physical, official or economic dependence.

On the face of it, throwing in this observation in the middle of a judgment about SM sex makes no sense. Wolfenden, of course, had had to couch the recommendation to decriminalize homosexuality in such offensive insinuations about gay lifestyles because that was the only way the reform movement could undermine the objections of rabid homophobes in Parliament and the legal profession at the time. Yet here was a contemporary law lord implying that being gay is somehow still the personification of indecency, and that gay people are a threat to public order, presumably because they go around exploiting people. By then drawing attention to Sections 1, 2, 6 and 7 of the 1967 Act (restricting the age of consent for gays to twenty-one; defining a gay sex act as public if more than two are present; and defining homosexual acts), Lord Templeman, however, revealed his purpose. He wished to undermine the Spanner defendants' third argument, that the law should not punish consensual achievement of sexual satisfaction, by playing off the fact that, as one Spanner participant had not attained the age of homosexual consent at twenty-one years, he, the youth K, had been 'corrupted' by the defendants by being encouraged in 'bondage affairs'. In other words, the youth could not really, legally, have given his consent. To emphasize the point, Lord Templeman repeated Lord Lane's comment about taking 'some comfort' to learn that K had now 'settled into a normal heterosexual relationship'.

Such comments clearly indicate some aversion to homosexuality *per se*, and indicate the use and excuse of homosexuality to override a viable legal submission which by implication might have been allowed otherwise. In this case, we are being asked to consider the involvement of K as proof that there was something unacceptable about the other defendants' SM sex scenes simply because one of the defendants introduced K to a bit of bondage.

Lord Lane had gone even further by mentioning K's physically harmless experience together with the fact that the defendant had also known other teenage boys, in order to suggest that: 'One cannot overlook the danger that the gravity of the assaults and injuries in this type of case may escalate to even more unacceptable heights'. Given that there was a viable dispute about whether or not any 'assault' took place, let alone injuries, as the public would understand these phrases, it is difficult to see what Lane was getting at. He did not spell out what he meant.

Was Lord Lane implying that the presence of a youth would encourage SM devotees to engage in the rarer acts more often, when the particular defendant's association with other teenagers had nothing to do with any of the SM acts he performed? Or was Lord Lane giving credence to the ridiculous police allegations suggesting that the defendant might have, at some later stage, introduced his teenage friends to the other participants who would then have taken the youths into the desert, shot some kiddy porn to sell, then made the odd snuff movie for rent, before chopping them up and feeding the flesh to the local child day-care centre to eat in the name of Satan? Since when have the perverted fantasies of fundamentalist Christians, or Vice Squad urban legends, been a suitable yardstick to deny a point of law on the vague possibility that other people, as yet unconnected with the defendants, might then have become involved? To deny SM sex the immunity against charges of assault currently enjoyed by far more dangerous activities, by using a vile stereotype to imply that SM sex is not really consensual, is scraping the barrel.

If the issue of homosexuality had nothing to do with the judgments, as is claimed, why did Lord Jauncey, having picked and mixed from half a dozen dodgy precedents, inform us that:

> I have not found it necessary to rely on the fact that the activities of the appellants were in any way unlawful in so much as they amounted to acts of gross indecency which, not having been committed in private, did not fall within Section 1(1) of the Sexual Offences Act 1967.

If he had not considered the question, why bother to mention it? Is Lord Jauncey implying that if he had not extracted a suitable sound-bite from a precedent he would have taken the groups' technically illegal gatherings for sex into account? What has a ridiculous legal restriction on three gay men meeting together for sex got to do with determining the legal status of SM? Quite a lot, according to the law lords.

Having asserted, against all the evidence available, that sadomasochism constituted 'the deliberate and painful infliction of physical injury', and having denounced the pleasure-enhancing acts of SM devotees as 'a perverted and depraved sexual desire', Lord Jauncey justified not granting SM sex immunity on the following grounds:

> Sado-masochistic homosexual activity cannot be regarded as conductive to the enhancement or enjoyment of family life or conducive to the welfare of society. A relaxation of the prohibitions in Sections 20 and 47 can only encourage the practice of homosexual sado-masochism and the physical cruelty that it must involve (which can scarcely be regarded as a 'manly diversion') by withdrawing the legal penalty and giving the activity an imprimatur.

So now we know. SM sex was not going to be granted immunity because three ignorant or prejudicial judges claimed that it promotes cruelty; that, like homosexuality, it is not 'conducive to the enjoyment of family life'; and because it is not comparable to 'manly sports' which can be called upon when the realm is endangered. The reason why all SM sex was to be outlawed was even worse. When considering the proposition that any exemption should be tested by considering the likely general effect of the activity, Lord Lowry's justification amounted to scaremongering. He was guided by the

> probability that some sado-masochistic activity under the powerful influence of the sexual instinct will get out of hand and will result in serious physical damage to the participants . . .

Not that Lord Lowry, any more than the others, could provide one example of where a consensual SM sex activity had got 'out of hand'. I know of a couple of cases where a faulty piece of equipment has caused a serious accident, but they had nothing to do with either party getting 'carried away'; but Lord Lowry did not need one example anyway. Who does, when you can wed a 1960s phobia with a 1990s panic to imply that SM sex causes death?

> some [SM sex] activity will involve a danger of infection such as these particular exponents do not contemplate themselves. When considering the danger of infection, with its *inevitable* threat of AIDS, I am not impressed by the argument that this threat can be discontented on the grounds that, as long ago as 1967, Parliament, subject to conditions, legalised buggery, now a well-known vehicle for the transmission of AIDS.

That snide disapproval of the decriminalization of homosexuality explains everything; and trying to justify outlawing all SM sex on the grounds that AIDS is not in the public interest shows that their lordships had no justification for doing so. As this judge clearly does not even know the difference between the HIV virus and AIDS, he is hardly in a position to assess the risk of HIV transmission in SM sex, let alone use it as *the* example of how SM sex constitutes bodily harm. Using AIDS as an excuse does not make legal sense anyway. If the transmission of HIV constitutes bodily harm, their lordships would have to explain why since 1888 giving someone else a sexually transmitted disease, of whatever kind – and back in those days syphilis was a deadly disease – has not been regarded as an assault. Indeed, such claims are expressly denied in British law precisely because the act involves sexual relationships and, in the words of the precedent *R. v. Clarence*, the 'circumstances [are] so completely removed from those which are usually understood when an assault is spoken of'. As AIDS and a single incident of branding were the only bodily harms referred to by their lordships that were clearly more than transient or trifling, it is not surprising that Lord Lowry fudged his concluding statement that:

> *If* as appears to be the fact, sado-masochistic acts inevitably involve the occasioning of at least actual bodily harm there cannot be a right under our law to indulge in them.

Given their feeble attempt to fix the legal precedents, and their inability to quote one authority who could demonstrate that SM sex inevitably occasioned actual bodily harm, this pathetic excuse about AIDS suggests that the law lords must have been desperate to make illegal hundreds of thousands of people's sexual proclivities and 'slap and tickle' games. But why?

A possible clue for this blatant attempt to police the nation's sexual habits with a political decision to outlaw SM sex can be found in Lord Templeman's endorsement of Lord Lane's comments about the escalation of SM sex to 'even more unacceptable heights'; for by redefining acts of sexual arousal enhancement as 'cruel tortures', the law lords were effectively endorsing the police's view that they had found something akin to a snuff movie.

When the police got their hands on the Spanner tape they were having serious problems solving the riddle of the Cooke–Bailey gang responsible for the murder of several children and a couple of teenagers. During the course of that investigation, codenamed Operation Orchid, several police officers, according to the press, believed that the gang responsible had filmed the murders and that the videos were now being sold at £500 a time to paedophiles from a distribution centre in the Netherlands.

Contemporaneously, Britain was in the grips of what Jeffrey Victor has called the satanic panic, whereby major 'children's' charities were promoting a series of bizarre allegations that a satanic cult with numerous branches was systematically murdering children and financing its activities by selling the snuff movies. Originally conceived by a group of money-grubbing 'therapists' who purloined the scenario from fundamentalist Christians who were convinced that the world was about to end, this sick fantasy led to hundreds of social workers and police officers wasting millions of pounds of tax-payers' money by raiding innocent people's homes and kidnapping their children, claiming that they were in imminent danger of being sacrificed.

Although the four main members of the Cooke gang were already behind bars on other charges while the nationwide search for them was on, it appears to have crossed the police's mind that the Spanner video's participants were part of this international satanic conspiracy. Given the fact that people like the Quaker family in Orkney were also being fingered at the time, perhaps we should excuse the police their foolishness when faced with an unusual home-made SM video. What is inexcusable, however, is that they continued with the case when it must have become blindingly obvious that there was no connection between the Spanner fifteen and the mythical satanists.

If this seems too far-fetched to be true, one has only to look at the way their lordships completely misrepresented what the Spanner fifteen were doing. The judgments are full of references to blood-letting, blood lust, buggery, cruelty, excrement, the fear of 'victims' who dared not go to the police, and 'a cult of violence'. Lord Jauncey was constantly inferring that something else was happening than a few friends getting together for sex; and then circumvented the consent defence by stressing that the failure of 'receivers' of this 'cruelty' to complain to the police was an integral feature of 'sex rings'. Unable to pass condemnation upon the home-made videos because they had never been intended for sale, Lord Jauncey then used that fact against the defendants by implying that such secrecy amongst the 'ring members' must have had a sinister motive. Likewise, having denied that the use of SM stop-words proved that those using them were consenting parties, he converted them into 'code-words' demonstrating the 'care and attention' the 'ring' took in order to carry out their secret activities in a 'highly controlled manner'. In this way, the well-ordered and private activities of the non-proselytizing Spanner defendants was turned into a sinister conspiracy. Apart from sacrificing and eating babies, the defendants were alleged to have done everything the mythical satanic cult was supposed to do; and that may explain why so much unnecessary emphasis was placed upon the youth called K, for he was proof the cult were after new recruits.

It was all very vague and all very convenient; at the very least, public fears, fuelled by the satanic panic, were being used to justify judicial sexual correctness. To use the case of a youth who had already expressed an interest in homosexual acts and then took up a suggestion that he might want to try something different as proof that the Spanner defendants were proselytizing and corrupting wider society is more than a means to imply that the activities were public as opposed to private; it shifts a lot of the prejudice once exhibited against gay people on to SM devotees; and that was handy given what came next.

Having used every single feature of the fifteen fall-guys' sexual habits they could find, no matter how rare or unusual, to present all SM sex in the worst possible light, the law lords then concluded that other SM sex devotees were even more dangerous. SM sex could not possibly be in the 'public interest' because as there was

> no suggestion that they and their associates are the only practitioners of homosexual sadomasochism in England and Wales, [we have to] consider the possibility that these activities are practised by others who are not so controlled or responsible as the appellants are claimed to be.

In other words, SM sex games, role-play, spanking and even love bites will now be illegal, because the law lords, having failed to find any evidence of real harm caused by SM sex in Spanner, want to *think* harm might be caused.

The absurdity of the hypothetical reasoning, whereby not one judge dared detail exactly what was so injurious, can be made clear by way of a couple of analogies. Imagine if you will a situation in which all acts of shooting, from gun clubs to water pistols, were outlawed on the grounds that a less responsible person might, some day, somewhere, kill someone with something that looks like a gun;

or that one was prohibited from driving a car because someone, somewhere else, might run someone over.

Asses have more sense than the law

The Spanner judgment may not be the most absurd in the annals of British law, but it will take a lot to beat it, given the failure to detail or define the activity the judges were making illegal. While their lordships' deductive reasoning proved nothing about the law relating to SM sex, they are some of the best arguments I have heard in twenty years for electing judges, or, at least, making them pass a test in elementary logic before their appointment. Far from providing a modern and rational judgment on the validity of consent defences for sex games, the law lords appeared to be determined to deny that right to SM sex, and merely set about making any assumption or assertion that justified breaking legal precedent.

The prosecution was a fix from the beginning. The sexual dimension was initially ignored simply because the defence of consent is not in doubt if the charge is indecent assault. Then the important questions like whether or not the prosecution were supposed to prove a lack of consent, and the viability of granting SM sex immunity, were considered by the judges as if they were separate subjects, when every aspect of the case was interlinked. Neither question was really answered anyway, as they always took second place to the determination to justify labelling SM an assault or an act of grievous bodily harm. Incredibly, the judges did not offer us an answer to that question either: they by-passed it. Rather than resolve, for example, the potential differences between Stephen's ceiling, Lord Lane's, and Lord Goff's belief that consent is a defence to battery in *Collins* v. *Wilcox*, Lord Jauncey simply announced that it was not necessary to resolve that problem in this case.

The ultimate reason why the judges could not supply any answers to the legal questions raised in Spanner is that they dared not. To have attempted to do so would have forced them to admit that denying immunity to SM sex is to defy both logic and precedents.

The law of consent to 'assaults', as it stands, is based upon an illogicality. The concept of assault in such cases rests upon the presumptuous term 'violence'. Judges do not like to consider let alone define the term despite its centrality because it would expose the anachronistic foundation upon which the law is based. In common usage, the term 'violence' denotes an act of *impetuous and unrestrained* forcible action, but its essence also follows from the concept 'to violate': i.e. to abuse, profane or defile. Consequently, to deny the Spanner appeal means that, when it comes to sex, the 'public interest' is served by making everyone's bodies inviolable *per se*; and that means one's body does not belong to oneself. So whose is it?

By upholding the ancient justification whereby 'manly sports' are granted immunity from assault prosecution because they apparently offered skills useful to Her Majesty's realm in times of war, the law lords are effectively saying that everyone's body still belongs to the Crown! Yes; it's that stupid. According to British law, British subjects are not allowed to ask their spouse to spank them because to do so offers no 'manly' wartime skills, and presumably reduces their ability to acquire them. That's why despite using modern-sounding definitions like the 'public interest' the judges dared not proffer any definitions: they did not have any. And all that talk about AIDS and 'cults of violence' cannot hide that embarrassing fact.

In reality, the so-called 'established' exceptions have never been 'established' by anything. Over the last three hundred years numerous activities have been added to the non-existent list simply because no one has questioned them. While I know of some legislation covering acupuncture and tattooing, for example, I am still looking for a statute or a case covering the introduction of ice-hockey or bungee-jumping into Britain. In truth, all activities denied immunity, except unregulated fighting, are those which a judge finds offensive.

It is, therefore, more than of academic interest that the sexual aspects in the Spanner case were all but ignored when it came to the selection of the precedents used to bolster up this illogicality. Rather than look at what SM sex really consists of, the judges simply insisted that SM is akin to a fist-fight, and that all 'blows' are experienced as and cause an injury or hurt, rather than enhancing the participants' pleasure. Such precedents and arguments are, therefore, meaningless; they can have value only if we deny the well-'established' fact that SM sexual acts promote and enhance pleasure rather than produce pain. So we are forced to ask by what right the Crown presumes to inhibit the arousal-enhancement properties of SM, and presumes that the recipients do not know their own minds.

Throughout the appeals, the fact that SM sex is innately pleasurable was deliberately repressed by the judges' determination to associate SM sex with illegal prize-fighting rather than compare its standard features and level of risk with the kind of 'blows' received in sport. Yet, even if one treats the analogy with fighting seriously, there are good reasons why it should be abandoned, and why SM sex is a good candidate for immunity from assault charges. First, the ancient justification for allowing violent 'sports' immunity can no longer be justified. Second, as surgery or other legal activities from tattooing to ear-piercing, which never shared the 'sports' justification and can hardly be compared to the obvious one in the case, clearly demonstrate, other reasons are acceptable in law. Third, the *Donovan* precedent, if applied systematically, provides its own justification. At the very least, if one decides that pleasure-enhancing acts are unlawful and malicious, the country deserves a clear reason why similar acts in contact sports are not regarded as such, especially when they cause far more harm; but the judges cannot do this either.

The distinctions in British law between the different types of physical 'blow', like those between different activities, rested upon the Crown's requirements in time of war; but whereas the distinction between activities is being retained in order to make exciting sex illegal, the law has been steadily abandoning the rationales concerning 'blows', and this raises an awkward question about the law's inconsistency.

Several hundred years ago, as the law sought to maintain consistency between lawful and unlawful consensual assaults, decisions were based upon the extent of the injury caused, and a fairly clear distinction was drawn between 'maiming', a bodily harm whereby the person was deprived of the use of any limb which could be needed in order to fight, and a bodily injury which merely disfigured the body and after a short period would not inhibit a person's ability to fight again. Maiming was unlawful because the Crown was deprived of the services of an able-bodied citizen in the defence of the realm. Nowadays the law makes no distinction between maiming, wounding or grievous bodily harm, except with regard to the sentence; and the reason for this change is instructive. Whatever the Crown and the law might think, juries were reluctant to convict people for duelling or prize-fighting, even when a maiming occurred, because the British public were very tolerant when it came to consensual activities. Consequently, judges, who like most politicians are pretty lousy fighters, began to insist that even those guilty of a mere bodily injury should be convicted despite consent, and began to invent reasons like a breach of the peace to trap jurors into returning 'guilty' verdicts.

In other words, the judges created the contemporary confusion within the law, because they did not like the ancient sense of fair play, and wanted to override popular decisions. But once the judges, and law makers, had conflated the different kinds of bodily harm, this obviously had ramifications for other justifications in law, especially those concerning 'manly' sports. Not content with that mess, later generations of judges have been further confused by the fact that several fortuitous cases of prize-fighting, where maiming was a likely outcome, were then used as an excuse to distinguish between 'blows' in violent but friendly contests, where skill was the major rationale for taking part, and those where anger was a motive and where injury was intended.

The problem the law caused for itself, therefore, follows from the fact that in order to stress the distinction between assaults and non-assaults, the law incredibly suggested that friendly contests were not only bereft of the intent to do harm but were unlikely to do so either: which is, of course, factually incorrect. Moreover, as everyone knows, there are many people who, despite being engaged in a friendly contest, deliberately set out to injure others with malice aforethought. Yet look what happened when the law tried to promote friendly boxing compared to prize-fighting.

When making his judgment in the Coney case, Justice Stephen not only provided a list of acceptable activities, he gave two specific reasons, which do not apply to contemporary SM activities, why prize-fighting was being targeted. First, the 'injury' was deemed an assault because it was injurious to the public as well as to participants. In turn, this public 'injury' was supposedly caused by the fact that it was against the public interest that the lives and health of the combatants should be endangered, that the fights were disorderly exhibitions and that they were mischievous on other grounds. Justice Hawkins and Lord Coleridge offered the circular reasoning why this was so in their judgments: as prize-fighters' blows could cause a breach of the peace, and because a breach of the peace was unlawful, the blows were taking place in an unlawful activity and were thereby assaults, not defendable by consent. But they also spelt out the current state of judicial thinking about the Crown's interest too. Justice Hawkins asserted that the Crown was securing the public interest in the maintenance of good order, and Lord Coleridge insisted that 'an individual cannot by such consent destroy the right of the Crown to protect the public and keep the peace'; and in doing so, they were making up a new rationale for lawful activities. Instead of being useful for the defence of the realm, the exceptions were seen as peaceful activities which helped to keep good order within the realm. On this basis, *consenting* SM, unlike Mr Donovan's selfish action, could not be illegal, as it would hardly cause a breach of the peace; not that the judges probably conceived that the means of keeping discipline in British schools would evolve into a popular sexual activity.

The second new feature of the ruling was that sports' immunity would henceforth rest upon their supposed lack of premeditated injury. Sports and even dangerous pastimes were allowed because life and limb are exposed to no serious danger 'in the common course of things', which, together with Justice Stephen's qualification that *in all cases* any injury up to maiming caused by the application of force is a question of degree depending upon circumstances. In other words, *no* 'sport' or any other activity was automatically lawful; they were *all* liable to prosecution if a maiming occurred, and, depending upon the circumstances of the particular case, if a lesser injury occurred. Although, other judges quickly abandoned this distinction when it did not fit their prejudices, there was no logical reason why that test, perfectly permissible amongst the available precedents, could not be applied to SM sex. The Donovan case *did not* alter this fact. Justice Swift had merely found a very good reason for declaring that a one-sided caning was not consensual.

Consequently, the law lords' failure to apply Justice Stephen's test, like Lord Lane's *Attorney-General's Reference*, can be seen for what it is: a simple excuse to define an activity as an assault because a judge does not like it. Their lordships attempted to define SM as innately 'injurious to life and limb', despite all evidence to the contrary, because they wanted to make a legal activity illegal.

While no one would deny that SM is subject to a risk of injury, even when one of the minority methods is used, SM sex is far less likely to cause an injury in the normal course of things than many activities granted immunity. The vast majority of SM acts, like the humble spanking, carry no or little risk. Given their lordships' reasoning, there can be no justification for maintaining that dangerous exhibitions are 'needed in the public interest'. In my home town several years ago, a stuntman died while undertaking an extremely risky enterprise solely for the benefit of a TV programme which was reconstructing how another stuntman had died when performing the same feat.

Having spent all that time ignoring the sexual aspect of the alleged assaults in order to make analogies between SM and fist-fighting, the law lords promptly used the sexual nature of SM to justify avoiding analogies with a 'game', and to invent a bogus fear, HIV transmission, to establish an innate capacity for bodily harm and a new form of public interest. The self-serving nature of this excuse is simply demonstrated by Lord Templeman's assertion that 'The violence of sadists and the degradation of their victims have sexual motivations but sex is no excuse for violence'. Since the description of SM acts as 'violence' rests solely upon SM being defined as an 'assault', we are faced with a circular argument. Yet how on earth the lords of England can denounce harmless consenting SM sex games by such means while upholding the right of a bunch of adults to enforce the ritual mutilation of little boys' foreskins is frankly beyond me. Every single one of Lord Templeman's complaints about SM, such as the absence of doctors or referees, obviously applies in these cases. Moreover, the 'victims' do not give their consent, are not asked for it, and are of an age when they could not freely give consent even if they wished.

This kind of mad distinction in British law has far less to do with any threat of AIDS or violence and much more with moralistic directives such as those based upon homophobic fears about 'the possibility of proselytization and corruption of young men', who may now be able to choose to ditch 'manly' sports in favour of sexual enhancement following the reduction in the male homosexual age of consent. The intellectual capacity of those making such decisions in the law's name can be judged by the most idiotic rationale advanced in the case by Lord Jauncey. At one point, determined to infer that there was more to SM sex than sexual arousal and satisfaction, he posed the inane question: 'If the only purpose for the activity is sexual gratification of one or both of the participants what need then is the video recording?' The answer is obvious: the participants' further sexual gratification.

Ultimately, the law lords were not enforcing an existing law, whereby SM sex constitutes an assault, so much as making up excuses for defining it as an assault; and they answered none of the necessary questions, because they never really considered any. The justifications offered for their decision were less legal than moral. SM sex was denounced as *de facto* 'violent' not only in nature but more importantly in intent, because their lordships believed SM sex was 'degrading' to both 'body and mind'. In doing this, they did not so much assert that SM sex was 'on the wrong side of civilized behaviour' as redefine what 'civilized' behaviour is, by asserting that to turn 'pain' into pleasure is an 'evil thing'. Being completely out of place in a pluralistic society, it is hardly surprising that this moralism fails to produce rational reasons.

But this moralizing certainly explains why precedents appearing to be in their favour were regarded as general principles by their lordships, while those clearly working against them were not. Likewise, moralizing explains why their lordships stove to deny the obvious and repeatedly contradicted themselves in the process. And only moralizing can explain why, despite claiming that they could not change 'the law' relating to SM sex in their judgment, that is precisely what they did, by selectively applying previous test cases that had also changed the law.

The judgment amounts to a ridiculous attempt to confine sexual activity to an ideal romantic standard; and to assert that SM sex is not pleasurable but illegal when it is legal to engage in ritual genital mutilation for religious reasons, which is clearly not pleasurable, makes the law far more stupid than any ass.

Chapter eight

Mastering Slavery

THE obvious question to ask oneself about the Spanner case is: if SM was clearly illegal, where is the statute or case law which says so? As the statute does not exist, and as Mr Donovan was deemed to be guilty because Miss Harrison did not find the caning gratifying, consensual SM activities were legal until Spanner; a point easily confirmed by pre-Spanner SM cases.

In 1988, for example, a Mr Carter, who ran a hotel in Cumbria which opened its rooms to ordinary guests and the cellar to SM devotees, was found guilty of assault during SM sex play only because he pleaded guilty. Mr Carter had been charged with causing actual bodily harm, after the police had intercepted his pictures depicting a couple of women being spanked and caned. Although the two women had both consented, had travelled some distance in order to participate, and one was later to marry Mr Carter, the accused was fined £100 for each 'assault' after he decided to plead guilty in order to avoid the media publicity that would follow the trial. Four years later, however, a chief petty officer facing similar charges at Portsmouth Crown Court went ahead with the defence and won. Although his 'crime' involved using nipple clamps and nipple piercing during bondage games, Judge John Whitely directed the jury to acquit the man when his girlfriend told the court that she had consented to every act.

Consequently, as the consent defence had proved successful in the past, and convictions had followed from other reasons, the legal motivation behind the Spanner judgment was to remove one's legal right to have an accusation of this kind judged on the specific merits of the case. Rather than consider whether or not there are circumstances beyond consent which may make an act *de facto* illegal, the law has decided that, when it comes to SM sex, it does not need an overwhelming reason for denying consent. In order to do this, the law argued that there were good legal reasons for doing so; yet when one examines them, there are good reasons for doubting this.

A *question of sport*

Whether you realize it or not, the only reason you cannot bring a charge of assault when you are rammed from behind by a reckless shopper with an overladen shopping trolley in a supermarket is that the law assumes that everyone who enters a supermarket has consented to that risk. The same applies to any similar 'assault' you may suffer in an underground station or busy street; for the law, in its wisdom, has decided that these accidents, while inevitable, are devoid of hostile intent. The law, however, does not want to make this obvious test to determine whether or not you have suffered an assault into a standard, because it would not be able to enforce certain ethical views upon the public if it did. This is obvious in cases like suicide and euthanasia, where the law wishes to enforce the idea that one's life belongs to the State and/or God, by refusing one the right to determine to end one's own life by one's own hand or solicit the help of others; but the same applies to SM sex too. By ignoring the attempt of previous precedents to ensure that every circumstance was taken into account when the courts faced a potential exception to the law of assault, we have become locked in a time-warp whereby the exceptions rest upon their benefit to the Crown when the realm is endangered. They did so because the case of SM sex raises fundamental questions about the nature and purpose of the law of assault and the so-called 'recognized' exemptions.

Whatever the original reason for offering some activities exemptions and not others, most share common facets which make their status logical. In most exemptions there is a lesser risk of injury to the participants than in a hostile attack. As long as everyone holds to the original purpose of the activity and takes due care, there is no risk of public disorder. To a lesser or greater extent the activity improves the health or well-being of the participants, and, in the case of sports, any spectators too. This logic extends beyond the participants' rationales. The cathartic effect many contact sports afford to spectators, and the various pleasures offered by tattooing, clearly show that the law recognizes that the 'healthy' effects are not confined to a direct biological gain such as fitness. Conversely, the law is even willing to allow serious injury beyond the obvious benefit of legal surgery, as in the case of professional boxing. The illogicality of not recognizing these facets in SM sex and not extending the exemption to it is proved by considering the case of boxing — though I would not wish to see boxing suffer as a consequence.

Professional boxing involves two participants attempting to win a fight by seriously injuring their opponent by rendering them unconscious through a powerful blow to the head, or physically incapacitating them through a series of body blows or inducing bleeding above an eye to inhibit their sight. These blows would all be prosecuted under Section 20 of the 1861 Act if it were not for the immunity given to boxing. Yet contemporary professional boxing bears a much greater resemblance to illegal prize-fighting than the 'friendly sparring' between amateurs which was granted immunity from prosecution by cases like *R. v. Young* and *R. v. Orton* during the nineteenth century! Prize-fighting was declared illegal because it caused injuries 'in the normal course of things', and because it was conducted for the purpose of making money and raised the audience's 'blood lust'; and as Lord Mustill, one of the two dissenting judges in the Spanner case, pointed out, this means that professional boxing makes a nonsense of the reasons for its exemption:

> For money, not recreational personal improvement each boxer tries to hurt the opponent more than he is hurt himself, and aims to end the contest prematurely by inflicting a brain injury serious enough to make the opponent unconscious, or temporarily by impairing his central nervous system through a blow to the midriff, or cutting his skin to a degree which would ordinarily be well within the scope of Section 20 [of the 1861 Act]. The

boxers display skill, strength and courage, but nobody pretends that they do good to themselves or others. The onlookers derive entertainment, but none of the physical and moral benefits which have been seen as the fruits of engagement in manly sports.

In the normal course of things, professional boxing clearly carries a higher risk than SM sex, and can hardly justify its status as a 'manly sport' which aids the defence of the realm. The same applies to many other contact sports. Given that the serious injuries in ice-hockey games have been justified in Canada by *R. v. Ciccarelli* on the grounds that the contestants have given their consent, the mind boggles at the law's inconsistency. While people are now at risk from an assault for playfully spanking their partners, 'sports' enjoy the luxury of the highest injury 'ceiling' imaginable.

Consequently, not only is it completely illogical to make the inevitable injuries in dangerous sports legal while outlawing SM sex play, but these 'sporting' exemptions do not have any logical rationale, let alone a consistent legal theory of consent to support them. As Lord Mustill pointed out, the majority judges' failure to explain why contemporary professional boxing is immune exposes the fiction of 'established' exemptions. It makes no sense to use precedents concerning prize-fighting to outlaw SM sex, as the other law lords did, as long as professional boxing is immune.

This inconsistency is further compounded by the failure to allow SM sex exemption status under the provision for 'rough horse-play'. While the nearest established exception to SM acts like spanking and caning is lawful correction, whereby a vindictive adult can beat a child with impunity, the vast majority of SM acts could readily be encompassed within the concept of 'rough horse play', to which the law has also established a high injury ceiling in the horrific case of *R. v. Terence Jones*. This gave children's playground peers the 'right' to throw them around without their consent up to and including serious injury. The law asserted that the children's presence in the playground amounted to consent.

In short, the law as it stands has no consistent theory of consent, or set of justifications for establishing exceptions to a charge of assault; and that is precisely why the major precedents alluded to in the Spanner case all insisted that any case involving a consent defence had to differentiate between the issue of consent and innate unlawfulness. Unfortunately for the Spanner defendants, the law lords utilized the law's general inconsistency to avoid following the advised procedure, in order to enable those who will follow them to impose the law any way they see fit.

In all cases, including SM sex, the issue should be simple: consent should be a defence to what is regarded as an assault when hostility is present, up to a certain level of harm. As Lord Mustill suggested, the infliction of bodily harm, especially in consenting privacy, should not automatically be criminal. Each individual category of violence, from a tackle on the soccer field to being spanked over rubber sheets, should be judged on its own merits, in the light of the situation as a whole. As circumstances will clearly alter cases, the issue of consent is vital in determining whether or not a malicious or non-malicious act should be prosecuted. The point of law the House of Lords were supposed to consider was:

> Where A wounds or assaults B occasioning him actual
> bodily harm in the course of a sadomasochistic encounter,
> does the prosecution have to prove a lack of consent on
> the part of B before they can establish A's guilt under
> Section 20 and Section 47 of the 1861 Offences Against
> the Person Act?

Since the precedents clearly suggested that the prosecution had to do this, and the House of Lords refused to judge the merits of SM sex within these precedents, they must have had a good reason for doing so. By simultaneously refusing to define what a sadomasochistic 'encounter' was, they have effectively criminalized any kind of sex act which could be labelled sadomasochism; and that highlights the real issue in this case.

A question of sex

The reason why so many judges asserted that none of the existing precedents were helpful was that SM sex, being sexual, is hardly analogous to prize-fighting. The fact that the Spanner defendants were not prosecuted under any statutory sexual prohibitions also demonstrates that it would have been difficult to secure a prosecution because no sexual crime had been committed. The 1861 Act was not used because the activities were violent so much as because it was the only Act that could, in any way, be used to prohibit SM sex. To have used the Sexual Offences Act of 1967 or an anachronistic Conspiracy to Corrupt Public Morals charge ran the risk of failure. Even if the authorities had succeeded in such a charge, the conviction would probably have led to a public outcry that the case was not in the public interest. By misrepresenting the nature and effects of SM sex as a 'cult of violence', however, they avoided this problem, they could by-pass the important legal caveats, and slot SM in with all the others which have been denied the right to a consent defence because serious bodily harm was involved. Along the way, they raised a smoke-screen to obscure the fact that the only precedent which links sex to violence outside sex crime legislation, the *Donovan* case, required their lordships to rule in favour of the Spanner appellants. In doing so the law lords were clearly deciding, as a matter of public policy, that SM sex should be criminalized – when they should have had no right to do so. That right, in the first instance, should belong to a jury; and any major change in the law should be considered and suggested by bodies like the Law Commission or the Criminal Law Revision Committee and then be determined by Parliament. But why take this right upon themselves, and outlaw SM sex?

At first sight, SM sex hardly threatens the public interest. It no more leads to social or public disorder than consensual acts of oral or anal sex, and can no more corrupt a youth than attendance at a soccer or boxing match. Conversely, by interfering with the right of citizens to choose their private sexual tastes the State will not inhibit one act of real anti-social violence. On the contrary, by running around looking at people's video collections and rummaging through their wardrobes, the State will tie up the very resources that would be much better spent on controlling anti-social violence.

Part of the reason why the authorities have decided to outlaw SM sex can be found in some judges' prejudice against homosexuals and hedonistic sex in general, and sadomasochism in particular, reflecting the views of various interest groups in society. Yet neither judges nor these groups can justify their fears.

Sexually orientated flagellation has been around for a long time. John Henry Meibomius's treatise on the medical use of rods, and its various translations during the eighteenth century, claimed that the Greeks believed flogging could cure melancholia and what we now call anorexia; that the Romans thought whipping women's hands was believed to aid conception; that married women in Persia and Russia took a flogging as a token of their husbands' love; and that from antiquity flagellation was regarded as a cure for impotence. Whether or not these claims are true, people believed them; and one of the reasons they did so was because they *knew* that 'flogging' could enhance sexual arousal. But while it is fairly common knowledge that flagellation was widely practised, here and there we also find an SM devotee:

> Perhaps the oddest whim amongst whipping anecdotes is that of a certain nobleman, who flourished in the reign of George II. This singular character rented a house in St. James's Place, and made an elderly good-looking woman housekeeper. It was this woman's business one day of each week to provide every article for scrubbing out every room, and to engage two pretty women to meet him there on the day – one to represent a housekeeper and the other a chambermaid. While he was scrubbing the room, he fancied himself a *Parish girl*, and he did his work so very bad, that one or the other of the women, or both, whipped him in the same unmerciful manner those poor girls are whipped by cruel mistresses.

Even if this particular anecdote is false, the idea that people could engage in SM role-play has clearly existed for some 250 years. Consequently, the real question to ask is not what is wrong with SM sex and role-play, but what right anyone has to stop other people doing it.

The most common excuse is that SM is painful, and that real loving relationships would never involve pain. Yet the idea that SM relationships are full of pain, and others are not, cannot stand up; as 'Juicy Lucy', a member of the American lesbian SM group SAMOIS, pointed out in *Coming to Power* (1982):

Pain is . . . the inevitable result of unacknowledged power roles. I have never known lesbians to say to each other something like 'let's start a relationship and hurt each other a lot, OK? You be needy and demanding and fearful and manipulative, and I'll be cool and tough and withdraw farther from you while meanwhile becoming completely dependent on you. Then you fall in love with someone else in secret and leave me with no warning. We'll both be broken for months with grief and guilt. Sounds like a good time?' It's never this consensual, though the roles are often this clear. These pain dynamics show up in friendship and political work as often as in lover relationships.

All relationships are capable of being painful, in one way or another; so this is no excuse to single out SM couples.

A more 'sophisticated' reason rests upon Freud's silly assertion that men's (*sic*) instinctive drive for pleasure, eros, has to be sublimated in the cause of civilization; and then that civilization will collapse if we allow people to become 'obsessed' with sex, because this reflects a regression to pre-civilized forms of behaviour and an immature form of sexual development. This argument never made any sense. By placing all the blame upon the child's psyche, which is merely a secular alternative to original sin, Freud effectively negated his own argument. As all sexual 'perversions' are actually invoked by the vagaries of 'civilized' child-rearing practices, the more controls one places upon children the more perversions civilization will produce, and the sooner it will bring about its own downfall. The related argument that people who become sadomasochists are sick is easily debunked. As we saw, the real problem with contemporary psychiatry is that it has never considered the possibility that the symptoms associated with sadomasochism frequently follow from a patient's failure to buy some rubber and PVC clothes, join an SM club, find some like-minded friends and have a good time.

Unable to find a devotee who causes anyone a problem detractors sooner or later prattle on about de Sade – not that they know anything about him, – and 'escalation theories'. Escalation theories have no basis in fact. The assertion that SM devotees will 'need' to inflict, or wish to suffer, ever-increasing amounts of 'pain' is merely a repetition of the simplistic Sunday School warning that little sins lead to big sins in a secular guise. Like the claims that soft-core pornography leads to hard-core consumption, escalation theories are actually disproved by people's behaviour. Even Dolf Zillmann has pointed out that one's reactions to different kinds of erotica are highly variable. People tend to stick with what they like; and SM pornography, in particular, is far more likely to reduce most people to mirth. Interestingly enough, the only people it appears to provoke to anger are those with restricted forms of sexual socialization and experimentation. As Zillmann and numerous other researchers have demonstrated, time and time again, when 'violent' pornography increases experimental subjects' aggressive reactions in laboratory circumstances, it is those who feel guilty or embarrassed about being aroused by the material or find it disgusting who record this response. Those who find this kind of pornography arousing and pleasing do not become aggressive. Why this should be so, we do not know exactly; but these results strongly suggest that those who vehemently oppose this material may find it arousing, and are possibly projecting their personal problems on to harmless devotees.

In any event, as these complaints have a long history, they can hardly explain why the Spanner case arose when it did. To uncover why it occurred we need to look at social trends and the politics of sex.

Bondage is back

The real problem contemporary SM sex poses for its opponents is not that SM sex is a threat to society but that it threatens to undermine their forms of prejudice. As more and more men and women discover that SM sex is not the province of perverts and weirdos and that it can be fun for some, the fewer people there are who will be convinced by moralists' attempts to stigmatize people.

As *Options* magazine pointed out in April 1992, one cannot even be sure, these days, that those happy smiling couples spending their Saturday afternoons in do-it-yourself superstores are going to use all those little chrome attachments solely for bathroom fittings. The only certainty, as far as *Options* was concerned, is that

> Bondage is being openly recognised as having a right to a place in every normal, sexy person's normal sexual repertoire, because people are finally willing to take a peek under the carpet of conventionality and do a bit of Spring-cleaning of their own . . . Accepting as perfectly ordinary what has previously been thought of as kinky perversion for low-life scum is not . . . a sign of the rapidly degenerating morality of contemporary society: it is a new and exciting phase in the way people can feel comfortable declaring themselves to be multidimensional beings full of complexity and contradiction.

A woman, Kimberley Leston, told the author:

> Being tied up spread-eagled across the bed or the dining-room table and being fucked stupid is a real release of energy for me. I'm in the typical modern woman's position of 'having it all' which is bloody hard work, so to let all that control go completely is a very affecting experience. It's like being outside myself somehow and yet in touch with something very fundamental and animal at the same time. Basically it's just a huge turn-on. I love it.

Likewise, during the late 1980s and early 1990s Madonna and Kylie Minogue helped to demonstrate that corsetry, see-through fabrics, fishnet and PVC can be enjoyed for their innate charms rather than as so-called 'fetish' items: a substitute for procreative sex known as the 'lingerie look'. Almost every fashion house began to offer its customers colourful designs and materials stripped of their 'perverse' image which would, as the author of the above article noted, grace a dinner party, let alone a trendy disco dance floor. The tabloid papers also began printing features in which one celebrity would claim that another was 'into fun and games in bed. All the really horny things that I get off on, like spankings, handcuffs, whips, and polaroid pictures', and people heard that Germany even has its own lesbian SM MP, Christina Schenk. Kinky fashions and sex became normalized, and people realized that they had nothing to fear from being more open about their desires and tastes.

This development obviously would not appeal to crusading Christians, separatist feminists and disapproving therapists. It was bad enough losing their arguments about homosexuality, soft-core pornography and satanic abuse; now their millenarian messages about SM were being ignored and disproved by hundreds of thousands of happy couples too. The biggest disappointment they faced, however, was women's willingness to abandon their fears about sex. Women have always had more to lose by wishing to fulfil their sexual desires, let alone being labelled perverts, than men have; and these groups have always attempted to maintain 'the fear'. Consequently, until recently women had to keep their fantasy lives a very closely guarded secret. This has often meant that their attempts to gain some fantasy fulfilment was restricted to SM-like incidents in Mills & Boon romances and 'bodice-rippers'.

Incredible as it seems, women's romantic fiction is full of the stuff; and, as Spencer Woodcock pointed out in a marvellous article in *Fetish Times* (No. 3, 1994), whilst these books steer clear of the thrust-by-thrust descriptions of sex found in hard-core pornography, they pull no punches when it comes to violence, and sexual violence in particular. Take, for example, Beth, the heroine in Anne Mathers's *To Tame a Vixen*. Never having forgotten the way a neighbour, Chad Barrett, once paddled her backside, when she was younger, Beth returns home to provoke him into repeating the act. Rhoda Seville's *Compelling Captor* offers readers an old gypsy advising her daughter:

> 'When your father stole me away from my tribe he used to beat me at least once a day and bed with me three times daily!'
> 'That sounds terrible!' Marie gasped.
> 'I loved every moment of it' the older woman smiled.

In 'bodice-rippers', it is the hero rather than the villain who does the ripping; and, whether the moralists like it or not, an incredible number of women seem to pore over page after page of abductions, rapes, spankings and enforced submission. Some feminists have been complaining about the likes of Mills & Boon for years; but, in their haste to claim it is part of a patriarchal plot, they have missed the point completely.

Yes, the gender roles and sexual orientations in this kind of fiction are fixed, unquestioned and presented as both natural and normal. In *The Savage Deception* by Lynett Vinet, for example, Diana marries the wrong half-brother, the dastardly Kingsley, who has a habit of giving her savage beatings which leave her with permanent scars. Believing Kingsley dead, she then marries his brother, Tanner, who soon compels her to strip whilst toying with a crop:

> God he was a merciless cad, and the words to deny him nearly slipped past her lips but he leaned back and tapped the crop in the palm of his hand. Diana stared hypnotically at the beastly thing, so thin and seemingly harmless, but so very damaging when applied to tender flesh ...
>
> At the moment she was little better than a slave ordered by the master to strip for him and she stripped down to nothing because he held the crop.

As Woodcock points out, there is some recognition in the text that there might be something perverse in this situation, for Diana wonders:

> Why did she suddenly, almost pervertedly, crave the sensual movement of the blasting tip across her body? The very instrument of torture was now causing a melting feeling at the centre of her womanhood.

Tanner is not slow to recognize this:

> 'Perverse am I? Well, my darling wife, I'm not the one who turned into a mass of quivering flesh at the touch of a riding crop. In future you'd do well to curb your perverse responses, otherwise a man might believe you're used to such odd pleasuring.'

I will not bother the reader with Fitzgerald's *Royal Slave* and *Slave Lady* group of novels. Suffice to say that the Turks' rape and murder of nuns, concubines and seven-year-old boys is, as Woodcock discovered, far more horrifying than anything SM pornography has managed. Contrary to the crusading feminist claims, however, women are not taught how to be passive by taking the stereotypes for granted; they have used this kind of material as a springboard to cross the divide and experiment with real SM sex; and that is what is really horrifying the crusaders. Now that women are no longer hiding their tendencies, and are exploring various ways to put their fantasies into practice, the crusaders cannot claim that women are being forced to do so against their will. And the more women who become involved, the more there are who know that they have little to fear from sexual diversity, and the less they are likely to back the crusaders in a desperate attempt to deny their desires. No wonder we have seen a growing number of campaigns against SM and other forms of sexual diversity in the last decade. As J.R. Gusfield (1963), the American sociologist of moral crusades, discovered: moral crusades are launched when those promoting them fear that their traditional supporters are defecting.

Unfortunately for the Spanner defendants, the crusades to dissuade 'normal' people from experimenting with SM slotted in with the priorities of certain police officers.

Illiberal nonsense

The futile Obscene Publications Squad must have thought that Spanner was manna from heaven. Throughout the 1980s as new technology made possible the rapid dissemination of sexually explicit materials despite the law, the Squad must have begun to feel redundant. In a desperate attempt to prove their worth and justify their existence they forged links with various moral crusaders attempting to outlaw soft-core pornography, on the grounds that because pornography was addictive on a soft to hard continuum it would inevitably lead the consumer to commit sexual crimes, and that they were, therefore, engaged in crime prevention, be it rape or satanic abuse.

As they were unable to justify this claim by publishing a systematic record of their hauls and the percentage of material involving violent acts, they needed a 'good' case to prove their point. Once they uncovered the Spanner videos they could assert that their theory was true, and tried to do so by asserting that 'The videos they produced were the worst ever encountered by this Branch. This was appealing for its sheer controlled violence: cold blooded, slow and ritualised.' The Squad, of course, had been saying this about any and every haul for years, but the emphasis upon the so-called 'ritualized' acts boosted their contemporary obsession with finding satanists at work.

But if the £500,000 Spanner investigation had initially begun as a means to prove that satanic snuff movies really existed, it quickly became an excuse to attack sexual diversity in general and SM sex in particular. As the Squad admitted in an August 1991 edition of *Police Review*:

> Actors in hard-pornography videos have become police targets following Operation Spanner, which netted more than a dozen homosexual sado-masochists. A successful identification could lead to assault charges, based on the evidence of the video itself.

The fact that criminalizing SM sex hardly proves that sex-video watching leads to 'sex crimes' did not stop the Squad, who also took the opportunity to assert, contrary to all independent evidence, that bizarre sex now accounts for two-fifths of the porn market:

> Ten years ago there was a little bit of urination, and a little bit of flagellation, but now the content is stronger, more violent and degrading. We're talking about real beatings to the point of bleeding, and heavy bondage.

Things have got so bad that the Squad, according to this article, were now investigating cases where the activities depicted lead to real deaths.

These bogus claims gave the ailing Squad a new lease of life, which is hardly surprising given that the likes of PC Len Yeoell, known in the Squad as S&M because of his supposed expertise in this area, have realized that 'What it's depicting are very serious offences of violence. If we see a crime being enacted in front of us – albeit on a screen – we have a duty to act.' Unfortunately, thanks to the Spanner judgment, not only do the Squad want to act, they are extending their remit. One unnamed officer, for example, told the *Police Review* that he found it highly suspicious that several of the women in one SM video he had seen were wearing 'collections of silver rings in their genitalia'; presumably because these women must have had their labia pierced at some point.

Any worries about where this police obsession will lead are hardly allayed by the Squad's insistence that 'Our objective is to protect people – not to criticise people's private behaviour. We're not going to burst into people's bedrooms as guardians of public morals', for the article's author, Ken Hyder, revealed that officers have already been poring over seized videos to pick out any woman who has had her nipples pierced! What else can this mean than that some police officers want to prosecute people who perform in sexually orientated videos? And once they have the power to seize anyone's private video collection, whether or not they keep it in their bedroom, the Squad *will* be acting as the guardians of your private morals.

Can there be anything more obscene than a bunch of police officers, having first gorged themselves on the very material they would like to outlaw, running around the country arresting people who perform in their own videos demanding that they reveal where and when they obtained their body jewellery? Yes; as I write, the government are going to give the same powers to trading standards officers.

Any suggestion that this is scaremongering is belied by the fact that the gay community has already suffered from this kind of policing. In June 1993, for example, one Hertfordshire man was raided at dawn by policemen waving around a warrant taken out under the Obscene Publications Act. Their haul? His sex toys, books and magazines, letters, an address book and his leather motor-cycling clothing! A couple of months later, another gay man from north London, who was an SM devotee, discovered that he could be harassed by the police with the aid of a child pornography warrant. No pictures of any child, let alone one in a pornographic pose, were found; but the officers took away every single video, magazine and photograph in the house, despite being unable to press any charges. When they fail to find any videos, the police have even taken to making their own. One caning devotee lost his teaching post when a video of his bedroom, highlighting a pair of stocks at the end of the bed and his cane collection, was shown to his school governors. These, and numerous other raids, including a 1993 raid on a private Yorkshire party, which netted thirty people, a couple of pairs of leather jeans and a pair of rubber shorts, show the lengths to which the police are willing to go.

During the summer of 1993, PC Len 'S&M' Yeoell even attempted to justify the Squad's role as enforcer of private morals by suggesting that they were really clamping down on violence, not sex. In a letter to *The Job*, the Metropolitan Police's own newspaper, he 'reasoned': 'The suggestion that SM is a sexual encounter, I believe, is an attempt to legitimise that violence by those who practise it.' And this man is supposed to be the police's expert on SM.

Sex is now what the Met say it is, and they are keeping everything they seize in these pointless raids, irrespective of its real purpose. When one man caught up in the Spanner Inquiry, but never charged with any offence, attempted to secure the return of his leather jeans seized by the Squad, he was told by 'S&M':

> Dressing up is very much a factor within the sado-masochistic scene, and is just as important as the restraints or torture implements to make the scene complete.
> Whether it is leather atire, gym wear, school uniforms, military uniforms, or even ladies' clothing, it all plays a part in catering for each individual's fetish or fantasy. It is for this reason that I am suggesting the clothing is used in the course of sado-masochistic practices, and as such I am retaining the items of clothing you refer to.

It would appear, therefore, that every couple who like to dress up for sex could now have their wardrobe seized on the bogus grounds that their garments may be worn during an assault. Some people have already had to take the police to court to secure the return of dangerous items like family photo albums and videos of steam trains. Yet every time the police go on one of these raids, the public are informed that the haul was full of sadomasochistic material.

Contrary to what the Squad would have us believe, the Spanner defendants *were* originally charged with conspiracy to corrupt public morals, which ensured that the case was referred to the Old Bailey and guaranteed maximum publicity even though the conspiracy charges were immediately dropped once the trial begun.

The cost to the Spanner defendants was high. They had been vilified in public, lost their jobs, been forced to move, and several fell ill with the strain. But the cost to the British public is even higher. Sadomasochism has now become the Squad's latest excuse to feed prurient sensibilities of tabloid news followers while spreading misleading information which is then ideologically exploited by moral crusaders in order to gain more legislation giving the police even more powers to invade Britain's bedrooms. This self-serving cycle of deceit has already turned Britain into the most sexually policed country in Europe; yet, far from doing anything about real problems like sexual assaults on women and children, crusading police departments are merely exploiting public concern over such issues to increase their power over people's private lives. To date, the gay community had been the main target; but if anyone thinks this has nothing to do with them, they should think again. There are several lessons one can learn from similar developments on the other side of the Atlantic, where SM sex has been prosecuted under American assault laws, gay or unmarried couples are forced to testify against their partners, and the sentences are high; a Kenneth Appleby, for example, was sent down for *ten years* for merely stroking his lover with a crop. But it is the political ramifications that are really alarming.

In 1976 the Los Angeles police used an obscure antique anti-slavery statute in order to raid a mock slave auction held in a gay club. The operation involved two phone-taps, several weeks' surveillance, sixty-five uniformed officers, two helicopters, and a dozen vehicles; all to bust a private party held in aid of gay charities, featuring the innocuous kind of 'slave auction' that is the highlight of numerous student charity rag weeks. The press had a field day, with the police's press release, and this vast waste of taxpayers' money and police time was hidden behind sensational headlines like 'Police Free Gay Slaves', implying that people were being sold into homosexuality against their will. While it is easy to be amused by the fact that the police detained everyone at the party for hours, did not remove the handcuffs, refused to allow them to go to the bathroom, and then subjected them to full strip-searches, the social costs incurred by this kind of policing are no laughing matter. This and other raids were promoted by people trying to convince the public that homosexual equality was undesirable, and they were effectively using public funds to push their morality upon others.

During 1981 a Californian TV station ran a four-part series on SM in order to represent SM as a public menace which was 'corroding the fabric of society'. To this end, SM was denounced as violent, sex toys were called 'dangerous weapons', and viewers were erroneously informed that the city's hospital emergency rooms were full of people with SM-related injuries. It was not long before these exaggerations and demands were subjected to their own inflation. Two weeks after the series finished, a local paper began to claim that ten per cent of the city's homicides followed SM sex. Then, when part of San Francisco's gay area was burnt down in July 1981, the police and moralists began a rumour that the bodies of unknown SM slaves who were chained to their beds in SM dungeons were burnt alive. The purpose behind this negative publicity was the proposition that any parents who engaged in SM sex should be relieved of the custody of their children, along with 'swingers', prostitutes, lesbians and gay men.

A similar crusade began in Canada during 1979 with the police raiding a gay sauna known as The Barracks, used by SM devotees. The owners were charged under the ancient bawdy house laws, and had all their sex toys confiscated. The gay community was nonplussed: no prostitution was taking place. The police, however, argued that as SM sex was indecent any building they suspected of being used for that purpose was therefore a bawdy house, and that they had the right to protect the public. The following summer, members of The Barracks Defence Committee were raided; and it was not long before anyone the police suspected of being a devotee found themselves charged, and any and every sexually orientated item they possessed taken by the police on the grounds that it might be used for an indecent act. Having gained several dubious convictions, the police then began to harass the rest of the gay community. Then the police started raiding gay businesses which made sex toys and designer leather clothing, which the police had reclassified as pornographic items. Having effectively redefined and extended Canada's sex laws, the police were able to circumvent the law of homosexual consent and prosecute prominent gay businessmen, lawyers and political activists for living off the proceeds of 'crime'.

Once one reviews the history of crusades against SM sex, the British case can be placed in context. The British police are engaged in a similar attempt to redefine the law, in order to arrest whom they want, rather than real criminals. In this respect it is interesting to note what happens to those who perpetuate real violence, compared to harmless SM devotees. Take the case of Andrew Sole, who helped his brother, Barry Mills, batter a Mr Williams for over an hour, because Mr Williams had dared to ask Mills to tone down his noisy all-night parties, and had refused to buy the stolen property Mills was peddling. Not content with beating him to a pulp, they then humiliated Mr Williams by making him clean up his own blood from the walls and the floors. He was beaten a second time before having to apologize to both of them before being released, and threatened that he would be killed if he dared to go to the police. Despite telling Sole that it was totally unforgivable to beat this man mercilessly, Judge Ian Starforth Hill QC gave him sixty hours' community service!

It should come as no surprise, therefore, that Britain is paying a heavy price both socially and economically for the latest bogus threat to the public, satanic ritual abuse, which also culminated in the crusaders trying to pass off an innocuous video made by a rock band as evidence of ritualistic satanic snuff movies. Having wasted several hundred millions of pounds on that one, the police officers and crusaders are now trying to justify wasting a similar amount on funding their crusade against SM sex in order to enforce their moral standards on the public.

Thankfully, I am not the only one to notice. A *Times* leader entitled 'Criminal Mischief' on 20 December 1990 accused the police and the Home Office, amongst others, of a conspiracy to delude the British public that they were in the grip of a crime wave. This was the day after the quarterly release of police crime statistics. *The Times* decided that, rather than fuelling the flames of panic, like the rest of the media, it would tuck the figures away on an inside page and consider the issue in an editorial. According to *The Times* the real problem was not the non-existent 'crime-wave', because the figures merely revealed 'a modest long-term rise, roughly commensurate with increasing wealth', but the fear generated by the sensational coverage of the statistics. *The Times* then used the

Spanner judgment to demonstrate the way in which such figures would inevitably 'be abused by the police, the media, and politicians':

> The beginning of such a statistical perversion also occurred yesterday, when 15 men received severe sentences from the Central Criminal Court for activities which most people would not have realised were crimes at all. What the police call 'sex offences' range from serious rape to acts between consenting adults in public places. Sex crime figures are largely a function of police decisions to raid public lavatories. The public has been led to believe that sex offences are mostly rapes, thus raising fear amongst women.
>
> Next quarter's crime statistics will now presumably reveal an increase in sadomasochistic 'sex crime'. Although the accused at the Central Criminal Court were adults acting in private, the Jury made a subjective judgement that the behaviour described was beyond the threshold of crime. *Thus an activity is criminalised, without any reference to Parliament, and the statistical crime wave is impelled ever onwards.*
>
> Police forces will now make it their business to seek out perverse sexual activity to which they think a jury would take exception. Judge Rant, QC, unwisely remarked: 'The Courts must draw the line between what is acceptable in a civilised society and what is not', thus bidding the police to enforce moral judgements and extending the always grey area between unpleasantness, immorality and statutory crime. The case, and the 'wave' to which it will give rise is an illiberal nonsense.
>
> If the police wish to collect figures on their own activities, that is their business and they can do with them what they wish. The Home Office should have nothing to do with this quarterly fiasco which is also a public menace.

The only criticism to be made about this rare piece of honest comment is that *The Times* failed to realize that the police were already doing their best to convince juries to take exception to things they might not otherwise object to, and that the law courts were taking the decision away from juries just in case they did not agree with the police.

When it comes to SM devotees, the future hardly bears thinking about. Unless they can secure a video, the police will have to induce one of the partners to grass-up the other; and couples could easily fall prey to blackmailers. It is highly debatable, however, whether the law should interfere in questions of private morality at all. As Britain is in the process of becoming a pluralistic society, there is no justification for using the law to impose one social group's morals on the others; and the state should abandon its irrational policing of citizens' private morals.

As a criminologist, I am worried by the efforts of the police, high court judges and the tabloid press to stir up public fear about SM sex. Britain is wasting far too many resources supposedly earmarked for crime prevention and control on nothing more than witch-hunts so that some people can impose their public moral standards upon others in private rather than tackle real social issues and problems, which they constantly exploit for their own ends.

If one is really concerned about eliminating violent sex crimes and inhibiting serial sex killers, to name just two, then one has to start by preventing the ideological exploitation of real crime and irrational fears; and we could all learn from the experience of the psychiatrist, the late Robert Stoller.

In 1991, having spent several months meeting and interviewing 'sadomasochists', Stoller had the guts to change his mind about SM sex. He then set out to warn his colleagues about the mistakes he had made, and suggested that their convictions, especially when based upon a belief-system like Freudianism, could deny them the opportunity to learn about the phenomena they claimed to be studying. His own explorations revealed that there was no sado-masochistic perversion, because there were over a hundred different kinds of sexual activity that could be classified as SM sex, and very few included pain. Like the sociologists before him, Stoller finally realized that consensual SM was play-acting, practised by perfectly 'normal' people, who just happened to prefer sexual excitement to other hobbies. Amongst the devotees he saw, he found no one who was psychotic, pre-psychotic or latently psychotic; but he did find far more understanding and compassion than one finds in many other kinds of relationships. Amongst the SM crowd the constant, high attention to one's partner's experience is more caring and safer than the blundering, ignorant, non-communicating obtuseness that governs so many 'normal' people's erotic motions. So, though I find my informants' games unappealing . . . I no longer extrapolate and think these people are freaks. We should distinguish those who harm from those who, in trying to undo the effects of harm inflicted on them early in life, play at harm. I believe it is immoral for psychoanalysts to hide their moralizing in jargon-soaked theory.

So if one of the world's leading psychiatrists can find nothing wrong with SM once he decides to take a real look, no one, be they judges, policemen, moral crusaders or tabloid newspapers, have any grounds for condemnation. SM sex is merely the logical extension of the recreational sex made possible after the arrival of the birth control pill and economic affluence. For most people, it amounts to little more than an extended form of foreplay which is directed towards heightening one's partner's sexual arousal before the digital stimulation of erogenous and genital zones, which ultimately lead to orgasm. Claiming anything else is an illiberal nonsense.

The Law Commission

As this book was being written, one of the Spanner defendants was preparing a submission to the European Court of Human Rights. Meanwhile, the Law Commission issued Consultation Paper no. 134 covering *Criminal Law: Consent and Offences Against the Person*, which sought advice on, amongst other issues, SM and the law.

Like the law lords before them, the Commission are under the misapprehension that existing precedents are contradictory, and completely ignored the procedure to be followed in court cases laid down by the judges in *Coney* and *Donovan*. They do, however, offer two major possibilities of dealing with SM. Either it could be made an exception to the general rule covering assault, or the level of 'injury' to which individuals can consent could be raised so that the consent defence can be extended. Yet, in order to avoid the possible absurdity of denying SM devotees the same 'rights' enjoyed by boxing fans, the Commission simply excluded boxing from their remit.

Given that every legal judgment – apart from the *Attorney-General's Reference* – which led to denying one's right not to consent to an act of 'bodily harm' was highly contextualized, the obvious legal solution is not only to raise the level of 'injury' to which one can consent, but also to exclude all consensual SM acts from prosecution. SM sex has nothing to do with violent intent and causes far less 'injury' to those taking part than participation in any contact sport does. As the most severe SM acts are on a par with ear piercing, there is no justifiable reason for criminalizing it.

The core issues in the Spanner case – why the law is trying to impose its ideas about the 'public interest' and 'good reasons' without defining either, in order to punish people who had not caused, and were not likely to cause, a breach of the peace or promote any hurt calculated to interfere with the health or comfort of the participants – were not addressed.

While admitting that the 'desirability and legitimacy' of SM acts were really 'incidental to the question that the House [of Lords] had to determine', the Commission justified the actions of the judges in the three cases by claiming that SM behaviour was 'controversial'. Yet SM sex is only 'controversial' because moral crusaders and the judiciary wish to outlaw it and impose their 'ideals' upon others, and use the law to do so. It can make no legal or ethical sense to do this when the Commission itself is recommending that religious flagellation and mortification are allowed to continue unhindered. In a sensible and sane society, there can be no justification for imposing one's ideals upon another; and when it comes to assault, the motive is all-important. Whether one is engaging in sport, thrashing oneself to get closer to God, or experimenting with excitation transfer, one should have both the right to be protected from malicious participants (whose further involvement can be curtailed by a prosecution) and the right to indulge oneself.

Unfortunately we do not live in such a society. The reason you are perfectly entitled to break someone's jaw deliberately on a rugby field and hide behind the fact that it is a 'manly' sport, but not to consent to being flagellated outside a religious ritual, is that certain sections of society are still obsessed about sex, and they are labelling

SM sex violent in order to justify restricting sexual acts that are different from their own. The right of consenting SM devotees to indulge themselves is not, therefore, an issue of violence so much as a right to their own sexual orientation. Far from protecting anyone, the moral crusaders are attempting to restrict one's choice and force others to conform to a rigid ideal. No wonder their friends in the law deliberately failed to define and justify the 'good reason' for claiming that this is in 'public interest'.

References

Adler, A. (1933), *Der Sinn des Lebens*, Wein, Leipzig, quoted in North, M. (1981), *The Outer Fringe of Sex*, The Odyssey Press, London.

Avery, N.C. (1977), 'Sadomasochism: A Defence Against Object Loss', *Psychoanalytical Review*, vol. 84, no. 1, pp. 101–9.

Bergler, E. (1961), *Curable and Incurable Neurotics*, Liveright, New York.

Berliner, B. (1958), 'The Role of Object Relations in Moral Masochism', *Psychoanalytical Quarterly*, vol. 27, pp. 38–56. Quoted in A. Rothstein, 1991.

Bloch, I. (1933), *Anthropological Studies in the Strange Sexual Practices of All Races in All Ages*, Anthropological Press, New York.

Blum, H.P. (1991), 'Sadomasochism in the Psychoanalytic Process, Within and Beyond the Pleasure Principle: Discussion', *Journal of the American Psychoanalytic Association*, vol. 39, no. 2. pp. 431–50.

Brenner, C. (1982), *The Mind in Conflict*, International University Press, New York. Quoted in Rothstein, 1991.

Breslow, N. (1989), 'Sources of Confusion in the Study and Treatment of Sadomasochism', *Journal of Social Behaviour and Personality*, vol. 4, no. 3. pp. 263–74.

Dally, P. (1977), *The Fantasy Game*, Quartet, London.

Dietz, P.E. *et al.* (1990), 'The Sexually Sadistic Criminal and His Offences', *Bulletin of the American Academy of Psychiatry and the Law*, vol. 18, No. 2. pp. 163–78.

Ellis, H. (1942), *Studies in the Psychology of Sex*, Random House, New York.

Eysenck, H.J. and Wilson, G. (1979), *The Psychology of Sex*, Dent, London.

Finell, J.S. (1992), 'Sadomasochism and Complementarity in the Interaction of the Narcissistic and Borderline Personality Type', *Psychoanalytic Review*, vol. 79, no. 3. pp. 361–79.

Ford, C.S. and Beach, F.A. (1951), *Patterns of Sexual Behaviour*, Harper, New York.

Frankl, G. (1974), *The Failure of the Sexual Revolution*, Kahn & Averill, New York.

Friday, N. (1982), *My Secret Garden*, Quartet, London.

Friedenburg, F.S. (1956) 'A Contribution to the Problem of Sadomasochism', *Psychoanalytic Review*, vol. 43, pp. 91–6. Quoted in Breslow, 1989.

Gebhard, P.H. (1968) 'Fetishism and Sadomasochism', Winter Meeting of American Academy of Psychoanalysis, New Orleans, 13–15 December. Also 'Fetishism and Sadomasochism', in J.H. Masserman (ed.) *Dynamics of Deviant Sexuality*, Grune & Stratton, New York, 1969.

Gibson, I. (1979), *The English Vice: Beating, Sex and Shame in Victorian England and After*, Duckworth, London.

Goffman, E. (1974), *Frame Analysis*, Harvard University Press, Cambridge, Mass.

Gosselin, C. and Wilson, G. (1980), *Sexual Variations: Fetishism, Transvestism and Sado-Masochism*, Faber & Faber, London.

Greendlinger, V. and Byrne, D. (1987), 'Coercive Sexual Fantasies of College Men as Predictors of Self-reported Likelihood to Rape and Overt Sexual Aggression', *Journal of Sex Research*, vol. 23, no. 1.

Greene, G. and C. (1974), *S-M: The Last Taboo*, Grove Press, New York.

Gusfield, J.R. (1963), *Symbolic Crusade: Status Politics and the American Temperance Movement*, University of Illinois Press, Urbana.

Hadfield, J.A. (1967), *Introduction to Psychotherapy*, London; quoted in M. North, 1981.

Hamilton, G.V. (1929), *A Research in Marriage*, Boni, New York.

Hariton, E. (1972), 'Women's Fantasies During Sexual Intercourse with Their Husbands: A Normative Study with Tests of Personality and Theoretical Models', unpublished doctoral dissertation, City University of New York.

Hariton, E.B. and Singer, J.L. (1974), 'Women's Fantasies During Sexual Intercourse: Normative and Theoretical Implications', *Journal of Consulting and Clinical Psychology*, vol. 42.

Hirschfeld, M. (1971), *Sexual Anomalies: The Origins, Nature, and Treatment of Sexual Disorders*, quoted in Levitt, 1971.

Holbrook, D., quoted in Whitehouse, M. (1972) *Whatever Happened to Sex*, Wayland, Hove, but also see *The Masks of Hate*, Pergamon Press, Oxford, 1974.

Hunt, M. (1974), *Sexual Behaviour in the 1970s*, Playboy Press, Chicago.

Kernberg, O.F. (1991), 'Sadomasochism, Sexual Excitement, and Perversion', *Journal of the American Psychoanalytic Association*, vol. 39, no. 2, pp. 333–62.

Lederer, L. (1980), *Take Back the Night*, William Morrow & Co., New York.

Leigh, L.H. 'Sado-Masochism, Consent and the Reform of the Criminal Law', *Modern Law Review*, vol. 39, March, pp. 130–46.

Levitt, E.E. (1971), 'Sadomasochism', *Sexual Behaviour*, vol. 1, no. 6, pp. 69–80.

Linden, R.R. *et al.* (1982), *Against Sado-Masochism: A Radical Feminist Analysis*, Frog in the Wall Press, San Francisco.

Loewenstein, R.M. (1957), 'A Contribution to the Psychoanalytic Theory of Masochism', *Journal of the American Psychoanalytic Association*, vol. 5, pp. 197–234.

Lowen, A. (1976), *Bioenergetics*, Penguin Books, Harmondsworth.

Marcus, M. (1981), *A Taste for Pain*, Souvenir Press, London.

Mass, L. (1983), 'Coming to Grips with Sadomasochism', in T. Weinberg and G.W. Kamel, *S and M: Studies in Sadomasochism*, Prometheus Books, Buffalo, NY.

Meibomius, J.H. (1761), *A Treatise of the Use of Flogging*.

Menaker, E. (1979), *Masochism and the Emergent Ego*, Human Sciences Press, New York.

Mollinger, R. (1982), 'Sadomasochism and Developmental Stages', *Psychiatric Review*, vol. 69.

Moser, C. and Levitt, E.E. (1987), 'An Exploratory-Descriptive Study of a Sadomasochistically Orientated Sample', *Journal of Sex Research*, vol. 23, no. 3, pp. 322–37.

Naylor, B.A. (1986), 'Sadomasochism in Children and Adolescents: A Contemporary Treatment Approach', *Psychotherapy*, vol. 23, no. 4, pp. 586–92.

North, M. (1981), *The Outer Fringe of Sex*, Odyssey Press, London.

Novick, J. and K.K. (1991), 'Some Comments on Masochism and the Delusion of Omnipotence from a Developmental Perspective', *Journal of the American Psychoanalytic Association*, vol. 39, no. 2, pp. 307–31.

Panken, S. (1967), 'On Masochism – A Defence Reaction of the Ego', *Psychoanalytic Review*, vol. 54, pp. 135–49.

Patrias, D. (1978), 'The Sociology of Secret Deviation', unpublished Ph.D. thesis, New York University.

Playboy (1976), 'What's Really Happening on Campus', editorial, October issue.

Reich, W. (1927), *Die Funktion des Orgasmus*, Internationale Psycho-Analytische Verlag, Vienna.

Reich, W. (1972), *Sex-Pol; Essays 1929–1934*, Vintage Books, New York.

Rhodes, D. and McNeil, S. (1985), *Women Against Violence Against Women*, Onlywomen Press, London.

Robertiello, R. (1970), 'Masochism and the Female Sex Role', *Journal of Sex Research*, vol. 6, no. 1, pp. 56–8.

Rothstein, A. (1991), 'Sadomasochism in the Neuroses Conceived of as a Pathological Compromise Formation', *Journal of the American Psychoanalytic Association*, vol. 39, no. 2, pp. 363–75.

Sadger, J. (1926) 'A Contribution to the Understanding of Sadomasochism', *International Journal of Psychoanalysis*, vol. 7, pp. 484–91. Quoted in Breslow, 1984.

Salzaman, L. (1971), Commentary on Dr Levitt's article, *Sexual Behaviour*, vol. 1, no. 6.

Socarides, C.W. (1958), 'The Function of Moral Masochism: With Special Reference to the Defence Purpose', *International Journal of Psychoanalysis*, vol. 39, pp. 587–97. Quoted in A. Rothstein, 1991.

Spengler, A. (1977), 'Manifest Sadomasochism of Males: Results of an Empirical Study', *Archives of Sexual Behaviour*, vol. 6, pp. 441–56.

Stoller, R. (1975), *Perversion: The Erotic Form of Hatred*, Dell, New York.

Stoller, R. (1991), *Pain and Passion*, Plenum Press, New York.

Szasz, T.S. (1974), *The Myth of Mental Illness*, Harper & Row, New York.

Tenenbaum, J. (1929), *The Riddle of Sex*, Pioneer, New York. Original version, 1929.

Thompson, B. (1994), *Soft Core*, Cassell, London.

Ullerstam, L. (1967), *The Erotic Minorities: A Swedish View*. Sphere Books, London.

Weinberg, T. and Kamel, G.W. (1983), *S and M: Studies in Sadomasochism*, Prometheus Books, Buffalo, NY.

Weinberg, M.S., Williams, C.J. and Moser, C. (1984), 'The Social Constituents of Sadomasochism', *Social Problems*, vol. 31, no. 4.

Zillmann, D. (1984), *Connections Between Sex and Aggression*, Lawrence Erlbaum Associates, Hillsdale, New Jersey.

Legal references

The Law Commission, *Criminal Law: Consent and Offences Against the Person*, Consultation Paper, no. 134, HMSO, London.

Attorney-General's Reference (No. 6 of 1980) [1981] QB 715.

R. v. *Boyea* (28 January 1992), unreported (Court of Appeal) Criminal Division.

R. v. *Brown* [1993] 2 WLR 556; [1992] 2 All ER 75 (the Spanner case).

R v. *Ciccarelli* [1989] 54 CCC (3d) 121.

R. v. *Clarence* [1888] 22 QBD 23.

Collins v. *Wilcock* [1984] 1 WLR 1172.

R. v. *Coney* [1882] 51 LJMC 66; 8 QBD 534.

Director of Public Prosecutions v. *Smith* [1961] AC 290.

R. v. *Donovan* [1934] 2 KB 498; [1934] All ER Rep 209.

J.J.C. (a minor) v. *Eisenhower* [1983] 3 All ER 230.

Mowatt [1968] 1 QB 421.

Wilson v. *Pringle* [1987] QB 237.

Emphases in the quoted passages are the present author's.

Further Reading

IN a book of this length it is impossible to include everything one would like to. As my task was to question the viability of the Spanner judgement, there are several aspects of SM that I have not been able to cover in any depth. For those who wish to know, I can suggest the following.

The Lesbian S/M Safety Manual, while written for leather dykes, contains a vast amount of essential information about playing safe. London's Lesbian and Gay Switchboard (tel.: 071 837 7324) have produced a *Rough Sex: Safer Sex* guide, available from lesbian and gay bookstores, etc. Those who wish to know more about the contemporary SM community, publications, fashion, equipment and activities will find the glossy fashion-orientated *Skin Two* magazine available in some newsagents. Niki Wolf's wonderful *Fetish Times* is best secured through subscription from BCM Box, London WC1N 3XX. Numerous articles and features on SM appear in the monthly *Forum Journal*. *Whips and Kisses*, published by Prometheus Books, is one woman's personal history, and covers the American professional and non-professional heterosexual scene. Robert Stoller's *Pain and Passion*, published by Plenum Press, contains interviews with several heterosexual devotees. The gay and lesbian community is covered in Mark Thompson's *Leatherfolk* and SAMOIS's *Coming to Power*. Both published by Alyson Publications, these provide a wealth of historical information and contemporary accounts by devotees. You can meet many contemporary devotees in person, at least on video. *Skin Two* offers several covering numerous aspects of the SM/fetish scene, and *S&M: Sociolistic Metamorphosis*, produced by RWP, consists of interviews with young devotees. These are available from major stores like the Virgin chain. A wealth of detail about Victorian flagellation fantasies can be found in the reprints of *The Pearl* published by The New English Library and numerous titles in the Starr Collection of Victorian pornographic classics. Donald Thomas's *The Marquis de Sade* provides a detailed account of de Sade's life and works, which goes a long way towards dispelling many of the myths surrounding this much-maligned marquis. For those who insist upon exploring the psychoanalytic and therapeutic approaches, the best book is Susan P. Schad-Somers, *Sadomasochism: Etiology and Treatment*, which is available from Human Sciences Press Inc., 72 5th Avenue, New York, USA.

Index